Light and lighting

Light and lighting

David Kilpatrick

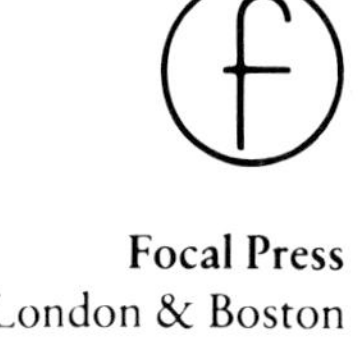

Focal Press
London & Boston

Focal Press
An imprint of the Butterworth Group
Principal offices in London, Boston, Durban, Singapore,
Sydney, Toronto and Wellington

British Library Cataloguing in Publication Data

Kilpatrick, David
Light and lighting
1. Photography – Lighting
I. Title
778.7′2   TR590

ISBN 0-240-51203-0

Library of Congress Cataloging in Publication Data

Kilpatrick, David
Light and lighting

(The photographer's library)
Includes index
1. Photography – Lighting
I. Title.   II. Series.
TR590.K54   1984   778.7   83-11623
ISBN 0-240-51203-0

First published 1984

Series designed by Diana Allen
Cover photograph by David Kilpatrick
Photoset by Butterworths Litho Preparation Department
Origination by Adroit Photo Ltd Birmingham
Printed in Great Britain by Robert Stace Ltd,
Tunbridge Wells, Kent

Contents

Acknowledgements

I would like to thank Keith Johnson Photographic Ltd., Minolta (UK) Limited, Ilford Limited and Paterson Products Ltd for help in various fields during the production of this book. I would also like to thank our portrait model, Tracie, and customers and staff in our studio who lived patiently with the more laborious bits.

The illustrations in this book have been produced mainly using Minolta 35mm, Pentax 6 × 7cm and Toyo 5 × 4 cameras with Ilford black-and-white and Kodak colour films. The lighting equipment used for all studio pictures was Multiblitz Vario, Mini Studio and Profilite mains flash.

Light and images

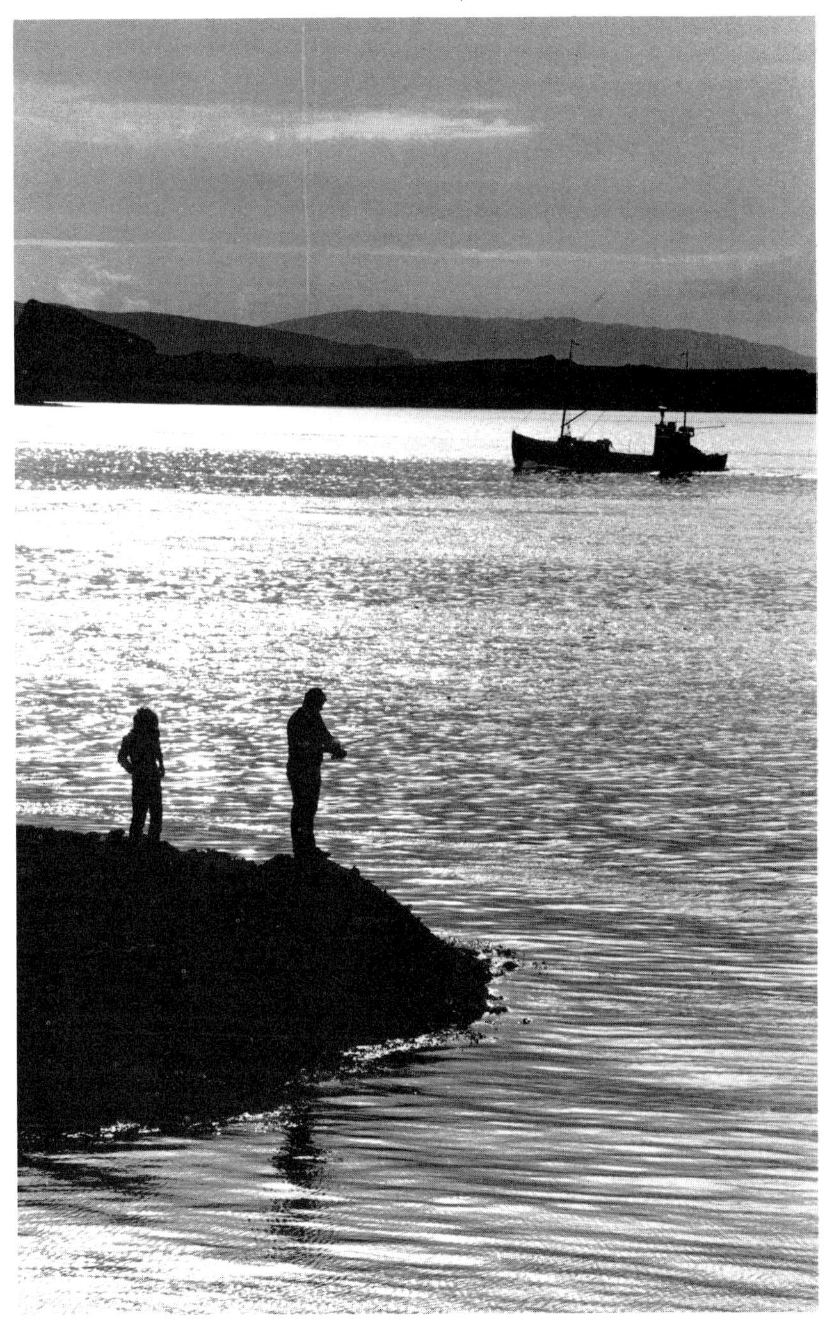

Visible light offers us the most informative view or reconstruction of physical reality. The human eye feeds far more data into the brain than any of the other sense organs, and our ability to interpret visual information is highly developed. To overcome the brain's one major failing, inability to store visual memories in full detail, we have progressed from cave drawings to photochemical (photographic) and electronic (video) recording.

We depend today on photochemical and electronic visual images almost as much as we do on biological ones, the transitory movie seen through the lens of our eyes. All three rely on the same energy to record images: that part of the electromagnetic spectrum which we call visible light, extending from around 440 nanometres to 700 nm.

Light itself is more complex in nature and variability than an ordinary human, with a lifetime of seeing to judge from, would assume. Our eyes and brains conspire to adjust, correct, override or ignore many aspects of light. In contrast, photographic and video systems record faithfully. Their images depend entirely on the quantity of light available. Without a full understanding and mastery of light and lighting, you can not expect proficiency in handling image-recording systems.

Basic qualities of light
The intensity of light, or the luminance reaching an illuminated surface, is one of the easier aspects of lighting to learn to assess by eye. Many experienced cameramen can do so with great accuracy and are only out of their depth in artificial lighting conditions or unfamiliar geographical latitudes.

Absolute darkness does exist, and can be produced easily. Absolute light does not exist unless you assume it to be the brilliance of the surface or interior of the brightest star. On Earth, there is a natural peak in brilliance which can be found in theory at noon, on midsummer's day, on the equator, up in the stratosphere. In practice atmospheric moisture, pollution, clouds, reflection off layers of air of different temperatures and many other factors reduce this light level. We are left with a finite range of light values, from bright equatorial sunlight to a moonless night, which is well documented. Photographic and video systems are designed to be able to cope with the brightest light, tackling low-light conditions according to their sophistication and cost.

Nearly all the factors which alter light levels can be identified, recognised, even predicted. Varied though weather conditions are, it is possible to calculate the light level given nothing more than latitude, time of year, time of day, and sky condition (clear, overcast, heavy cloud, etc). Obsolete photographic-exposure calculators using this principle prove very accurate.

Spectral composition, or the mixture of wavelengths making up visible light, is harder to assess. White light is composed of a fairly good and even mixture of the colours of the spectrum from violet through to red; in photography and video, the full range of colours is recorded using a comparatively restricted sensitivity to bands of blue, green and red. This is also how the human eye works. Instead of being equally sensitive to every wavelength, it has peaks of sensitivity and opposing flat spots. Individuals vary, as colour-blindness shows, either in their colour sensitivity or the way the brain interprets the signals.

Some light sources which appear 'white' to the eye are not. The brain compensates for slightly blue, yellow, pink or other alternatively tinted light when this is the only light-source available. It balances back to white. Other light sources appear to be a true white, even when compared with daylight, but are not – there are gaps in their colour mixture which the eye does not notice, but film and video detect. Fluorescent tubes are the most common examples of such light sources with a 'non-continuous spectrum'.

Instruments are made to measure the colour content of light, so that adjustments can be made, and modern film emulsions and picture tubes are deliberately designed to be tolerant, allowing final visual adjustment of the image to match colours as apparently seen. A little understanding of the subject can help a great deal, however, in improving images from the start.

The remaining qualities of light are easier to understand but infinitely variable. The physical size or area of the illuminating source in relation to the subject makes enormous differences to the image rendering. The two extremes are a completely white, cloudy bright sky over snow-covered ground, and the light from a single concentrated spotlight at night. Between these, anything is possible.

Distance is related to light-source size. A $1m^2$ light source positioned 10 cm above a small subject is similar to the open sky in light quality; positioned 10 m away, it would resemble the light from a small high window. The angle of the light as it falls on the subject (naturally linked to your viewing position) is also important. The maximum amount of light is reflected back, from a typical subject, when the light source is very close to the viewing position. If the light is to one side, then half the subject is in shadow; if it is the other side of the subject, facing the viewer, then only small surfaces and edges may be lit. There may also be several light sources, not just one, building up the pattern of illumination and shadow in the scene viewed. Some light sources may appear simple but are complex. The sun in a clear blue sky is one of these; a point source of white light in a large diffused source of slightly blue light.

White light, or daylight, contains a mixture of wavelengths which the eye sees as white. The distribution of lengths is not perfectly even, and the eye can compensate for changes. All these types of light can be seen by the eye as 'white'.

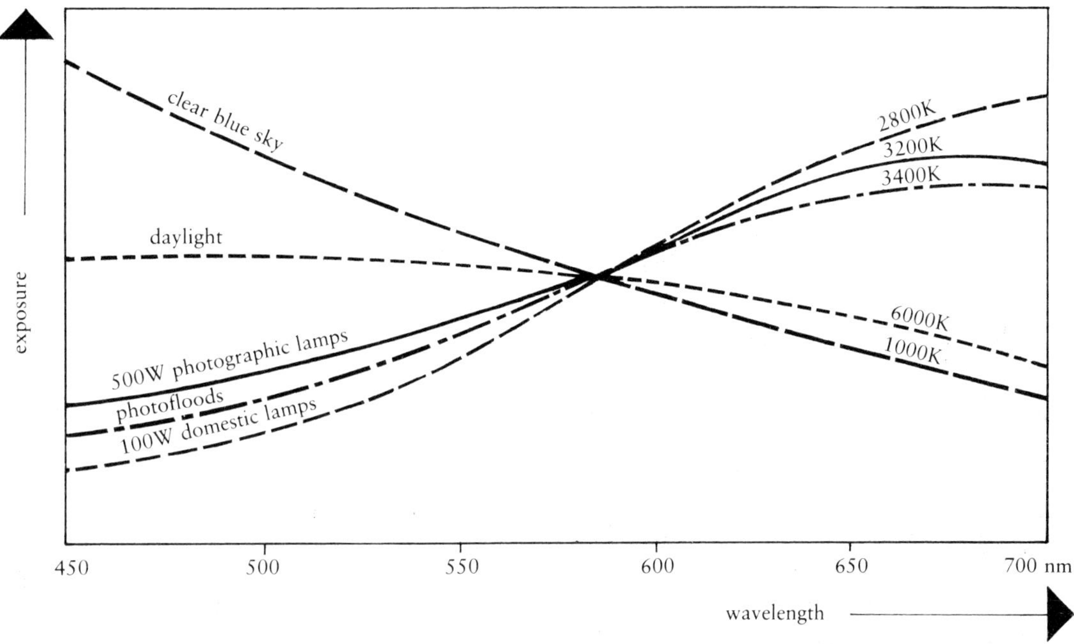

What we see as 'light' can also conceal changes in continuity. A fluorescent tube flickers at the frequency of mains electricity (50 or 60 cycles per second). A very fast stroboscopic lamp may seem to give continuous light but in reality gives hundreds of individual flashes in a second. A photographic flashbulb seems instantaneous, but burns for a comparatively long period, perhaps 50 milliseconds; an electronic flashgun giving roughly the same visual effect may fire for just one fiftieth of a millisecond.

Information from light
We can tell much about the physical properties of the world around us from the information given by light. It reveals colour, shape, texture, three-dimensional space, relative size, consistency and physical state. Because light travels so rapidly, and bridges distances 'instantly', we rely on visual information to tell us about changes in subjects, movement and actions. It is much more reliable than sound; you see a finger pull the trigger long before the sound of the gunshot reaches you. Because our atmosphere is effectively transparent, and absorbs little light, it also extends human awareness much further; transmitted sound and heat also travel, but are absorbed very quickly and do not go far. Human reliance on visual data depends on these qualities of light, and this helps explain why visual images are such an important medium today. Pictures reach our most highly-tuned, key sense.

Any object can absorb, reflect or transmit different proportions of various regions of the spectrum. A deep black object absorbs most visible wavelengths. A pure white sheet of paper reflects about 95 per cent of all the rays reaching it. The clearest window glass transmits a similar amount. The colour of objects is determined by the wavelength bands reflected or absorbed. A red scarf reflects long wavelengths which we see as red, and absorbs short wavelengths which are blue. A green glass bottle

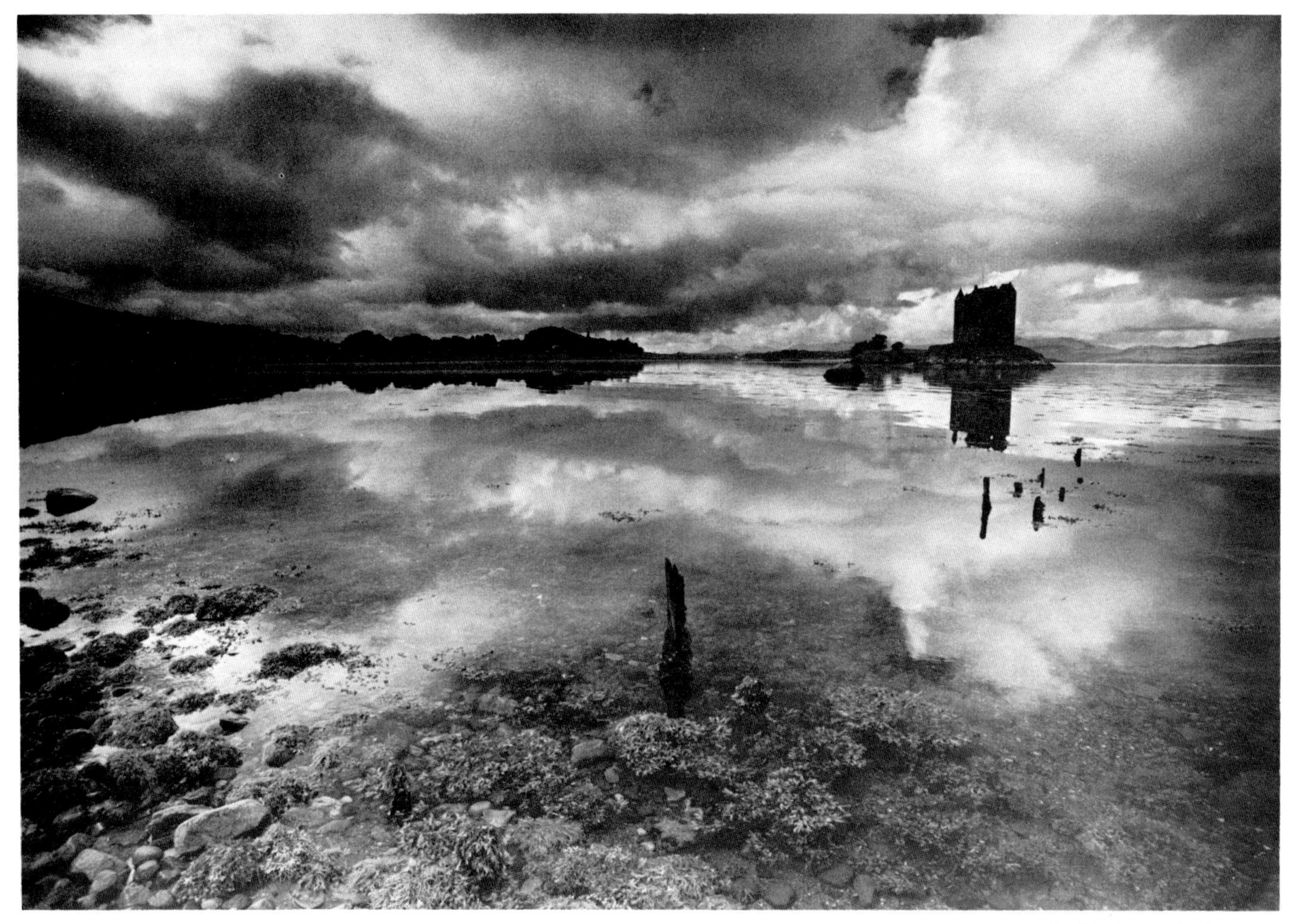

In this shot, reflection, absorption and transmission of light all combine in a complex range of tones.

both transmits and reflects wavelengths in the area of the spectrum which covers blue, green and yellow; it absorbs violet and orange-red wavelengths at the extreme ends of the spectrum.

Texture is revealed mainly by the opacity or reflectivity of a subject casting shadows or forming highlights in a fine pattern, showing up irregularities in surfaces. Shape is shown in much the same way, on a larger scale. Distances, three-dimensional shape and size are shown by the way that shadows are cast. In open landscape views, slight haze may also give distance information. Physical qualities of objects are judged by the combination of opacity, transparency, reflectivity, texture, shape, size and so on; we do not confuse the surface of a still lake with a sheet of glass, or human skin with a waxwork model. Human perception and judgment of physical qualities is finely honed, and we carry this ability through to judging visual images in photography or video formats.

The importance of light in pictures
It must be clear that light not only forms our visual media physically, but provides all the vital wealth of data which images convey to the viewer. Before you press and shutter or aim a video camera, the way that light and lighting modify the scene in front of you must be fully understood. Often you will encounter lighting conditions which, although adequate from the standpoint of mere illumination, do little to enhance or help the final picture work. The bad cameraman shoots without thinking and accepts the result as inevitable. Some after-work may be done to improve things.

The proficient camera operator, on the other hand, looks critically at existing light. There may be particular approaches to photography which can use whatever light is there and do so effectively. Perhaps correction, in the form of filters to change the light colours and reflectors to bounce directional light in new directions, can be used.

Perhaps the entire scene needs to be lit with purpose-built light sources: floodlights, spotlights, electronic flash or even flashbulbs. Today's trend is towards natural or existing light, even to the extent of capturing the strange colours created by industrial sodium and fluorescent lighting. When lighting is added, it should enhance the existing 'feel' rather than override it. Modern technology does not need the overkill of early Hollywood movie lighting.

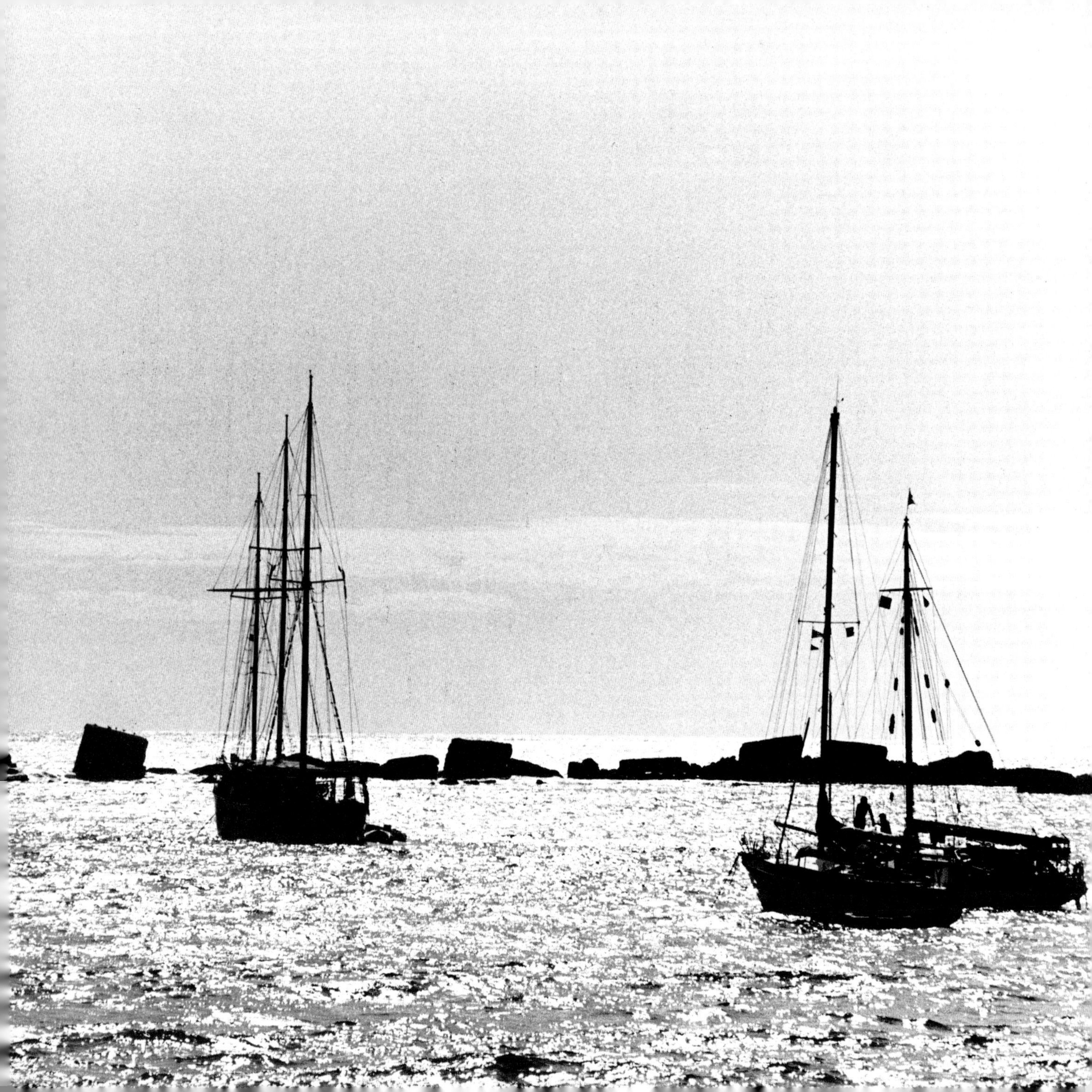

Light intensity

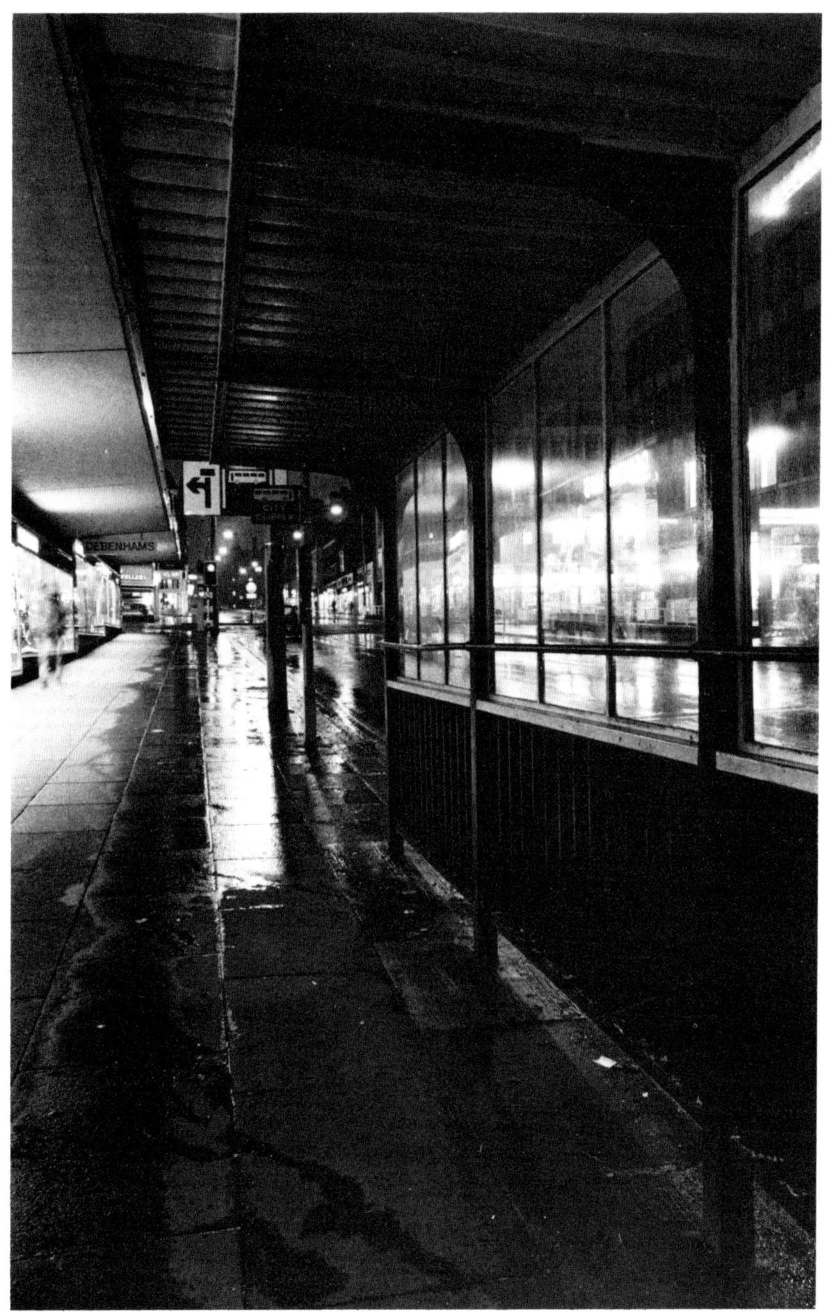

The fixed scale of light values found on Earth has already been mentioned. Under normal conditions, the working range of a photographic or video system is unlikely to be exceeded. However, some older cameras used with the latest films may be unable to cope in bright sunlight.

Despite a large vocabulary devoted to light and its measurement, no-one has yet devised a scientifically accepted simple value for brightness. The terms lux, lumens per square foot, and foot candles all refer to measurements of light intensity reaching a surface but have no convenient instant conversion to photographic values. A value of 2000 foot candles – bright overhead equatorial sunlight in a reflective, light scene – would be understood by a physicist but not by a photographer. The video cameraman has little use for any kind of light values; beyond knowing that a particular camera is either designed for low light or not, adjustments are so easily made that exposure metering plays no role.

The photographic scale normally used is the Exposure Value, or EV, scale. The technically more relevant Light Value or LV scale is hardly ever referred to. LVs are absolute; EV figures depend entirely on the film 'speed' or sensitivity which they are quoted for. As EV figures are always quoted for ISO 100/21°, historically the 'medium' sensitivity for photographic film, they are as consistent as LVs.

The EV scale at ISO 100/21° (which we will take for granted from now on) runs to an effective maximum of EV20. Most cameras reach their cut-off point at EV18 or 19, and bright summer sunlight is EV15; brilliant sun on snow or white sand can reach EV16; sun augmented by rays reflected from mirrors or similar surfaces might reach EV17. Each step is a doubling in brightness. A comfortable level for domestic room illumination, on the other hand, would be 5 foot candles; one five-hundredth of bright outdoor sunshine, or EV7. A simple automatic camera would reach its limit at about this brightness. A good single-lens reflex with a built-in metering system will meter 'down to EV1' which is equal to about 1/32 000th of bright outdoor sun. It is also a level where the human eye begins to find things definitely dim.

Values lower than EV1 on the photographic scale are 'seen' by most video cameras only by boosting sensitivity and sacrificing colour, sharpness or absence of unwanted effects like after-image ghosting. The eye sees them with less colour distinction, and poor resolution. Photographic film can be given an infinitely extended exposure and will therefore continue to resolve detail and colour clearly, regardless of the light level. The practical lower limit of photographic light-metering is around EV -7 to -10; late dusk to moonlight. It is sobering to consider that the brightness encountered here is less than one 50-millionth of our original bright outdoor sun.

The limits
Such a set of extreme figures, combined with comparatively meaningless numerical values, has little to do with light and lighting. It serves to emphasise the nature of the light we are dealing with. Unless you consider how and why light varies and how it is measured, you do not grasp the sheer scale of the finite range of possible light values encountered.

In practice, it is only necessary to accept that by using 'neutral density' or grey filters in front of lenses, any image system can cope with brilliant light. Such filters are freely available from major manufacturers in strengths of up to 100 000× − that is, cutting light down to 100 000th of its

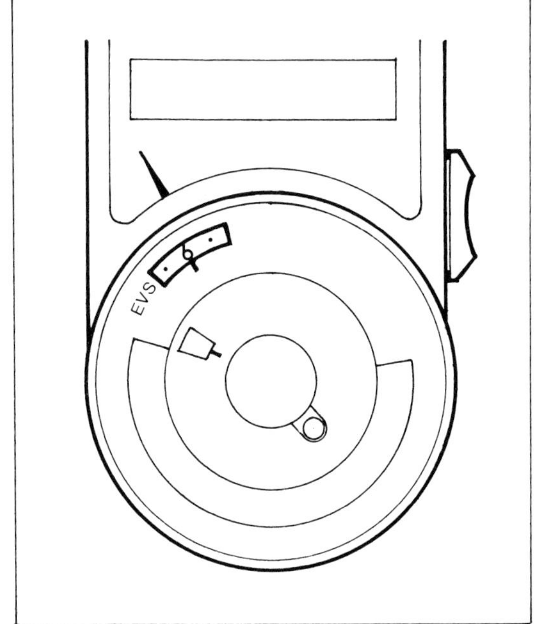

brilliance. Secondly, accept that it is rarely necessary to produce images when the eye itself is unable to see properly. When this is the case, light and lighting become secondary considerations and the sole object may well be to see clearly where the eye can not. The infra-red night-sight is a well-known device which does just this.

Your main problems will happen because the human eye is very bad at judging light *quality* when the *quantity* is extreme, in either direction. Exposure meters, video monitors, colour meters and other devices are put to best use when their ability to *compare* rather than just *measure* is understood. Measurement can almost be replaced by rules of thumb or simple tables and calculators; comparison can not.

Daylight
The position and distance of the sun change with the seasons and the time of day. Its brightness does, in fact, vary, but only to a slight degree, of more

Many exposure meters have a scale showing exposure values or EVs, which give an indication of the level of illumination without referring to filmspeeds, shutter or aperture settings.

Page 12: extremely bright light over water in a subtropical location. Courtesy Sunair Holidays Ltd, *David Kilpatrick*.

Page 13: a very low light-level in a city street at night.

A simple pictorial exposure guide for an ISO 64/19° colour film out of doors. The aperture/shutter-speed combinations given are for average scenes with the sun coming from behind the camera.

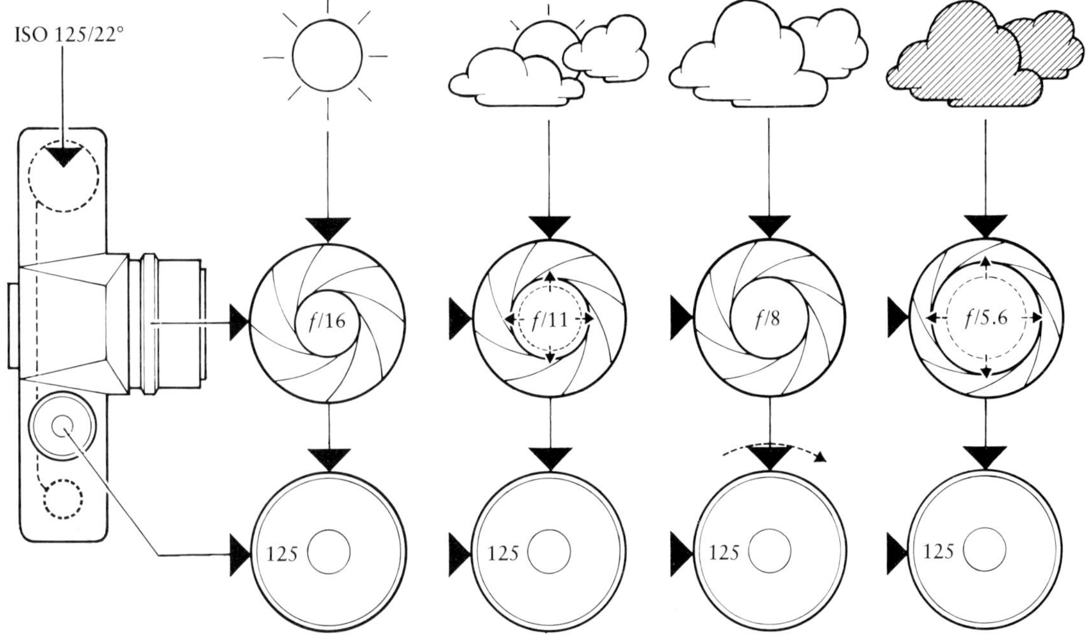

interest to astrophysicists than photographers. When the sun is high in the sky, during the six hours around mid-day in summer, it is possible to set a very accurate fixed value on its light. In photographic terms this is equal to an exposure needing $f/16$ when the shutter speed is set to a value numerically identical to the ISO/ASA film speed in use; for ISO 125/21°, set 1/125 on the camera; for ISO 1000/31°, set 1/1000.

'Hazy sunlight', a term found on film instruction leaflets, is often due to a thin cloud layer in the upper atmosphere. It needs twice as much exposure ($f/11$). 'Cloudy bright' is the next step down, and that means definite clouds through which the disk of the sun can still be seen though no sharp shadows are cast on the ground; double it again ($f/8$). 'Overcast' is more difficult to assess. Clouds should not be heavy, but the sun's disk is not visible; double the exposure once more ($f/5.6$). 'Dull' means the clouds are now grey, not white: $f/4$. 'Rainy' or 'very dull', and the clouds are

decidedly dark or low: $f/2.8$. There has to be a dramatic, black thunderstorm to get any dimmer than this during midday hours in summer.

Exposure calculators and tables, even down to the ones supplied with rolls of film, work on this rule of thumb. It has ramifications; two to three hours after sunrise or before sunset, open up one stop (double the exposure); one to two hours ditto, two stops; winter season, add an extra doubling all round; streets or enclosed areas with dark surroundings, do the same; close-ups, same again; snow or light sand, go the other way and halve the exposure. Special conditions, which no calculator can cope with, include low cloud, pollution, sunsets and dusk light (highly variable).

Most photographers prefer a camera able to cope with all reasonable light levels. A video photographer taping wedding ceremonies in churches soon finds that it pays to have a camera with extremely good low-light performance. An aerial photographer is more concerned with bright light levels because low light and visibility restricts flying and makes aerial views impossible. For the rest, the extremes of the setting range remain unused. Most photographs are taken on the lens aperture and shutter speeds 'in the middle'; most video systems remain on fixed-lens apertures and fixed-brightness adjustments, with only minor changes. As modern systems all incorporate forms of adjustment or light metering, often fully automatic, you do not need to carry the rule-of-thumb values in your head. Remember that they do help cameramen spot when equipment is malfunctioning, and some grasp of them can be useful should anything go wrong.

Man-made light

Our problems begin as soon as the sun is left behind, and the fixed values of season, time of day and weather conditions no longer apply. Artificial light sources are infinitely variable; they have shades and covers, bulbs of various ages, all manner of wattages and outputs. They are sufficiently small and localised for their illuminating power to depend entirely on light-to-subject distance. No common artificial light sources bear even a remote relationship to sunlight in brightness. They may seem very bright to the eye, and when used to cover a small subject at a close distance they may match the sun's illuminating power. But the sun lights entire continents at one go.

Indoors, you may be forgiven for seeing artificial light as 'bright' when it is not. A ceiling consisting of nothing but fluorescent panels can seem very brilliant. This is because your eyes adapt to the room and to the level of brightness reaching the desktops or the floor; compared with this, the light source itself does look bright. Take the fluorescent tubes outside into sunlight and you might not even be able to tell if they were switched on.

Never try to judge indoor lighting by eye. It is impossible; the eye accommodates, its pupil opening up to admit more light. Comparisons are impossible, too, because the pupil changes between looking across a room and looking out of a window. Great differences in light level are evened out. The colour and continuity of artificial light are also impossible to judge by eye. You may think that a factory sodium lamp seems rather yellow and a fluorescent tube slightly blue; on film, they could appear as bright orange and a lurid green.

Simple technical solutions exist to both problems: for light levels, a good exposure meter which is also capable of measuring relative values, and for colour quality a colour temperature meter which gives a reading converted easily to coloured filters. Continuity of light, whether it flickers or not (at however high a frequency) has no effect on conventional still photography, but may have adverse effects with certain types of cine and video work. It is not advisable to work with any moving image system using a frame or scan time in excess of 32 frames per second with discharge, fluorescent or artificial light other than tungsten. Normal film and video (from 18 to 24/25 frames per second in effect) pose no problems.

The inverse square law

To understand any type of artificial light, whether continuous or pulsed (flash or strobe), you need to know the inverse square law. This basic law of optical physics is also useful when taking extreme close-ups using special equipment, and when working in the photographic darkroom. The inverse square law describes (perfectly) how light from a theoretical point source behaves in terms of distance from the source and relative illumination. Here is the law, restated for clarity as some previous definitions have been inaccurate and ungrammatical:

Relative illumination at any radial distance from a point source of light is inversely proportional to the square of the distance itself.

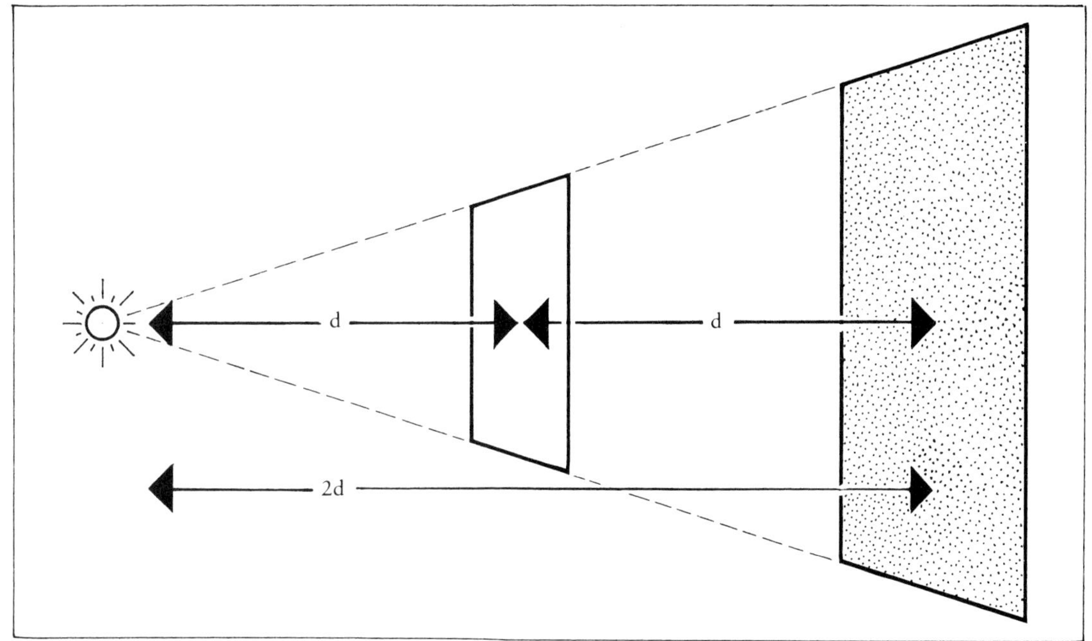

The important key word in this law is *relative,* as the law itself is only of real value when used to compare illumination level at two different distances. Moreover, actual units of measurement, like feet or metres, are only of value if the light-emitting power of the light source is known *in relation to those units.* In practice, the inverse square law means:

Double the distance = one quarter of the illumination.

Treble the distance = one ninth of the illumination.

Halve the distance = four times the illumination.

Few light sources approach point source in quality, but as far as exposure and illumination levels go, floods, cine lights, flashguns and other lights smaller than 100 cm^2 in radiant surface or reflector area can be treated as point sources for all distances greater than 1 metre. What the inverse square law really means is that small differences in relative subject distance from an artificial light source can make big differences in illumination. The law, used in the field, tells you that to double the light reaching a particular part of the subject you must move the source 30 per cent closer. It also tells you that the closer the light is to the subject, the greater the differences in illumination within the depth of that subject will be.

This knowledge helps you decide to position a powerful light source a long way off from a 'deep' subject, rather than a weak light source much closer in. It also tells you that if you are forced to stand close to a subject like a group of people and use a portable light or flash, it pays to arrange the people at an equal distance from you in a slightly concave line.

Diffuse light sources do not behave like point sources, particularly when they are much larger than the subject and used fairly close. The inverse square law is degraded, and its effect reduced, so that illumination in depth is much more even, and small changes in the light-to-subject distance do not affect exposure much. For this reason, as well as for the quality of lighting, reflections and minimal shadows produced, large reflectors, diffusers and light-boxes are often used in studios. As they do not obey the inverse square law, controllable output is very important. Even with comparatively small light sources, like portable flashguns, the law ceases to work at very close distances, as for macro photography, because the reflector may be far bigger than the subject and relatively very close.

Guide numbers
Guide numbers were devised to state the actual power of photographic and movie lights, in relation to film-speed figures and lens apertures. They are not used for video work, but any general-purpose photographic light bought for video may have a guide number stated, and those with higher figures are more powerful. Guide numbers use the inverse square law and the fact that lens apertures, as a factor of the *area* of the lens which transmits light, also depend on squares and form a binary-number series 1, 1.4, 2, 2.8, 4, 5.6, 8, 11, 16, 22, 32, 64, 128 and so on.

To find the required lens aperture number in this series (*f*-stop) you divide the guide number by the light-to-subject distance. Thus a light with a guide number of 110 metres used at a distance of 10 metres needs aperture 11, or *f*/11. This setting will be found marked on the lens-aperture scale and it is only necessary to set it, without further calculation.

Guide numbers for continuous light sources are stated in a table which has to cover three criteria: first, it is either a metric or imperial (feet) guide number table; secondly, each different ISO film speed ranges along one co-ordinate; thirdly, each shutter speed from 1 second to 1/1000 ranges along the other co-ordinate. By reading the table for the appropriate film speed and shutter setting, the correct guide number is found. Ciné filming speeds or effective shutter speeds can also be listed.

Guide numbers for flash are stated according to two criteria only: whether metric or imperial, and according to film speed. Because no co-ordinate table is needed for this, most flashguns are able to have a calculator or table which takes over the work of calculating the *f*-stop. The film speed forms one co-ordinate, or moving scale, and the distance in feet or metres the other. The required *f*-stop is simply read off against the distance focused.

With both types of light source, what matters is making sure you know the guide number for the film type you are using, and that you never confuse feet with metres. It is common for manufacturers to state the guide number of a flashgun two ways: first, in metres for ISO 25/12°, and secondly in feet for ISO 100/21°. Recently both Japanese and DIN standards have made quoting for metres at ISO 100/21° more common.

To recap, the method for using a guide number is this:

Distance in units divided by guide number = *f*-stop number.

or

Chosen *f*-stop number × guide number = distance at which light source must be positioned.

Guide numbers are quoted for tungsten lights and studio flash units for a certain reflector only – normally the one which comes with the light. Changing the reflector alters the guide number, and using large diffusers or 'scrims' destroys its relevance for the reasons stated when discussing the inverse square law.

Guide numbers are very important when selecting the correct equipment for your needs. Even if you never need refer to them again, because you have access to flash exposure meters or your equipment gives fully automatic exposure, the manufacturer's stated guide numbers express the output. For

The inverse square law is used with flash and tungsten lights to turn a 'guide number' given for a particular light and filmspeed into the required aperture at any set distance. To find the aperture needed, divided the distance into the GN.

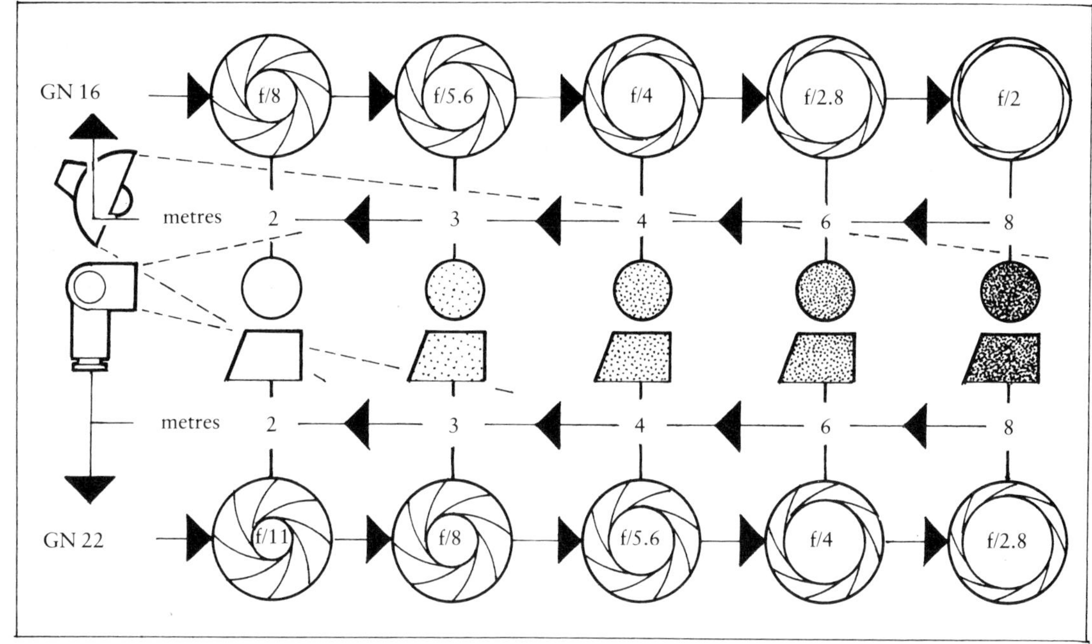

accurate judgment, also examine the stated field of even lighting coverage; a unit with a stated guide number of 100 covering 30° × 40° has a lower true output than one with an identical guide number covering 45° × 60°. The inverse square law and basic geometry will tell you that the unit with the wider coverage is between three and four times as powerful.

By way of final warning, it is common for manufacturers to state guide numbers for optimum performance, when in practice very few lamps or flash units achieve better than 90 per cent of designed output. Combined with advertising optimism and sample tolerance, real output may be down to 75 per cent of stated performance. For this reason, all buyers of new lights of any kind are strongly advised to make initial tests in typical working conditions with familiar equipment and materials, and to adjust the stated guide numbers in future if any discrepancy does show up.

Flash

Flash differs from continuous light like tungsten not only in its duration, but also in its colour. The xenon tubes used at high voltage to achieve short, intense bursts of light also yield high colour temperatures, similar to daylight.

Flashbulbs, which use aluminium wool electrically ignited in a sealed bulb full of oxygen, produce light similar to tungsten but are coated with a blue lacquer which matches their output to daylight. Unlike electronic flash, they burn up to peak and then die down, taking a relatively long time. Flashbulbs have to be used in conjunction with accurately-set firing synchronisation and precise shutter speeds. Their guide number figures may vary according to the type of camera and shutter speed used.

Electronic flash durations are invariably no longer than 1/250th of a second, with no significant build-up or decay in output. The shortest durations

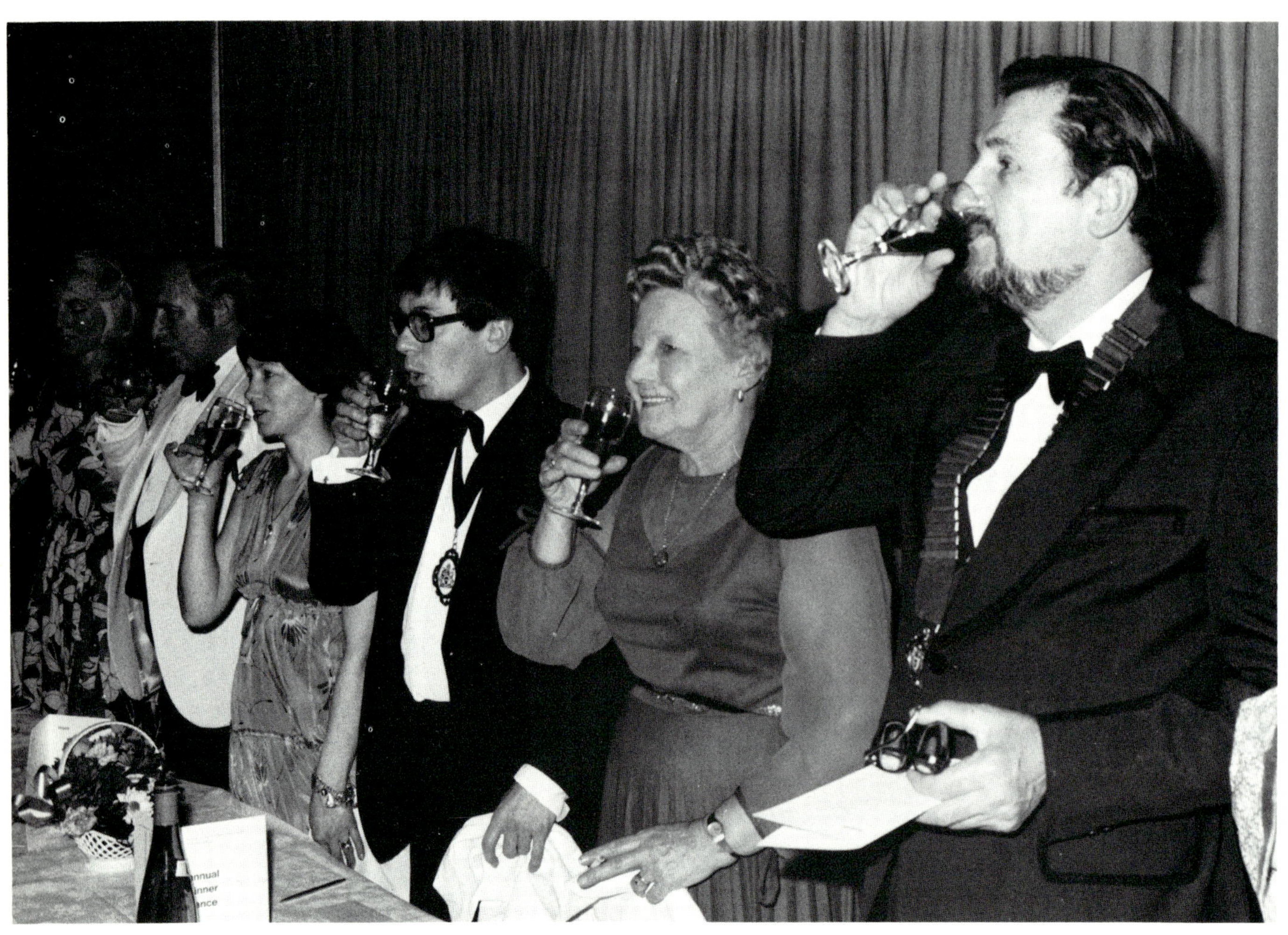

Annual
inner
ance

are around 1/50 000 second. Most popular flash units have durations between 1/750 and 1/2000 second. Large studio flash units have durations of 1/250 to 1/1500 second, mainly around 1/300–1/500 second. It is often assumed that with cameras giving 'full synchronisation' for electronic flash, shutter speeds of 1/500 or 1/250 second can be used safely in the studio. In practice, studio flash manufacturers warn against times shorter than 1/125, since some attenuation of output may occur. This little-known fact has been responsible for many assumptions that very powerful long-duration studio flash systems are 'underpowered'. Like tungsten lights used on thyristor dimmers, electronic flash units with variable power also change slightly in colour temperature when the power is changed. This similarity to continuous light is also infrequently recognised.

Because flash does not depend on the shutter speed used in most circumstances, and exposure is controlled only by distance, aperture setting and flash power, the effect of existing light can have variable results. With some cameras using larger film sizes, the flash-synchronisation speed (the fastest setting where the film is fully covered at one time) may be 1/30th of a second. This can be long enough for ambient light to add slightly to the exposure unless a room or studio is well blacked-out. Bright modelling lamps, used to judge the lighting effect of the flash when setting up and to aid focusing and composition when shooting, may also interfere.

Many cameras have faster synchronisation speeds of 1/60, 1/125 or 1/200 second. With in-the-lens shutter cameras, synchronisation at 1/250, 1/300 or 1/500 second is possible with portable flashguns. This does allow their use as controlled fill-in lights outdoors, even in bright sunlight. The simple but subtle calculations involved when mixing flash and other light will be dealt with later on.

Electronic flash is seen as a universal solution; good units stop action, freeze camera shake, allow small lens apertures without time exposures, avoid colour shifts, consume little power, and are remarkably consistent. Combined with a modern flash exposure meter able to read all the factors involved, including shutter speeds and effects of existing light, electronic flash does indeed offer almost foolproof quality but it is by no means the only light-source a photographer should rely on.

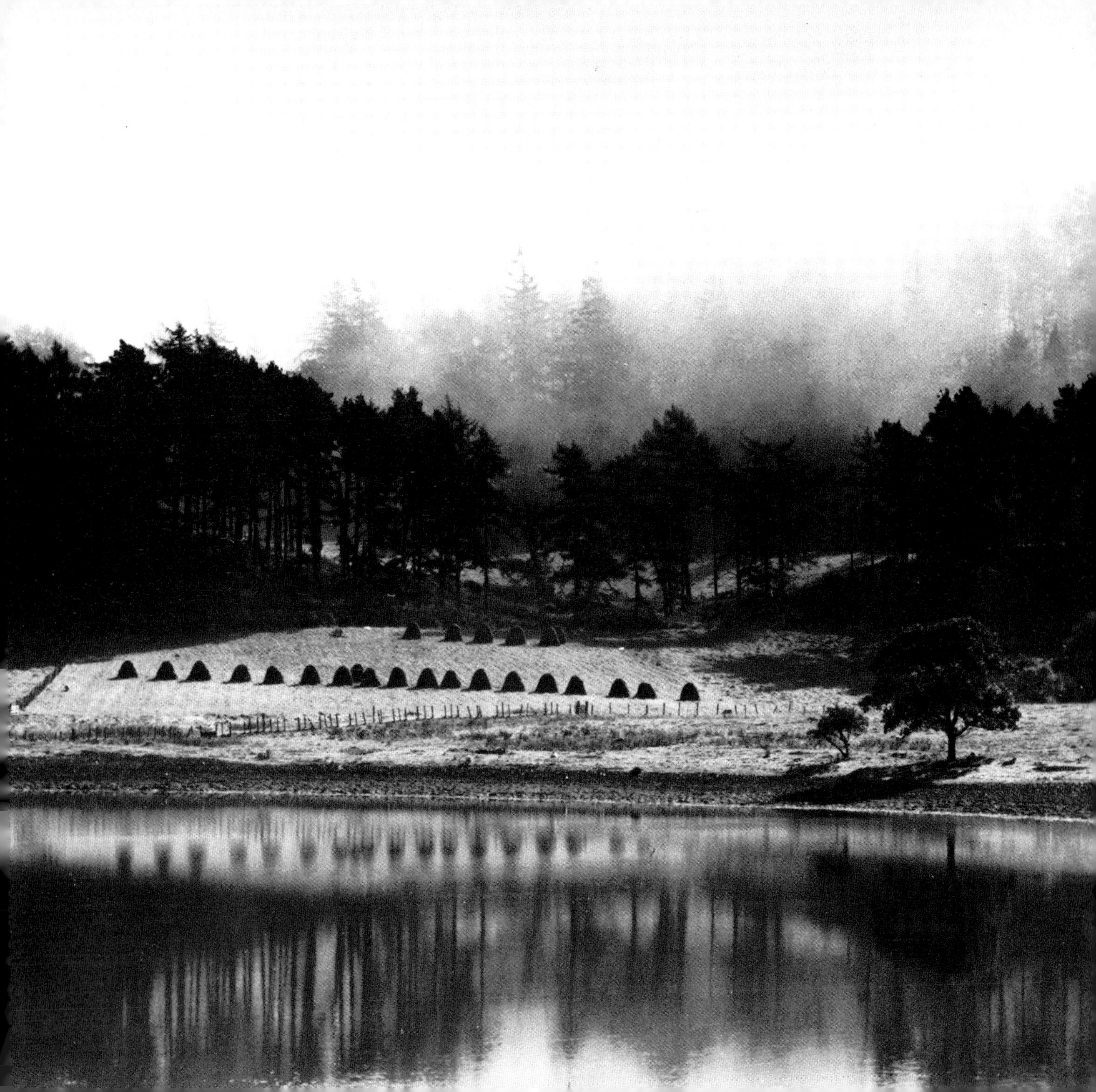

The quality of light

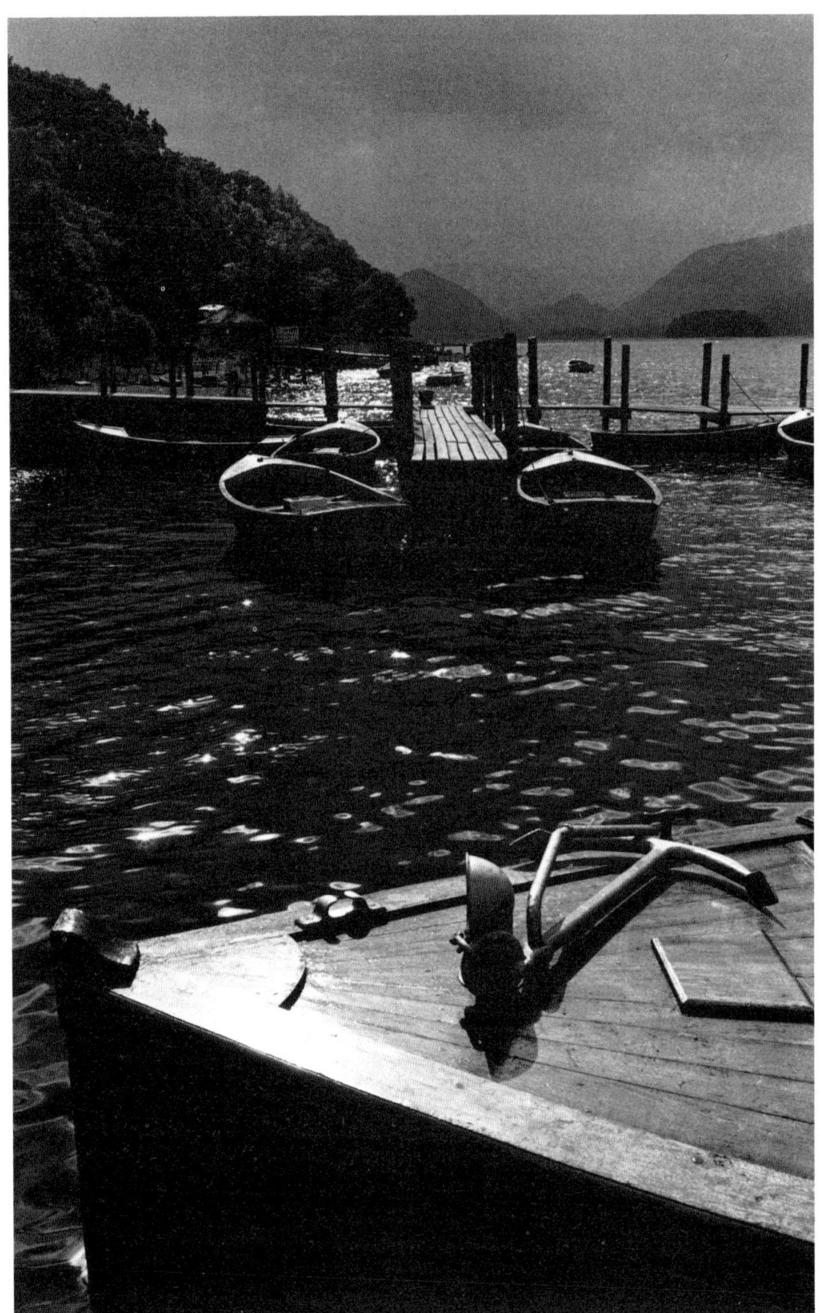

If the intensity of brightness of light was all that mattered in a photograph, direct flash would be the perfect lighting. What makes pictures unique and interesting is not the quantity but the quality of the light, and this is an infinitely variable factor. A cameraman working on location may choose to start the day at five in the morning, take a break of four hours for lunch, and resume shooting until sunset. To record a particular building, he may wait for an overcast afternoon; for another, the first rays of the sun in midsummer. Most of the time, photography has to cope with whatever light is available, within the time allowed for the session and the constraints of a normal working day. It is therefore worth looking at the course of an average day, and the kind of lighting encountered.

Dawn
First light, even in summer, follows the coldest part of the night. Dew will have formed on foliage, condensation on glass and metal. In cold weather, anything from a thin rime to thick hoar frost will cover the scene. Dawn and sunrise light changes rapidly. Just before sunrise, light tends to be comparatively blue unless the sky is clear and a red 'sunset' dawn is produced.

You will often find a combination of slight ground mist with high cirrus or stratus clouds. The effect is to turn a highly-directional low sunlight into a more diffused overall light, filling in shadows. If there is frost, the light, open effect is greater. Dawn light is ideal for photographing open landscapes, city roofscapes, and churches (because of orientation towards the east, and sunrise). The mist often lies in pools where the ground is low, and valley landscapes seen from higher vantage points looking east, north-east or south-east can be highly effective.

Cars, metal consumer goods, and anything with a
shiny or lustrous surface can be photographed on
the west shore of a lake or wide river, or east coast
of a country, at dawn. The quality of light from the
sky produces optimum surface sheen and
reflections in polished and painted surfaces.
Fashion and figure shots can also be taken using
this location/orientation, looking eastwards, but
for human reasons it may be easier to use sunset
and dusk light on with a west-facing shot, as
explained later.

Morning
During the first two hours after sunrise, the light
changes rapidly. The sun may disperse haze or mist
(in warmer months) or produce it (by evaporating
frost in colder months). In late summer, the clarity
of the air is likely to be best at around this time.

Slight rising steam from wet roads, rivers and
ponds can be very effective. When it has rained
overnight, the scene will not have dried out fully,
and the light will catch shiny wet foliage or reflect
off wet streets which are normally matt and dull.
Aerial perspective is produced by haze. Detail may
still be visible, perfectly clearly, but the scene
appears progressively lighter with increasing
distance. This is a valuable clue to the third
dimension in two-dimensional photographs and
video.

At this time of day, the colour temperature of the
light changes from a vivid warm golden yellow to a
warmish neutral. Skin tones photographed in
morning light look very smooth, aided by the fact
that skin tightens overnight and faces look better in
the morning. The sky is rarely a very deep blue until
later in the day, and this means that shadows do
not have the blue tinge produced by 'open skylight'.

Morning light, from an hour after sunrise, is
generally considered to be ideal photographic light.
It is standard professional practice when on
location to find the time of sunrise, and get up and

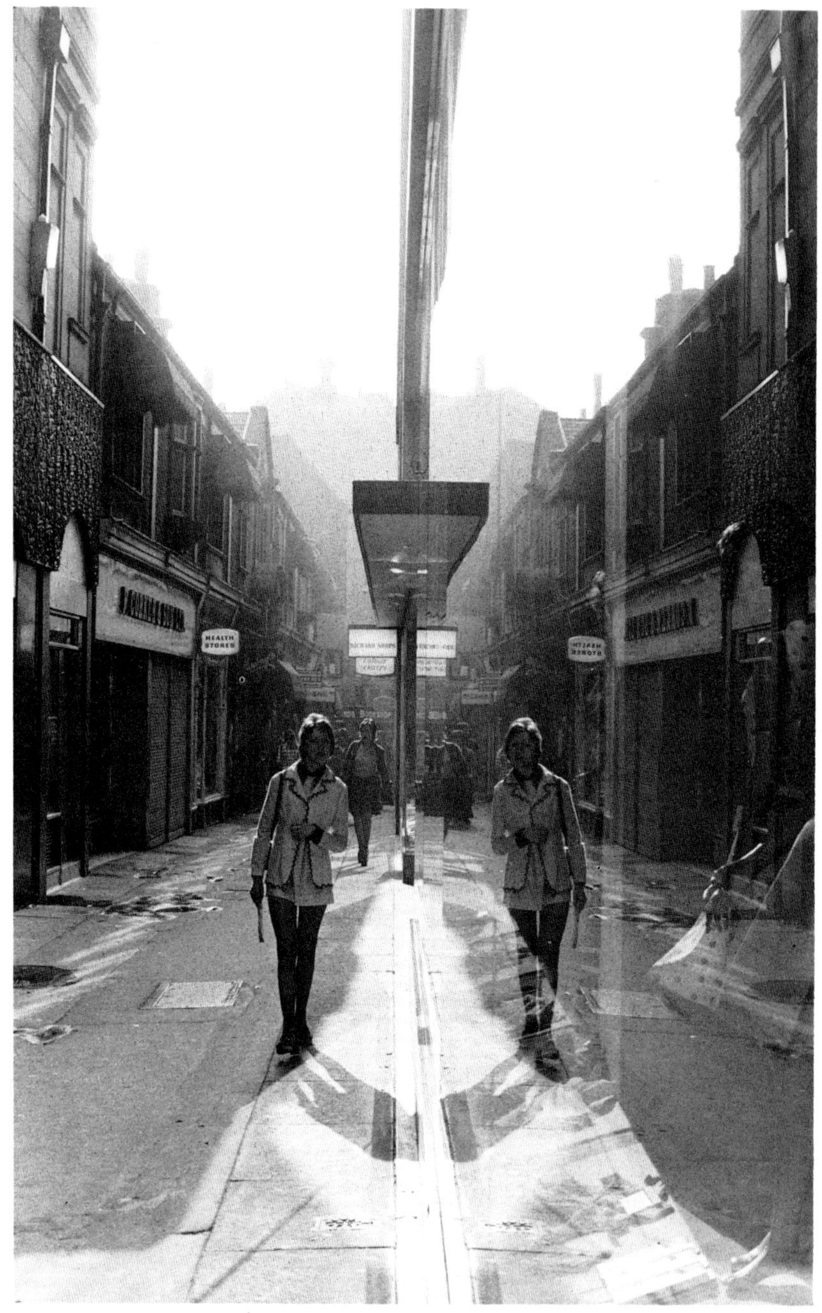

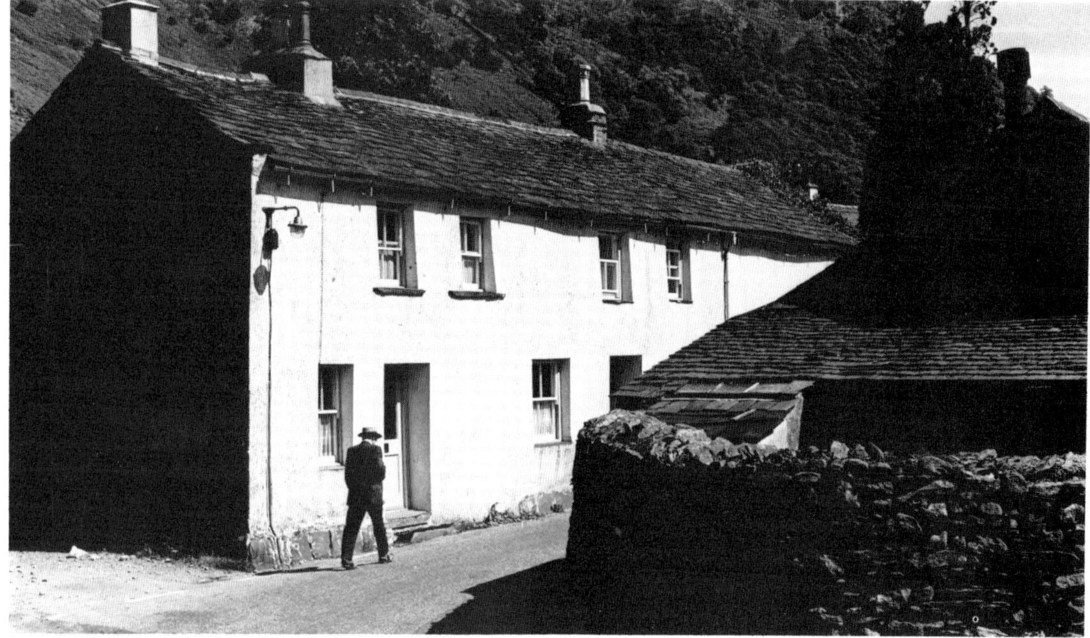

prepared well before dawn. Weather forecasts are of little value anywhere in the world, when exact photographic conditions are in question, and the only way to be sure of getting the best light is to be there for the whole period of daytime. There are other good reasons for being up and around during the morning light period. You may get a fair idea of how the weather is going, and you will be able to see from the angle of the sun what times of day may be ideal for certain shots.

Midday

How long 'good light' lasts depends on the time of year and the latitude; in the far north, where the sun never sets but does not rise far above the horizon, this kind of light is available all day and most of the night. In temperate latitudes (45°) the period of good light remains fairly constant in terms of hours, but the position of the sun changes. In winter, the sun may be low all day, with a period of four hours in the middle of the day which gives the best brightness. In summer, there may still be

four ideal hours – two hours morning and two hours afternoon, with a 'dead' period in the middle.

Midday sun only causes serious problems, making almost unusable light, in tropical and equatorial locations. Heat is partly to blame, and the nature of roads, landscapes and buildings designed to withstand heat; white or sandy in colour, reflecting light and heat together. The flat, featureless glare from overhead sun kills pictures. Large expanses of very deep blue sky do not help, because shadows become very blue and open shade, keeping out of the sun, may give a strong 'cold' colour cast. As the sun passes through its highest point, things begin to change which may affect conditions later on. The temperature will remain high for an hour or so after, as it depends on cumulative action, but will then begin to drop.

Rapid cloud formation, a dull aerial haze and sudden changes of wind to bring in sea-borne mist

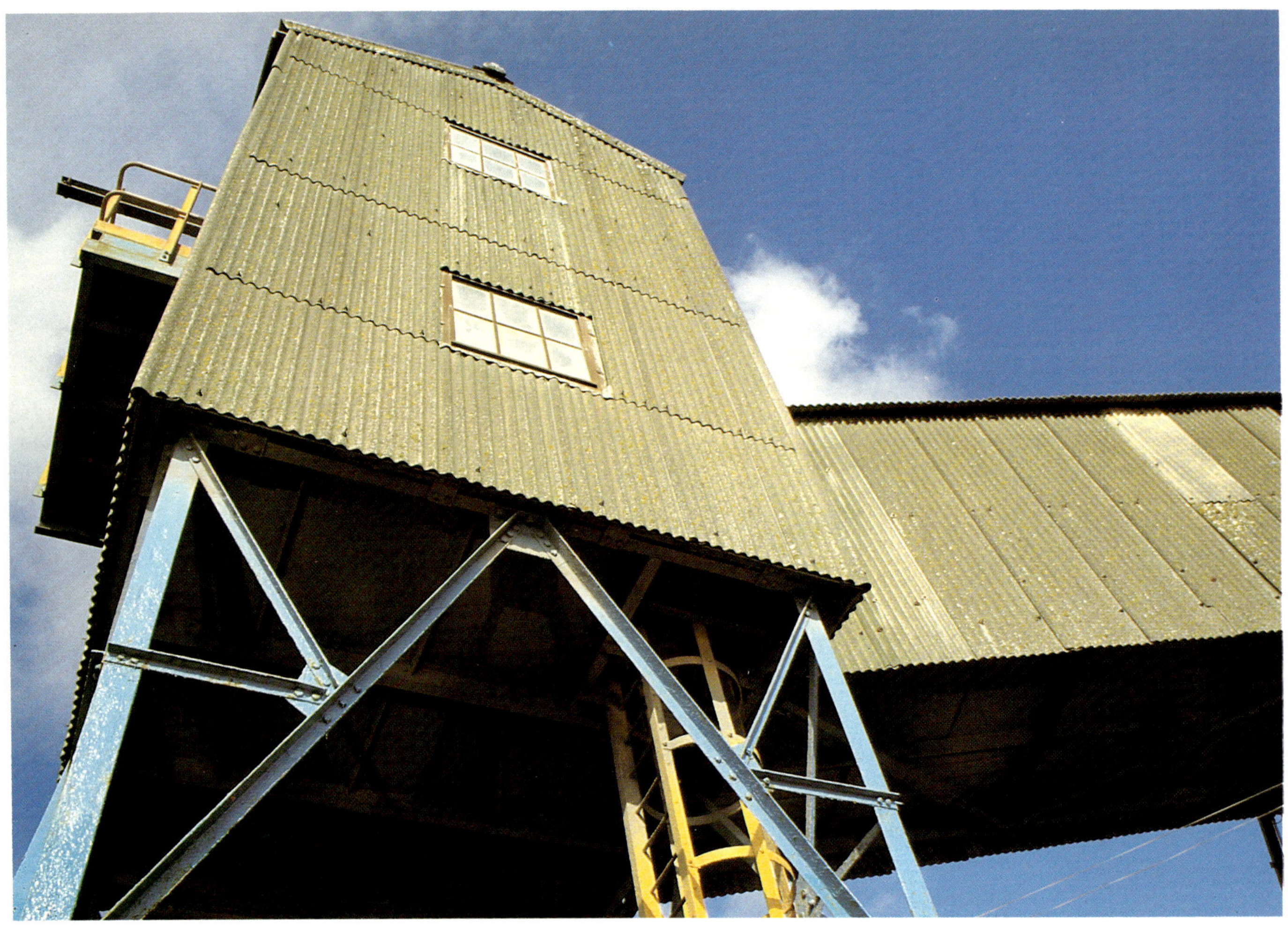

may be a predictable pattern. You will find this in mediterranean countries with a mistral or scirocco; the wind, mist and cloud hit the land-mass with absolute certainty and regularity during periods of several weeks at a time. In travel brochures it is traditional to have a totally clear blue sky, and the puffy white clouds of pictorial photographic merit have no place. The best locations are often south-facing shorelines; the best view of the hotel is often from the beach, looking north. To get the right number of holidaymakers on the beach, an

afternoon rather than morning shot may be needed; but afternoon brings clouds to the sky over the land behind the hotels.

This kind of situation is one which you can come to recognise and spot in advance, knowing that morning may be the *only* time that skies are clear, and late morning the only time with the sun facing the hotels and enough people visibly sunbathing. When photographers say they dislike midday light they usually mean the two hours after midday, for

Afternoon sunshine gives clarity without harshness, and is often considered ideal for colour photography.

26

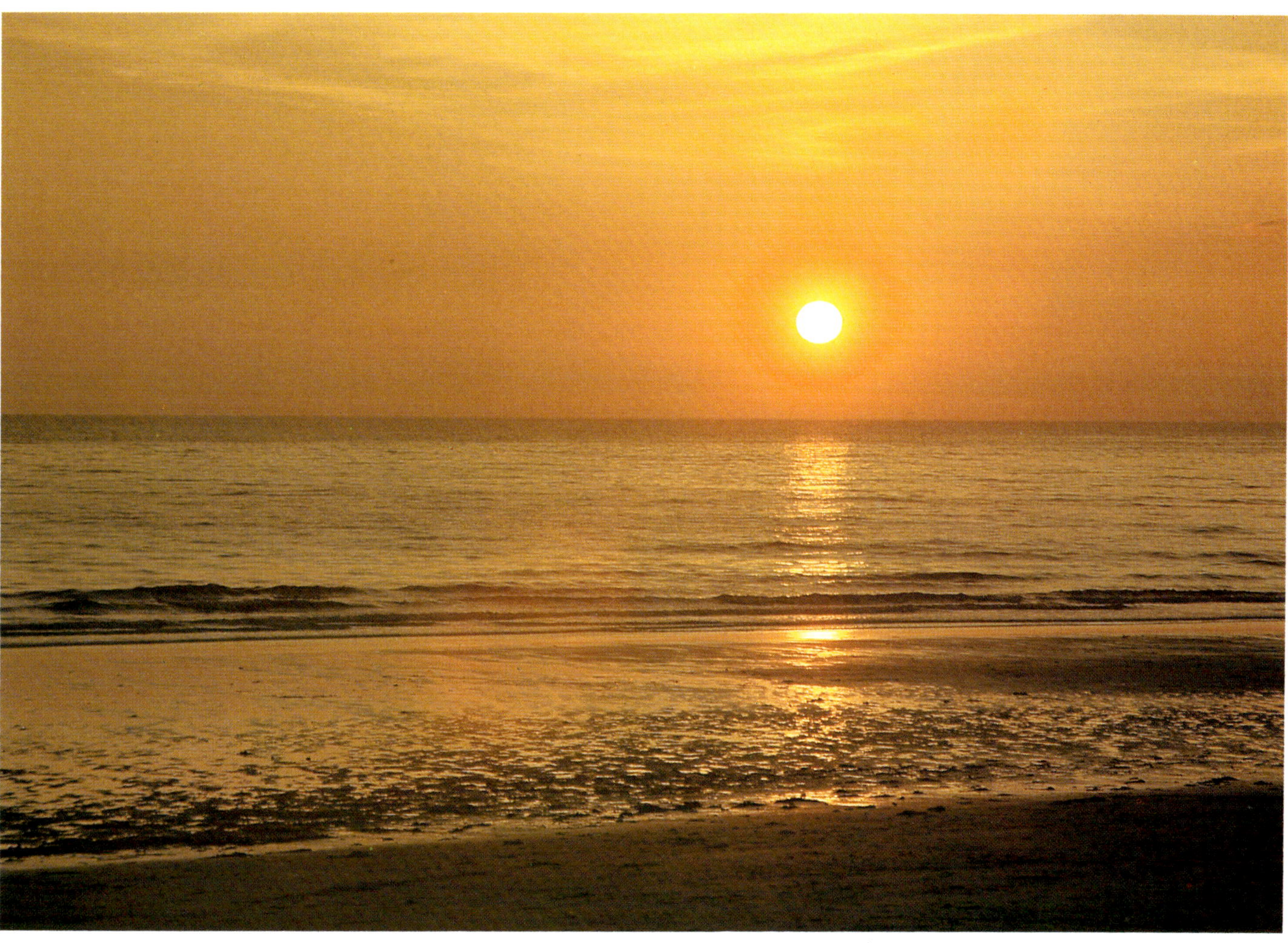

Sunsets fill the sky with warm colours from the yellow, orange and red zones of the spectrum. *Shirley Kilpatrick.*

this kind of reason. An early start and a late lunch both extend usable daylight.

Afternoon and evening

Because moisture is taken from the ground or water into the air if it gets warmer during the day, things happen to the colour of light in the afternoon which do not always happen in the morning. Warm air can hold a higher humidity. As it cools, with the sun dropping lower, the air can no longer hold the moisture. It condenses out, in the form of invisible droplets so small that they remain suspended. When there is a sudden drop in temperature, this produces fog or mist, typically over sea.

Most of the time, the mist is so thin that it forms little more than a slight haze. This can 'flatten' the light, making a summer afternoon seem grey or dull despite bright sun. In a photograph, this compresses the tones and colours giving a result best described as leaden. Things improve as the sun gets lower because it begins to strike through the thin haze, turning into layers of aerial perspective. The haze tends to trap dirt particles and holds these, too. City air on summer afternoons can be literally grey. View a small town from an aircraft and you may see a pall of thin bluish haze surrounding it. Apart from the effect on light quality, this can mean losing half a stop in exposure terms.

Moisture and dirt also scatter light-rays. When the sun is high, they scatter blue wavelengths and absorb red, so that the colour temperature becomes higher than normal. The cold, metallic blueness produced rarely looks good in the final image.

This is only a part-explanation of the difference between morning light and afternoon light. There are other things far more subtle, such as the typical orientation of architecture in different places. People on an east coast tend to build houses overlooking the sea, and the late afternoon sun does not fall on their facades; on a west coast, the reverse applies. Gardens are arranged to catch the sun in certain ways; plants and trees reach their final shapes partly because of the pattern of sunlight. On balance, morning light gives better results than afternoon light for many reasons including these, unless there are special circumstances such as a west coast location.

Sunset and dusk

Sunsets work because the low angle of the sun lets the atmosphere refract and reflect short wavelengths (blue), while longer wavelengths (red) can penetrate. Haze, which earlier in the day absorbed some of the red but scattered and emphasised blue, now receives very little blue light to scatter, and is penetrated by comparatively strong red. The upper sky, lit from a different angle, remains blue. The result ranges from smooth gradation to dramatic patterns.

Sunsets are a subject as well as a light source, but here we will look only at the quality of light they produce. Early on, when the sun is filtered through thin cloud or haze, it will become progressively warmer in colour (technically, a lower colour temperature). Most photographers accept this as a welcome atmospheric clue, giving pictures a sense of time as well as more colour interest. If necessary it can be corrected by placing a blue filter over the lens.

Just before sunset on a very clear evening, the sun may cast positively red rays, colouring everything a distinct pink. This tinge will only affect the side of the subject facing the sun, and unless there are heavy clouds above, the rest of the detail will be more or less normally lit. This is because the sun, as it sets, becomes a relatively low-power concentrated light source competing with a big, open sky. The sky, often pale blue, contributes three-quarters of the light to the subject. Facing the sun, the shadow side of silhouetted elements like figures or trees may be intensely black, far more so than normally, as the sky opposite the sun is fairly dark. The brightest sky area will be between the sun, and vertically overhead. If you had to create this type of light in a studio, you would need elaborate light-tents, filters, and a spotlight. The result is a very beautiful light, similar to dawn, but normally lasting longer and more frequently met, without early-rising problems.

The contrast between the warm light from low down the sky and the cool blue light from above creates subtle gradations of colour on any three-dimensional subject. Taken a step further, sunsets over sand, snow or sea are even more effective because the light is reflected and enhanced. West coast, west-facing locations are normally chosen for automobile photography at sunset or just after.

Dusk

Dusk light, after the sun has disappeared, starts off with a similar colour to midday sunlight but rapidly becomes very blue. It is around this time that

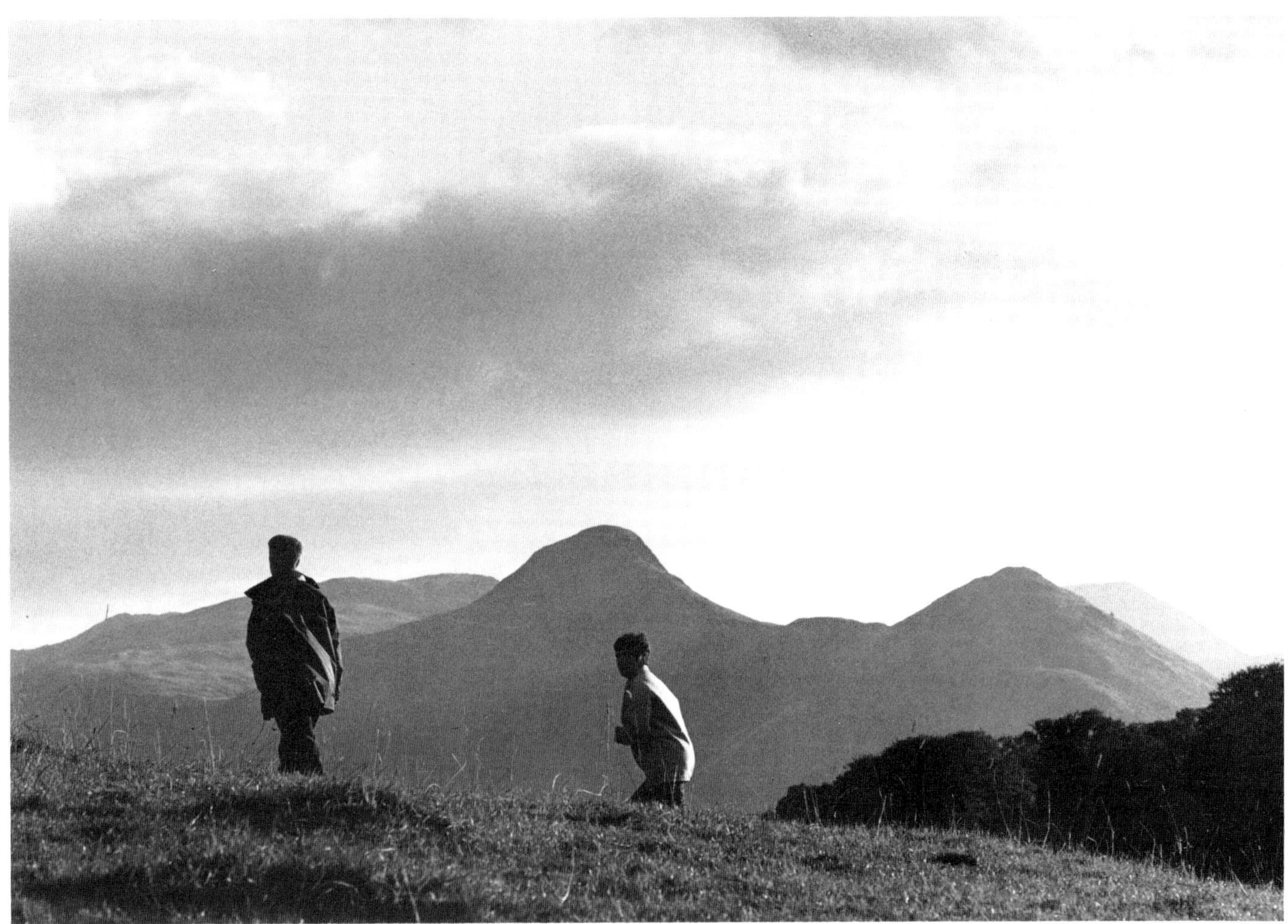

residual red clouds, lit by the sun after it has set, are likely to stand out in the strongest possible colour contrast. Over sea, the whole western half of the sky may diffuse yellow-red light, and then dusk stays very warm until the afterglow fades. Our eyes begin to lose colour sensitivity as dusk deepens, and pictures shot at this time may show greater saturation than you think exists visually. Street lights, lit-up shops, fires and fireworks balance perfectly with dusk light and look much better at this time than they do in total darkness.

Twilight

Before nightfall, you may still be able to take a meter reading although you see everything looking very grey. The camera will show colour, just as on a dull day. Video cameras may show poor colour, with a coarser image.

Moonlight

To create the effect of a moonlit picture, a blue filter is combined with underexposure. This is because the result corresponds to our visual

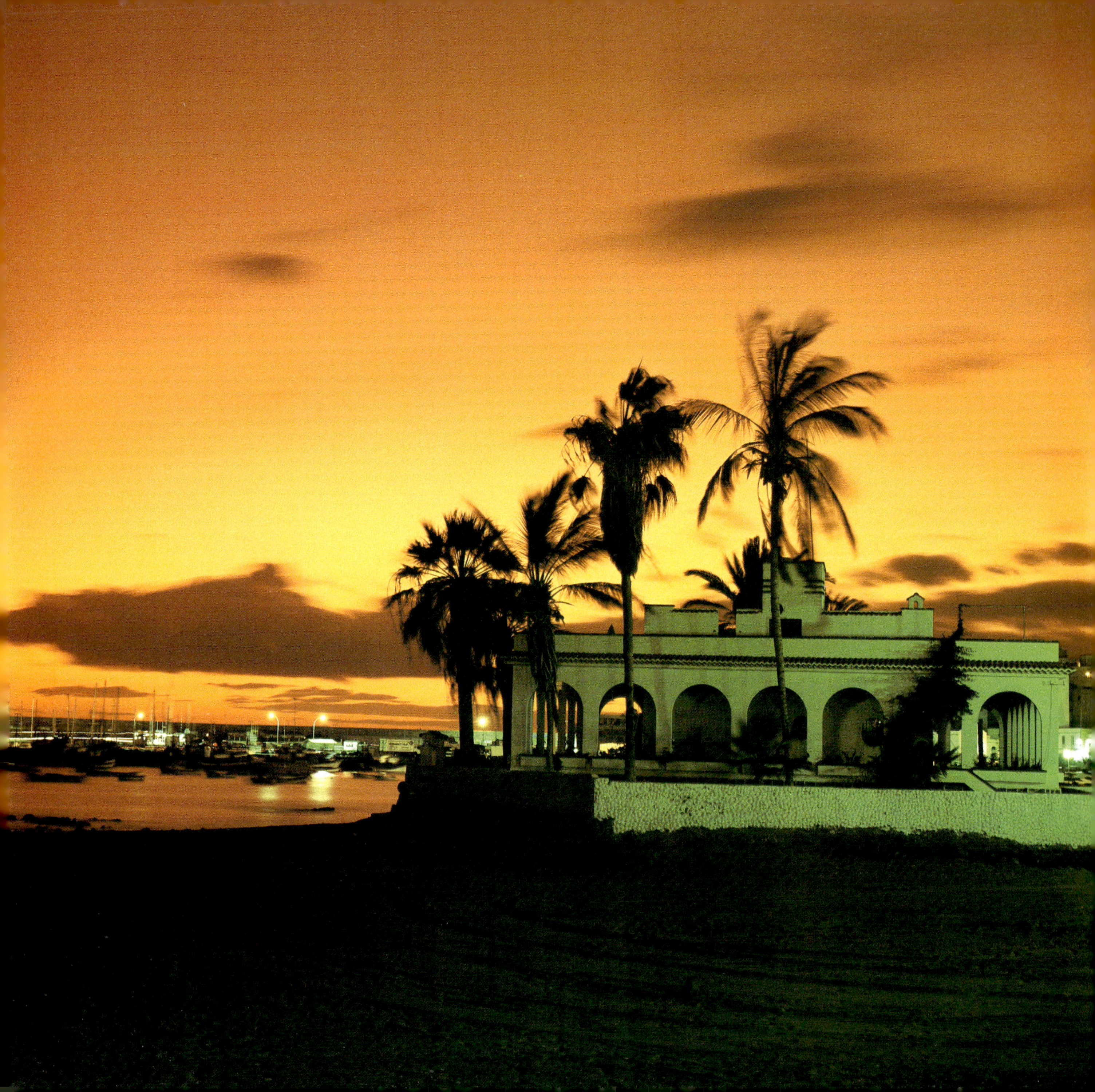

experience, which tells us moonlight is 'blue' and 'dark'. If you take a colour photograph using moonlight, and giving the correct full exposure, it will have the same colours and tones as a daylight shot. Moonlight is merely reflected sunlight, and it is human eyesight which produces the 'blue' cast, not the light itself. Exposures need to be in the order of 20 minutes to several hours for still pictures, and during such a period the moon itself moves significantly. You should not include the moon in any picture where the exposure is likely to exceed a minute, and when shooting the moon as a subject on its own, an action-stopping shutter speed is needed.

The movement of the light source produces a totally new effect, with soft-edged shadows, as if a large striplight was suspended in the sky. As the exposure times are so long, bracketing them to have some choice of final result is impossible except on successive nights or with several cameras, so few people tackle moonlight photography.

Night
Night without moonlight is effectively without light, though some exists. Photography is impractical and video or film are impossible.

Other factors
We have looked at haze and its effect, but physical surroundings have even more influence on the final subject lighting.

Reflective surroundings like pale sand, snow, whitewashed walls, sea or pale rocks reduce overall contrast and lessen the depth of shadows. Where the reflective surfaces have a colour (e.g. a pale-pink building), a cast is introduced. Some of the most attractive lighting is created when direct sunlight strikes a light-coloured wall, and the subject is positioned in shade to catch the reflected light.

Dark surroundings absorb light. They increase

contrast, and deepen shadows. They also lower the total level of light. In some circumstances the boost to the directional quality of light is enough to change an 'overcast' feel to a 'soft sun' feel, when the light reaches the subject from a small area of cloudy sky. Black panels are used in some outdoor lighting systems to control light using a 'subtractive' principle; starting with overall diffused light, the panels absorb selectively and create carefully controlled directional light. By combining reflecting and absorbing surfaces, both natural and purpose-built portable ones, you can exercise local control over the light quality outdoors. The size of area you can affect, and therefore the size of subject, is determined by the size of the reflecting and absorbing panels available.

Lighting contrast
One of the reasons why generally reflective surroundings, such as the whitewashed streets of Mediterranean villages, create good pictures is that overall lighting contrast is reduced. Bright, direct sun, which would produce very harsh results in other locations, can be used. Most films are capable of recording full detail in shadows when the level of the light in the shadow area is not less than a tenth of the level reaching the fully-lit areas. Video systems can be adjusted to record greater ratios accurately, and monochrome film processed individually can be made to 'hold detail' despite high contrast.

It is simple to take close-up exposure readings from the same surface in both areas, and compare them. You can use your hand or sleeve, as the actual reading does not matter. If the reading in the shadows is more than three exposure steps (stops or shutter speeds) less than the reading in full light, use reflectors or re-position the subject close to a reflective surface. A difference of four steps will still produce satisfactory pictures, but once five steps' difference is recorded, the result will inevitably consist of deep black shadows without detail when the fully-lit areas are correctly recorded. The

alternative is to expose to record detail in the
shadows and allow the highlights to become
burned-out, an effect most viewers find unpleasant.

Enclosed and open locations

It is wrong to assume that by working in very open,
unrestricted locations the lighting will be even or
low in contrast. The impression of 'airiness' you
feel is due more to open air, and visual perspectives,
than to light quality.

Where there are no vertical surfaces or natural
reflectors, the quality of the light is determined by
the sun and sky. In open moorland, direct sun can
be extremely contrasty. The ground is dark and acts
as a large absorbing surface. On an overcast day,
the light becomes top-heavy and gives an
unpleasant quality to shadows round the eyes and
under the chin. Any three-dimensional subject will
be badly lit; the topside of a rock will be bright and
the underside devoid of detail, and the same would
apply to a vehicle.

In an enclosed location, even without obvious
natural reflectors, a relatively greater degree of
fill-in from randomly-bounced and scattered light
will improve things. The quality of light on a dull
day in the streets of a town with plenty of
light-coloured paintwork, large shop windows and
light road surfaces can be much more even than the
light on the same day in open fields. On the other
hand, a very dark enclosed location may suffer
from the reverse effect; light entering a dense pine
wood through a gap in the trees may reach the
subject directly, but the shadows receive no
reflected fill-in whatsoever. Contrast then becomes
unmanageable.

Recognising natural effects

It should be clear by now that the possible results of
natural conditions and locations are infinitely
variable. Combined with changes in weather, time
of year, camera techniques, materials and subjects,
you have a vast range of possibilities. There are

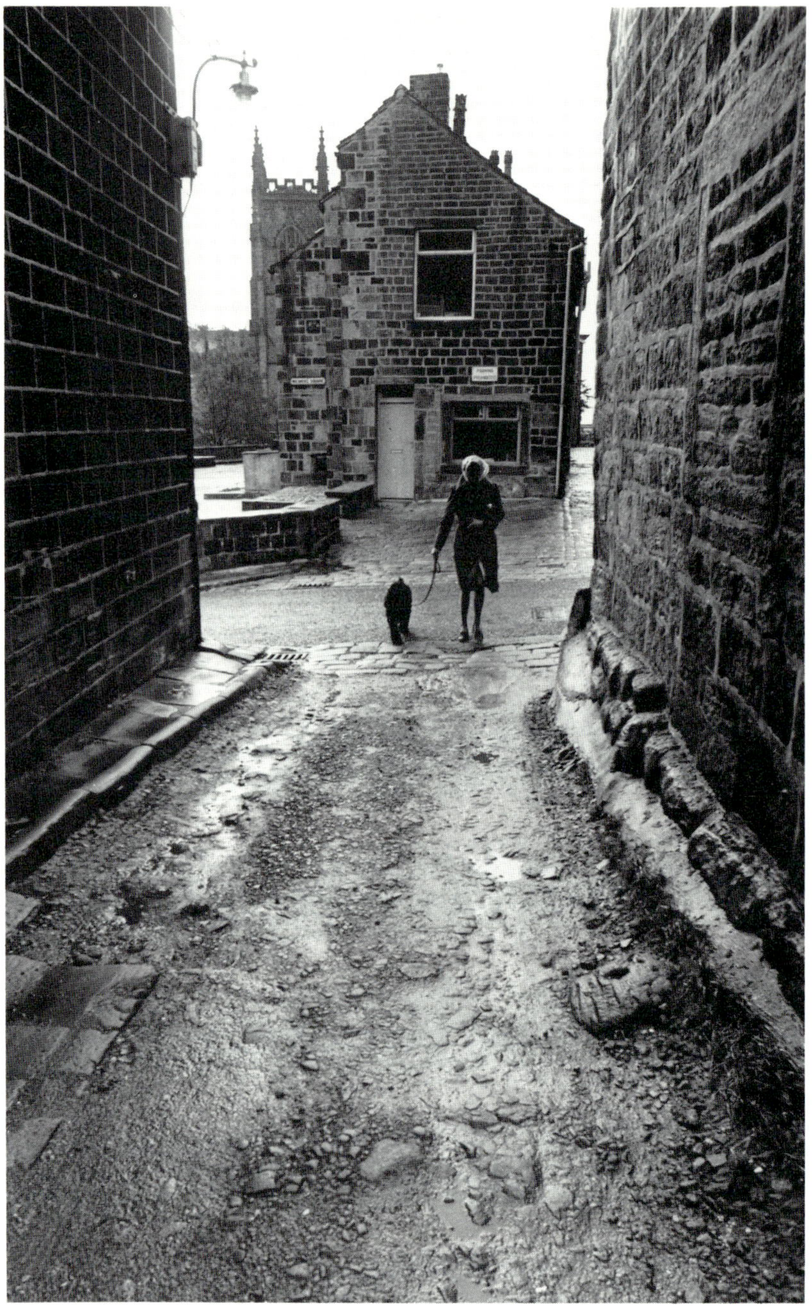

some general situations with which any competent camera user should be familiar. The most obvious ones are the great natural reflectors, which can change the whole contrast and directional quality of daylight. These are sand, snow, water, and clouds.

Sand (in its white to yellow varieties) is a diffused, low-efficiency reflector. It fills in directional shading from any kind of overhead light, and at the same time it imparts a warm colour-cast to the reflected light. This can be useful when the light tends towards coldness (blue).

Snow is the most efficient neutral natural reflector, and gives no colour cast. As a result, blue skylight reflected from it may make an entire picture excessively blue. This can be corrected by using filters or adjusting colour recording or printing settings later on.

Water only acts as a reflector when light strikes it at 42° or less, and then only when the water surface is between the light and the subject. Given these conditions, it reflects with efficiency like a mirror when smooth; any surface disturbance changes the quality of reflected light.

Clouds, normally acting as vast diffusers in the sky, become reflectors whenever they present a vertical surface to the sun. As a cloud is often a deep structure, like an iceberg, this happens frequently; large white cumulus clouds look white because they are being lit by the sun, and not because the sunlight passes through them. They are, like snow, neutral reflectors. Their effect is often to neutralise excess blue, because they reflect sunlight rather than the blue sky light. A sky with a squadron of large white clouds and brilliant sun gives generally excellent colour and contrast.

Natural absorbers are less easily recognised. There are none in the sky! Water can act as an absorbing surface when on the other side of the subject from the main light direction. Dark earth is the most obvious absorber, closely followed by coniferous foliage and dark-coloured rocks. There are few very dark man-made structures, but soot-blackened alleys or creosoted wooden buildings are examples.

Light quality: the source
There are four basic conditions apart from direct sunlight, which a non-photographer will simply call 'dull'. This is far from true. They are sky light, overcast light, diffused sun and directional overcast light. In combination with other environmental factors, all will produce pictures of a different lighting quality.

Sky light is 'dull light' produced when the sun, in an otherwise mainly blue sky, passes behind a dense cloud. The light will be very blue in colour, and is normally totally diffused. In these conditions subjects look very two-dimensional, and lack modelling or plasticity. For film and video users, there is the major disadvantage that sky light of this type is prone to change suddenly to full sun as the cloud passes. Therefore it is rarely used deliberately.

Overcast light results from a totally grey, even sky, when it is impossible to tell where the sun itself is. Without the blueness of sky light, results may be better. Slight variations in the cloud layer can give a hint of directional quality and better dimensional rendering. The light level in totally overcast weather is always low.

Diffused sun resembles overcast lighting, in that no shadows are cast, but the sun is clearly visible and there is a strong bright patch; overall light is likely to be fairly warm in colour, and bright. The plasticity and modelling on all subjects is greatly improved, and this can be the ideal kind of light for outdoor portraits. Diffused sun may be caused by cloud or mist. In the case of cloud, it only occurs during the middle of the day, as the sun has to pass obliquely through the thin cloud layer when low and the extra-effective thickness of cloud absorbs

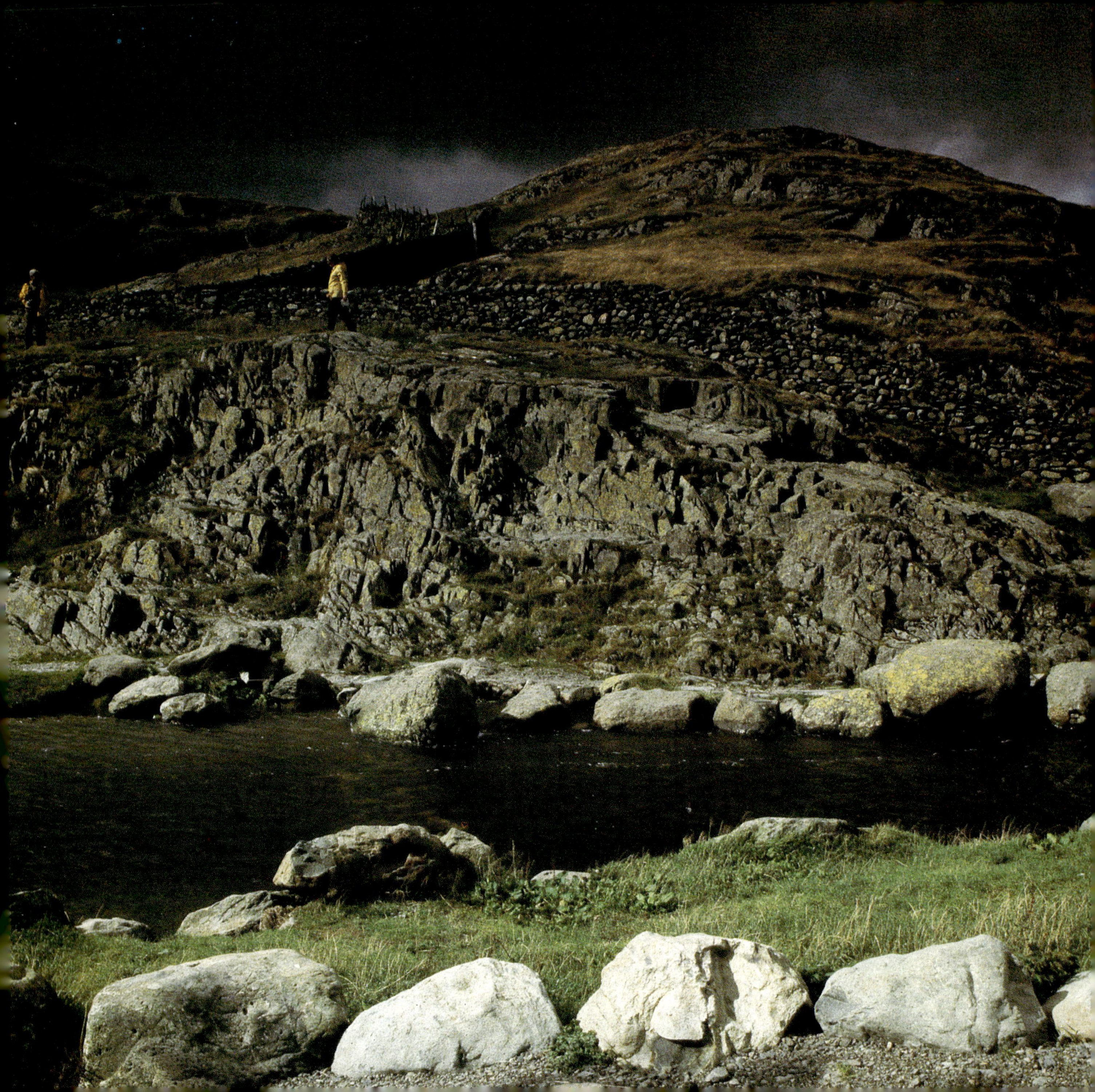

After rain, with storm clouds still masking the sky, fresh sunshine can create extrmely vivid colours. Locations like Watendlath in the English Lake District often have conditions like this.

the light. Mist can produce diffused sun (in contrast) at dawn and dusk, and only rarely persists through the whole day.

Directional overcast light is different, and unpredictable. It happens when the cloud layer is so irregular that large areas appear brilliantly lit through gaps in lower clouds, and some parts are almost black where layer upon layer blocks the light. Thundery weather, high winds and storms produce conditions like this. You can also find them on coastal areas where the prevailing wind off the sea hits the land, and creates banks of changing clouds. Because directional overcast light can come from almost any angle, in any combination, and may be combined with steel-grey skies or occasional shafts of sun (not to mention rainbows and distant showers) the possibilities for camerawork are endless.

Other conditions
In addition to the topography and weather outdoors, the physical state of the subject can affect the final image. After rain, when everything is still wet, contrast is greatly increased and colour may seem to be enhanced. In summer, a layer of dust or sand may have settled undisturbed for weeks; this has the opposite effect, reducing everything to flat monochrome. You should now understand why photographic and film crews travel to specific locations and avoid others. They have learned, from experience, where to find the elusive combinations which create well-lit pictures. There are others they avoid. This also applies to times of year. It is not possible to give a full guide to all possibilities, but here are some examples.

The west coasts of Europe, Scandinavia, Britain and the USA are considered excellent locations at almost any time of year for climatic, geographical and orientation reasons (the sun sets over a west coast sea, but rises over an east coast beach – simple logistics make it better to be up and around to catch an unexpected sunset than to anticipate an uncertain dawn). Florida and the Mediterranean are considered unusable for photography in the heat of midsummer (July and August) because the humidity, heat and haze destroy quality despite sun.

Scotland, part of Canada, Alpine and inland Scandinavian locations are exceptional in spring and autumn, where rapidly changing weather, the colour of vegetation and the clarity of the air make for unusually sharp, clear pictures. Most tropical and sub-tropical islands are at their best off-season, in spring or autumn as well as their 'winter', and should be avoided during the hot season.

All built-up areas with pollution may be prone to atmospheric inversion during the most interesting clear, sunny days in winter. This holds the smoke layer down and cuts light considerably, destroying the clarity and colour of city views.

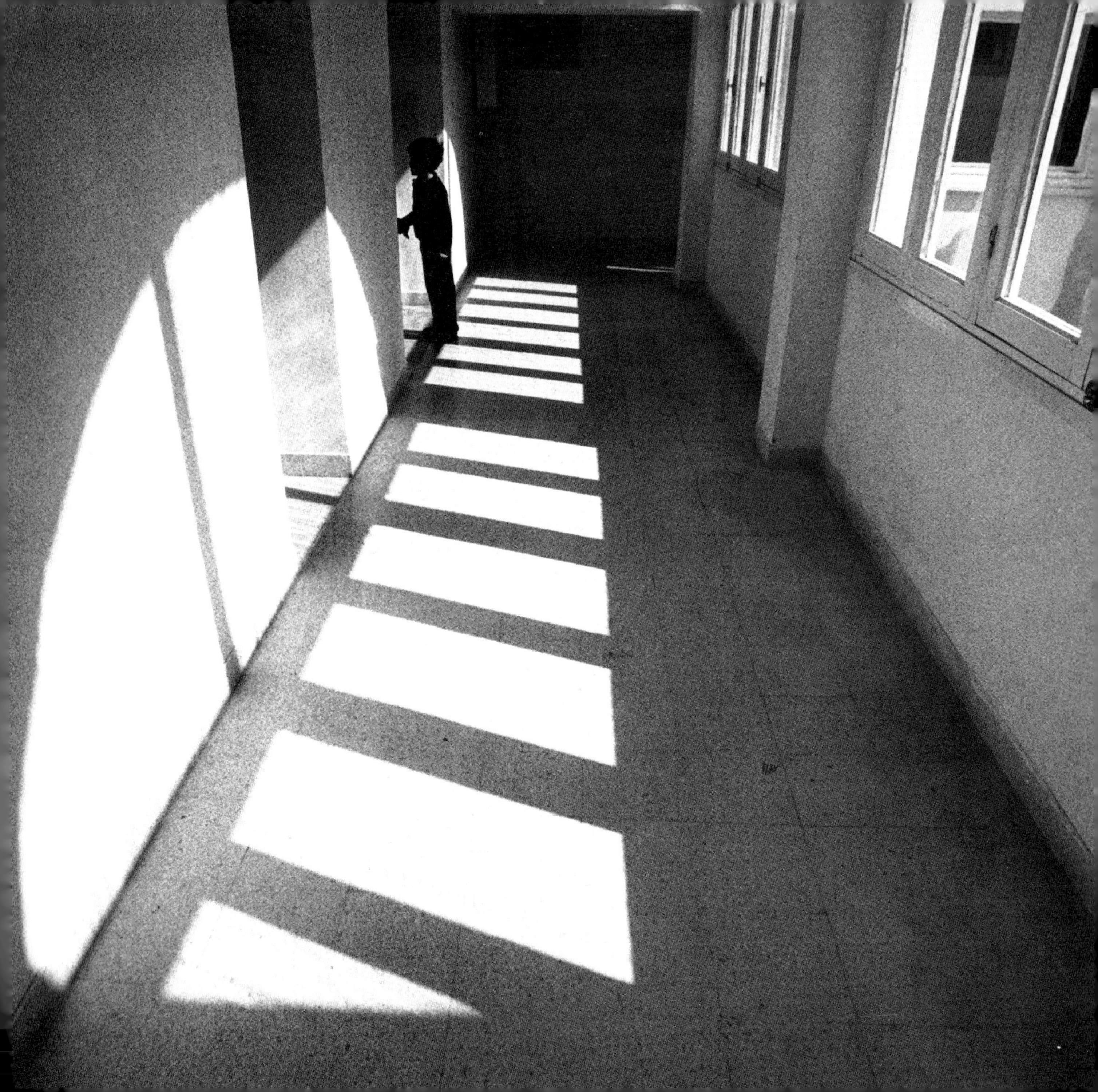

The effect of light

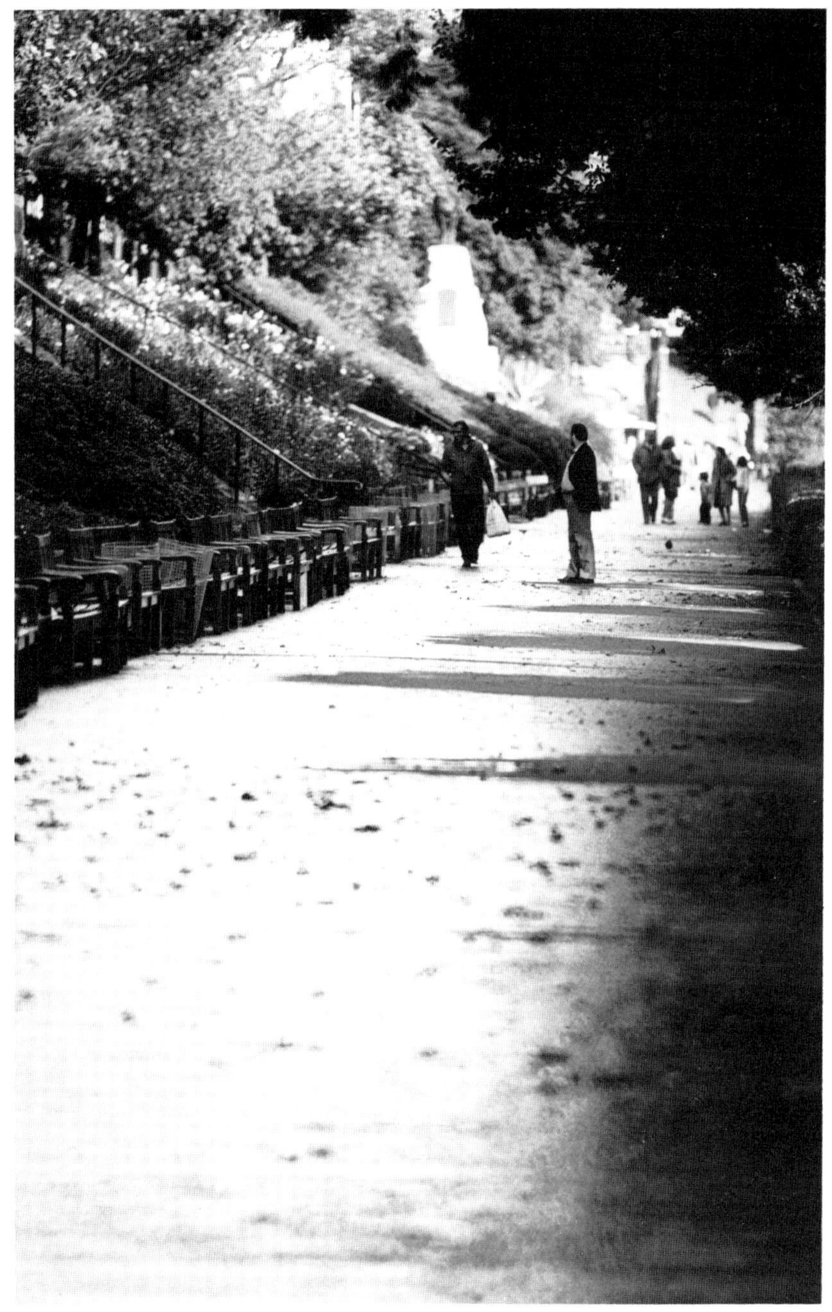

The final image cannot be a result of light alone, as light itself has no shape or form. Nor can it be an image of the subject without light, because without light (visible or otherwise) the camera system cannot record the subject. The image is a result of subject and light together, inextricably linked. The image is a result of the effect the subject has on light, rather than vice-versa. If a red light shines on a blue card, most people say 'look, the card has turned black', or 'the red light makes the card look black'. The assumption is that light has an effect on the subject.

The true story is that the subject has altered the light. Its colour remains blue, and is unchanged. Blue absorbs red wavelengths, and reflects little of the light falling on it, thus reducing the level of light leaving the subject compared with the amount reaching it. The subject affects the light, although our eyes assume that the light has altered the appearance of the subject.

The red light and blue card are extremes. Real subjects and scenes are complex mixtures of physical properties. Light is absorbed, reflected and transmitted variously by every different part of the picture. The human face is a simple example, and even that combines translucence, specular (sheen) reflectivity, normal reflection, and absorption.

Taking the possible qualities of subjects, we are confronted with a vast range of distinctions. If a subject reflects light, it can do so in any number of ways. Straightforward reflection (random reflection) is responsible for every image we see. All the light not absorbed by the subject is reflected by it, in every direction. A housebrick lit by a spotlight can be seen just as well from 60° to either side of the light as it can from directly beside the light. The light falling on the brick, from one direction alone, is reflected off in every direction.

Whenever a smooth surface occurs, some light may be reflected at an angle equal to its angle of incidence, with only a small amount of scatter. The surface must be smooth enough for a significant number of rays to hit identically orientated facets of the surface. This produces a specular reflection, or sheen, which is partly polarised. This is the kind of reflection that can be reduced by viewing it through a suitably orientated polarising filter.

Specular reflection can be found on the surface of foliage, on skin, smooth rock, almost anything wet, water itself, polished wood, plastic and many other common subjects. It ranges from a slight lustre to a mirror image, faint but sharp, as seen on the surface of a still lake. It has nothing to do with colour reflection or absorption, and the reflection is the colour of the light reaching it.

The distinction between light 'reflected' naturally from a subject which will not absorb it, and reflected in the literal sense by bouncing off due to its angle of incidence, is important. No shift in viewing angle, or use of polarised light or filters, can alter the quantity or colour content of light reflected by a surface as a result of its absorption/reflection characteristics. Changes in viewpoint and polarised light or filters can have a marked effect on specular reflections and sheen, altering the apparent brightness of a subject greatly. Sheen, even when very diffused, can mask the true colour or detail of a subject, which only shows in lighting where there is no surface reflection.

Transmission qualities should also be looked at. The skin on a human face is translucent; it transmits light, in a diffused form. The exact way a face is rendered in backlight, from a side view, may be a result of this translucence as well as normal reflected light. Plastics, foliage, liquids, flowers,

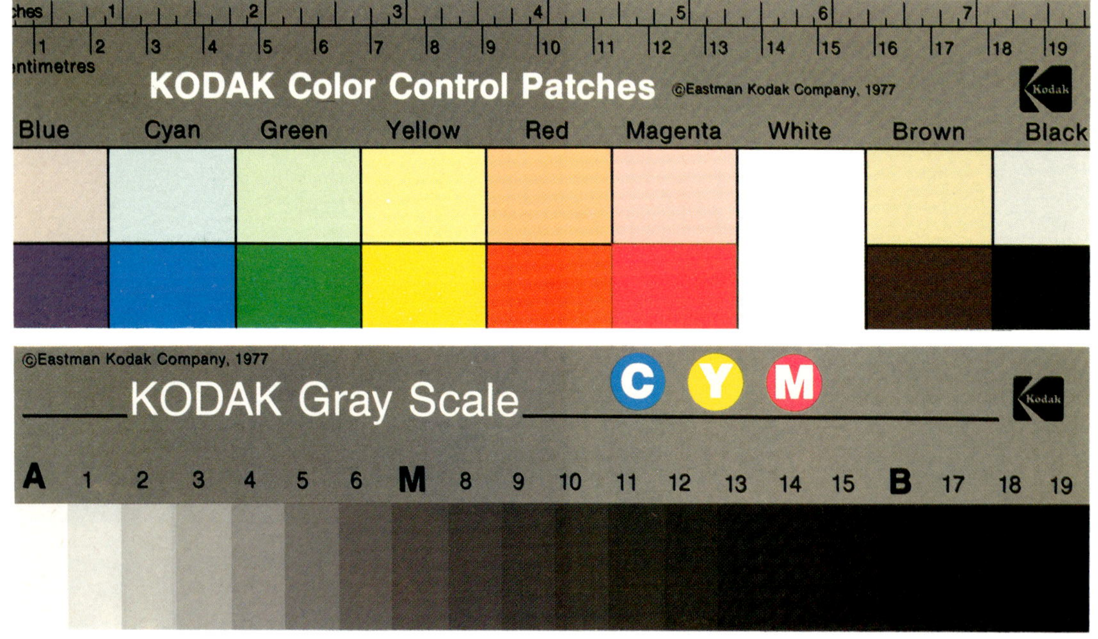

The standard Kodak Test Patches allow photographers to check both bright and pastel colour reproduction, contrast, and the effect of colour filters.

38

clothing are just a few of the many things that are translucent.

For a subject to be transparent, as opposed to translucent, the light rays must be able to pass through it and retain all or part of their original relationship. A clear image should be seen through the subject. Windows, cut glass, polythene sheet, clear water are all more or less transparent. Unlike translucent subjects, they may not become suffused with light through internal reflection and transmission at random.

The term 'opaque' does not mean absorbing all light; it may mean reflecting it all. A silvered mirror is perfectly opaque (unless designed for clandestine surveillance!). Opacity is a term referring only to the ability to block light off, either by absorbing it or turning it away.

Colour absorption

The colours we attribute to objects are a result of whatever light is reflected back off them to reach our eyes. Assuming that we start with a white light mixture, a red brick looks red because it reflects wavelengths round the red end of the spectrum. It may reflect a great deal of yellow and orange, some green, a little indigo, even some blue. But most of the blue, indigo and green will be absorbed. It is possible to measure, exactly, the colour reflection and absorption of a surface. Every imaginable colour has its spectrographic profile; every dye, every paint, every natural colour. Two colours which look almost identical to the eye might well have radically different profiles.

Pure or bright colours are normally a result of very selective absorption and reflection. They are produced by surfaces which reflect nearly all of certain wavelengths and absorb others, usually in simple ways. *Desaturated* pastel or pale colours are less selective; they absorb a small amount of light, reflecting a wide range of wavelengths with only slight preferences. They are like the brighter colours with more white light mixed in.

Muted colours have low overall reflectance, absorbing most wavelengths, with small peaks of reflectance at others. They can be thought of as resembling the purer colours mixed with black (in pigment terms). Photographically, it is impossible to turn either a pastel or a muted colour into a bright or saturated colour. A colour with too much white light mixed in can be darkened, but will then resemble a muted, sombre shade. A colour with too much neutral density (grey) in it can be lightened, but then becomes a pastel shade. Affecting all colours, as perceived, we find specular reflection or surface sheen present in the form of glare. A pure, saturated red may appear to be a pastel pink if it happens to be polished paintwork and is catching the light. Reflection is adding the unwanted dose of white light.

Relative illumination also has a strong effect. A colour in shade looks less vivid than one in full sunlight when the two are seen side-by-side. In a picture, both can be made to look equally colourful individually by varying the exposure. Together, the operator has to choose one or the other. The reason that many coloured surfaces look less colourful on dull days is because of glare, not because of light levels. The cloudy sky is reflected, and the overall diffused light gives overall diffused sheen. Direct sun gives no sheen from many angles, or a bright glare patch when the surface is seen 'against the light'.

Colour filters

Because of the effect things have on light, the sunlight which starts off white may end up a different colour by the time it reaches the subject. The most obvious 'casts' thus produced are towards blueness (sky light, high altitudes) or yellowness (late or early daylight). Other casts may be given by surroundings. Forest light may be green. The light within a redbrick quadrangle is

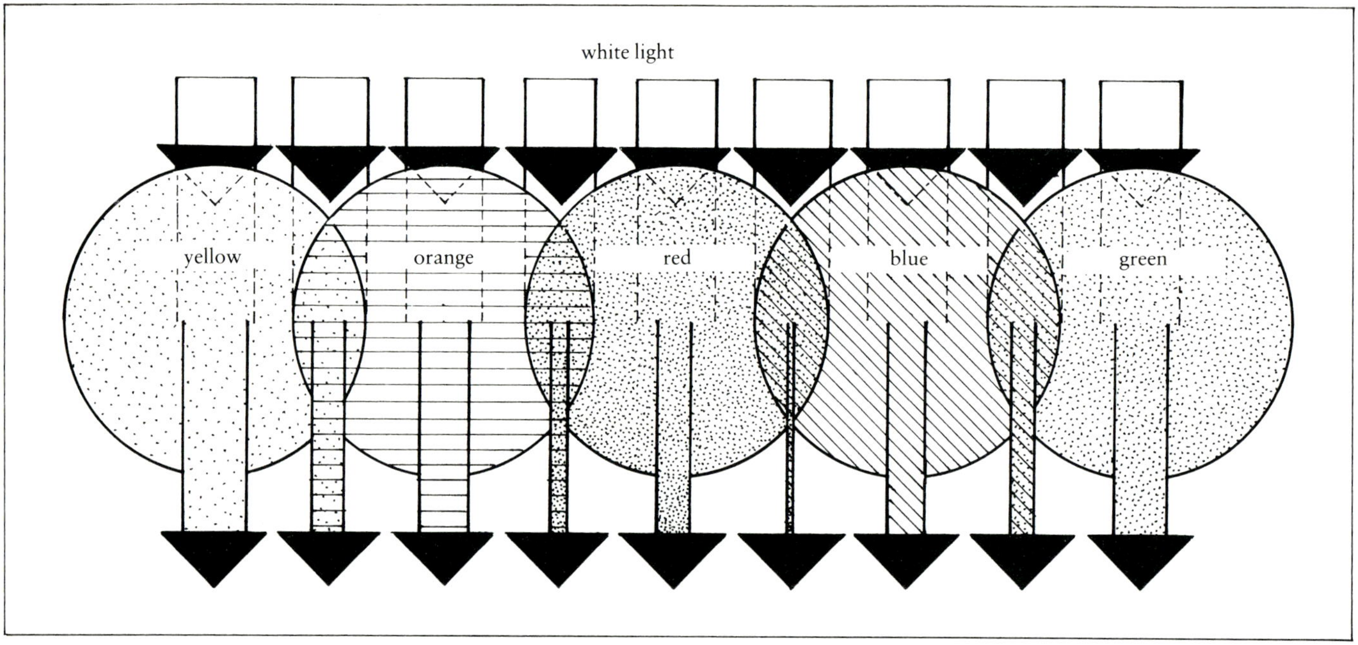

white light
yellow
orange
red
blue
green

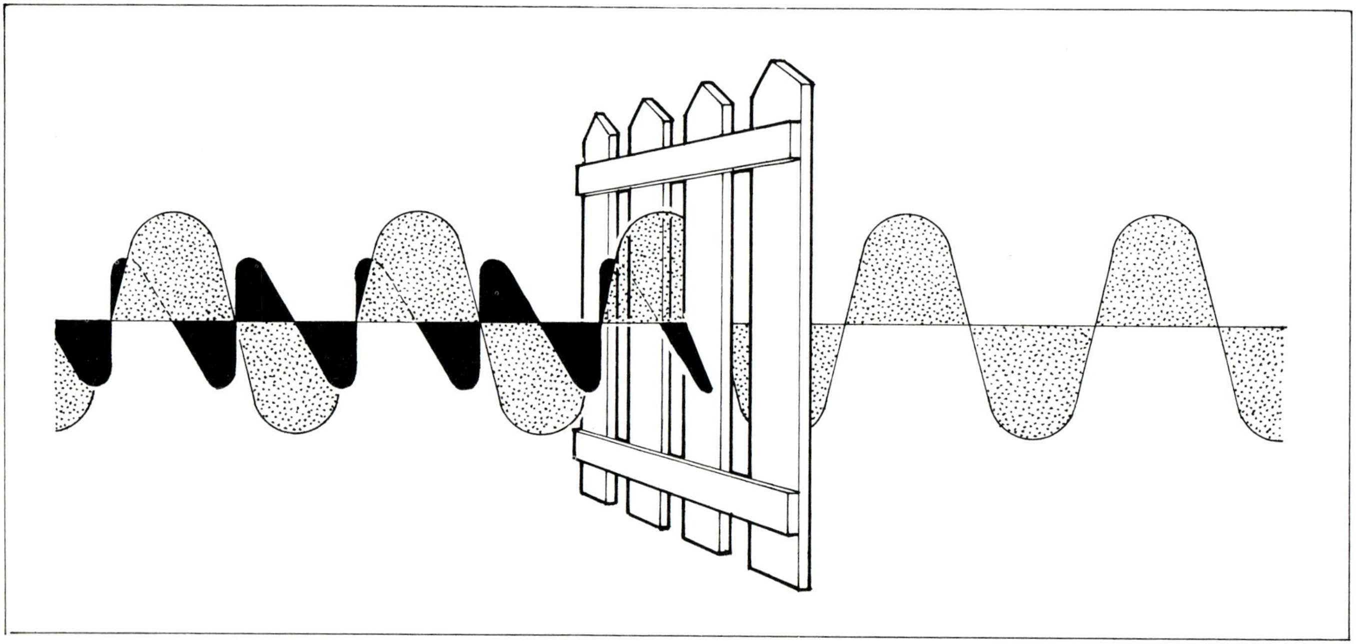

often pinkish. Old glass gives light a greenish-yellow cast. Industrial pollution turns it amber or brown.

When taking portraits, there is a specific requirement to avoid all 'cold' casts but to accept 'warm' ones. Green, neither cold nor warm, is anathema. Purplish or mauve skin is also considered undesirable. For other subjects, much depends on the nature of the photography. Some lighting casts add a great deal to effect; others do neither harm nor good. Some are destructive.

Colour filters and controls are therefore used on still cameras and video to adjust or compensate. A simple understanding of the complementary (opposed) colours helps: yellow is complementary to blue, magenta to green, red to cyan (blue-green). A green cast is corrected by using a magenta filter. A yellow cast needs a blue filter, and so on. These six colours are supplied as filters in a range of strengths for still and cine work. Video images can be adjusted using red, blue and green controls only, as combinations of these provide the effects of the other colours: +red +green = +yellow, +red +blue = +magenta, +blue +green = +cyan.

The details of how colour is measured and how the filters are used are covered in full in the chapter on light and colour. To begin with, it is important only to recognise that some correction for excess blue may be needed in open shade, under sky light, or at high altitudes. Correction for the warm light of dawn or dusk is rarely used because the golden colours are considered attractive. It is also useful to know that surroundings can, or will, influence the colour rendering in your work.

Polarised light

Polarised light has been mentioned when referring to the way in which surfaces reflect and absorb light, and how glare or sheen is created. The control and use of polarised light belong to an advanced level. Despite this, polarised light is all around us,

and makes major differences to the way things look. Anyone who has worn polarised sunglasses knows this, and the effects are even more pronounced in photographs and film.

Polarised light is not light which has been altered in any way. Unpolarised, random light vibrates in all planes; if you imagine a ray of light as a rope held between two people and actuated to produce a kind of sine wave, then in normal light there are ropes moving vertically, horizontally, and at every angle between. The wave-forms are vibrating at every orientation. If the people with the rope have to do their trick with it slotted between the vertical lathes of a paling fence, then the only direction the rope can be made to vibrate will be vertically. A polariser, whether it takes the form of a surface reflecting the light or a filter transmitting it, acts like the fence. Only light within a narrow limit of one orientation will get through.

As it happens, one of the effects of specular reflection (sheen or glare, or reflection off a non-metallic, non-mirror surface) is that most of the reflected light is polarised; its vibrations are all aligned in the same way. This is the reason it managed to be reflected in the first place; other rays, aligned differently, struck the surface in such a way that they were absorbed or reflected at random angles. A polarising filter, rotatable, can be placed over the camera lens and turned until sheen or glare is removed from important parts of the subject. Even in something as 'general' as a landscape, the effect on colour saturation and tonal contrast may be considerable.

Despite this, the use of the polariser remains little understood by many cameramen, and rarely associated with overall lighting contrast and colour rendering. Its more dramatic effects, of cutting out reflections and darkening skies, are well recognised.

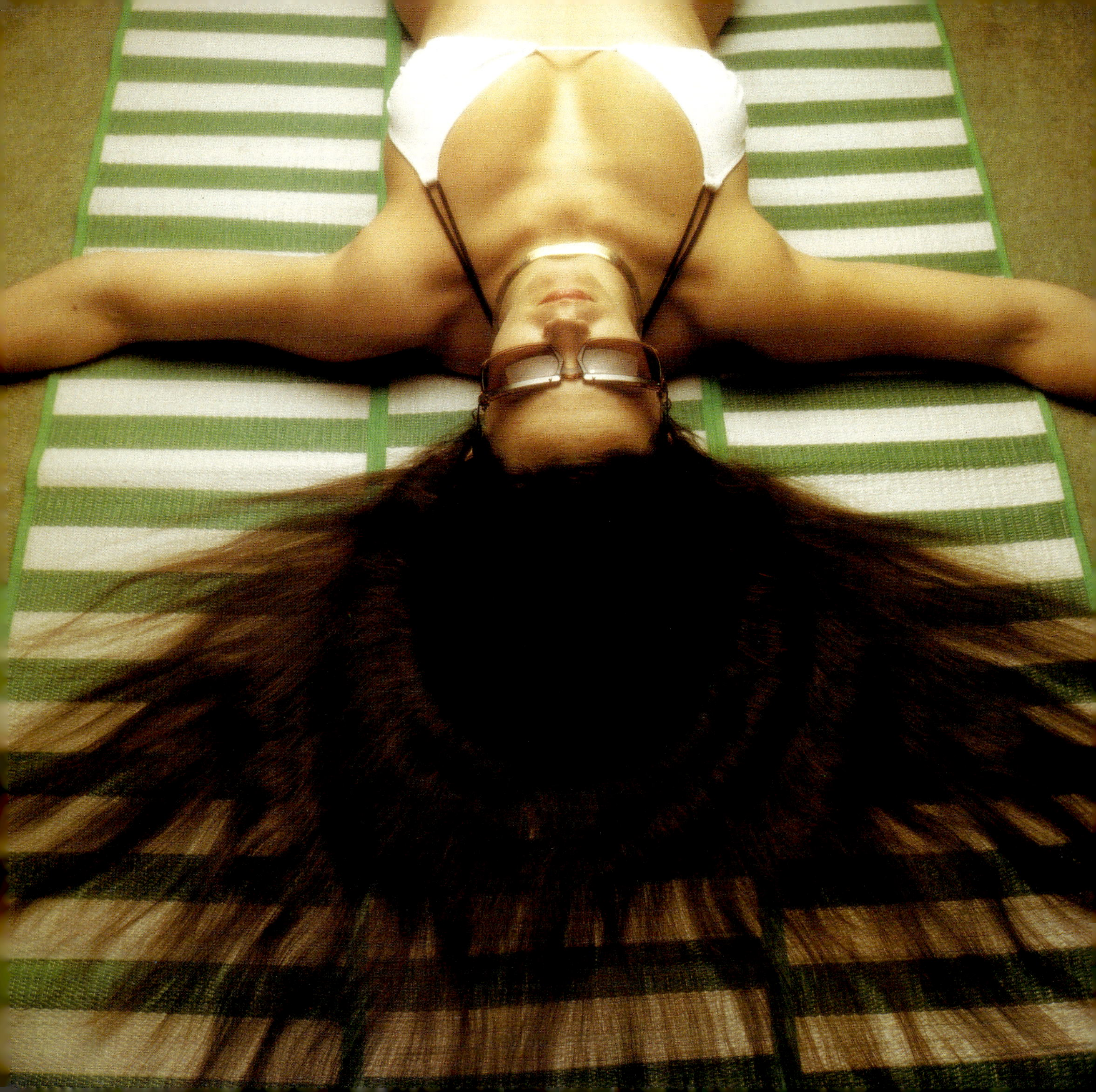

Light and the camera

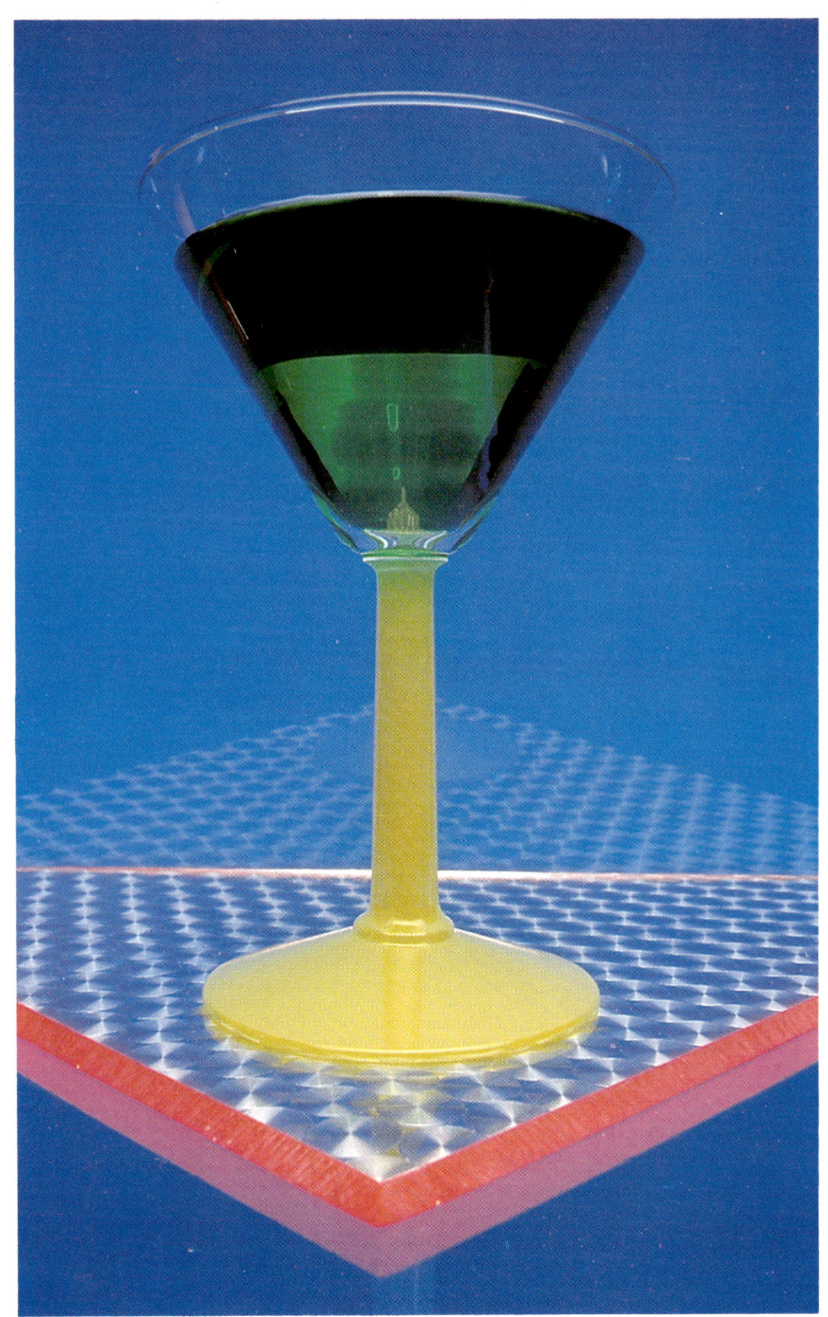

The basis of any photographic system is a fixed, direct relationship between tone and colour values in the subject scene and those finally created in the picture. A theoretically perfect imaging system would reproduce external reality exactly; every colour, every degree of light and shade would be reproduced without modification. In practice this does not happen. Colour is changed, slightly, and overall contrast is always reduced. The picture remains realistic because the changes bear a constant relationship to the original.

In black-and-white, colours are reduced to shades of grey which are more or less equal in visual density to the original shade. Tones, as opposed to colours, are reproduced on a slightly compressed scale, with either or both the highlight and shadow tones omitted. In colour, three basic primaries are used to produce the entire range of possible colours from dyes. They are intended to give the best overall effect, particularly with respect to common colours including fresh tint, grass green, sky blue, and neutral greys. This may mean that some pure reds look too orange or some mauve shades appear pink; each film or video system has its own characteristic rendering. As human colour vision itself varies widely between individuals, few people find any reason to dislike results unless there is some very strong bias. No photographic or video system can be considered an accurate means to record or assess colour values.

Sensitivity

Film or image tubes have to be given a fixed light sensitivity. A given dose of light must always produce a given effect. This may be adjusted when needed, in either film or video, by changing the processing or electronic settings respectively. At any one time, and at every point across the imaging material's area, this sensitivity has to be constant. This ensures that all light reaching the surface is recorded in proportion to its own relative values. If one point on the film's area was to be twice as sensitive as another, then the result would be meaningless.

Sensitivity also has to be matched to light transmission. In the case of electronic systems, light transmitted to the image tube is a function of scene brightness and lens aperture alone. In photographic systems, a shutter which opens for a set duration adds a third factor. Common shutter opening times run from 1/30th of a second to 1/1000th in practice for hand-held cameras; the range can be extended in most still cameras up to 1 second, and in some to as long as 30 seconds or as short as 1/4000th.

The reciprocity law
The law of reciprocity states that if you change the level of illumination reaching the film in a photographic system, an equal and opposite (reciprocal) change in exposure time will be needed to give identical final results. In photographic systems, this rule governs the use of four measurable values. They are the film sensitivity (film speed), the scene brightness (light value), lens aperture (*f*-stop) and shutter opening time (shutter speed). All are expressed in doubling scales of values, though the numerical figures may not appear to represent doubling steps in the case of the lens aperture. This is an extract from possible scales for all four values:

Film speed: expressed in ISO/ASA values –
12 25 50 100 200 400 800 1600 3200 6400

Light values: expressed in LVs –
5 6 7 8 9 10 11 12 13 14 15 16 17

Lens aperture: expressed in *f*-stops –
f/2 *f*/2.8 *f*/4 *f*/5.6 *f*/8 *f*/11 *f*/16 *f*/22 *f*/32

Shutter speed: in fractions of a second –
1 2 4 8 15 30 60 125 250 500 1000

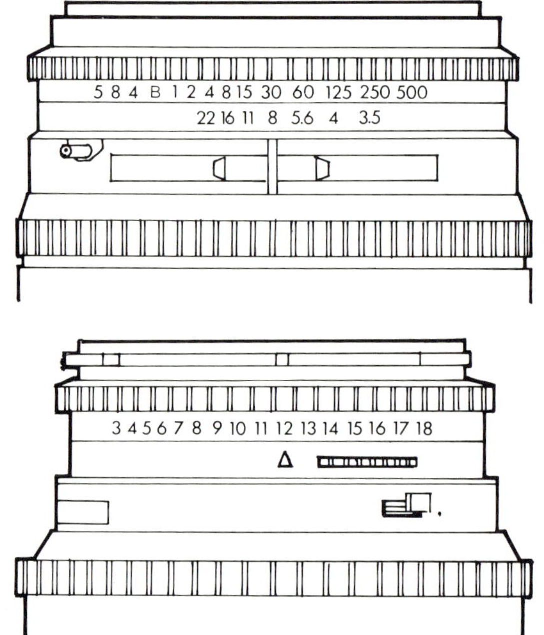

The two scales to control exposure on most cameras are shutter speed and aperture. On this lens, they run parallel to allow simultaneous adjustment.

On the underside of the same lens, an EV scale corresponds to the settings in use.

All these scales have been written to read in similar direction. Low film sensitivity and light values are at the left, high ones at the right. Aperture and shutter settings suited to low film sensitivity or dim light are at the left, those suited to fast (sensitive) film and bright light at the right. It is now standard practice to refer to any one-step change within any of these scales as a 'step'. Photographers often use the term 'stop', derived from the aperture scale, indiscriminately; they refer to a one-stop change in film speed, or losing two stops of light because the sun goes behind a cloud. 'Step' is a more accurate, less misleading term.

The photographic reciprocity law means that a one-step change in any one of the values can be counteracted by an opposite one-step change in any one of the others. As the shutter times and aperture stops are fixed, physical values, and the film speed is a constant value decided by the film you buy, an exposure meter can be designed which only needs

Page 42: light plays a strong part in this simple studio shot where everything is upside-down, including the overall light direction.

Page 43: the basic primary colours are used by putting strong lights behind perspex panels so that the subject itself is illuminated from the back.

to read the light level in order to recommend possible choices of setting. After setting the film speed, a light reading is taken. This value is transferred to an electronic system or visual scale. The shutter speed and aperture are then adjusted to match the visual scale, or the electronic value. This is the principle behind every exposure metering system, even fully automatic types built in to cameras; the difference is that with automation, an electronic system matches the settings to the input signal without human intervention.

In video systems, the reciprocity law does not apply as strictly. With a given sensitivity set on the controls, a one-step change in the light level (doubling or halving) calls for a one-step change in the lens aperture to restore the same image brightness. Most systems, however, work at a fixed lens aperture and use an automatic electronic exposure circuit which varies the sensitivity instead. As manually adjustable sensitivity has no fixed scale (unlike photographic film speed), this can not be quantified or even compared from make to make.

Restoring image values

There is no need to go deeper into how image-recording processes work, because once the exposure is made, light and lighting cease to have further effect. In essence, all photographic films work on a scale of reduced values to recreate the picture. For every doubling or halving of light intensity in the original scene, they may (for example) show a 60 per cent change in density on the final print. The contrast would then be said to be 60 per cent of the original contrast. Very efficient methods produce figures closer to 100 per cent, poor-quality ones closer to 20 per cent.

In negative-positive processes, rather than instant print or slide processes, the contrast of the negative itself may be even more reduced. To contain a full range of tones, 50 per cent can be considered 'bright' and 40 per cent reasonable. This is restored to a fuller contrast by the printing paper, which is matched to the film's tonal range, and expands everything back again to a more acceptable level. In practice, constant steps of contrast only occur in the middle range of tones. Values in deep shadows or bright highlights are usually lost or 'compressed', so that a much smaller difference is recorded. As long as the final printing paper does not also do this and worsen the situation, it is visually acceptable. It is also one reason why control of highlight and shadow values is one of the keys to good lighting and exposure technique.

In electronic imaging systems, much the same has to apply. Whatever values are stored or encoded, the final screen image must re-convert these back to an equivalent of the original scene. The ratios and relationships have to stay constant. The controls for brightness and contrast allow manual visual adjustment to be made, and in practice there is more freedom for personal taste than in photographic systems.

Exposure

'Correct' exposure means adjustment of controls to produce the best possible quality of image. However, there is some latitude in films, allowing minor errors in exposure to be corrected or simply accepted. Normally this is one step either way, towards over or underexposure. If overexposure is given, any loss of detail which occurs will be in the highlight areas. This is worth noting when working with skin tones, or when trying to ensure that a pale blue sky records pale blue rather than washed-out white. Underexposure tends to make shadows look blacker, and may turn delicate shades into slightly stronger colours than necessary.

Because photographic film is the least expensive part of the picture-making process, it is worth taking two pictures rather than one. The first should be the exposure as you measure it. The second should be adjusted one step in whichever direction seems most likely to improve the result. Professional users will often give three or five exposures in total, covering an even wider range of 'bracketed' exposures.

Contrast

We have already covered the way in which film contains contrast, reduces its scale, and may lose either shadow or highlight detail or both when the scene contrast exceeds a certain level. Deciding this level is more complex. The highest levels of contrast can be successfully contained on black-and-white film given special development. As a rule, films of *medium speed* are best suited to this. Films intended for low-light use will naturally prove able to cope with high contrast, but they should not be used in bright conditions.

Colour transparency films, for slides, are also able to handle contrast well. In general terms, the slower films (Kodachrome, Ektachrome 64) are lower in natural contrast. Fast slide films may be fairly high contrast, and thus unsuited to high-contrast subjects. Colour negative film, for prints, will not handle contrast well. Underexposure results in grey shadows, because printing systems do not normally produce an overall dark result, and lighten the print to 'compensate' for the error. Overexposure damages skin tones, so that they can never be rendered accurately. Extremes of contrast simply produce harsh prints. There are no means available to change the contrast of colour prints commercially.

Video systems can be adjusted to cope with high contrast. In practice, any important contrasts within one scene can normally be contained. The contrast control may also be useful when panning from a dimly-lit area to a brighter one, as it lessens the sharpness of the exposure adjustment made by the camera. The point is that photographic film must be chosen to suit its final use, or the lighting controlled to suit the film, but video can be adjusted within reasonable limits.

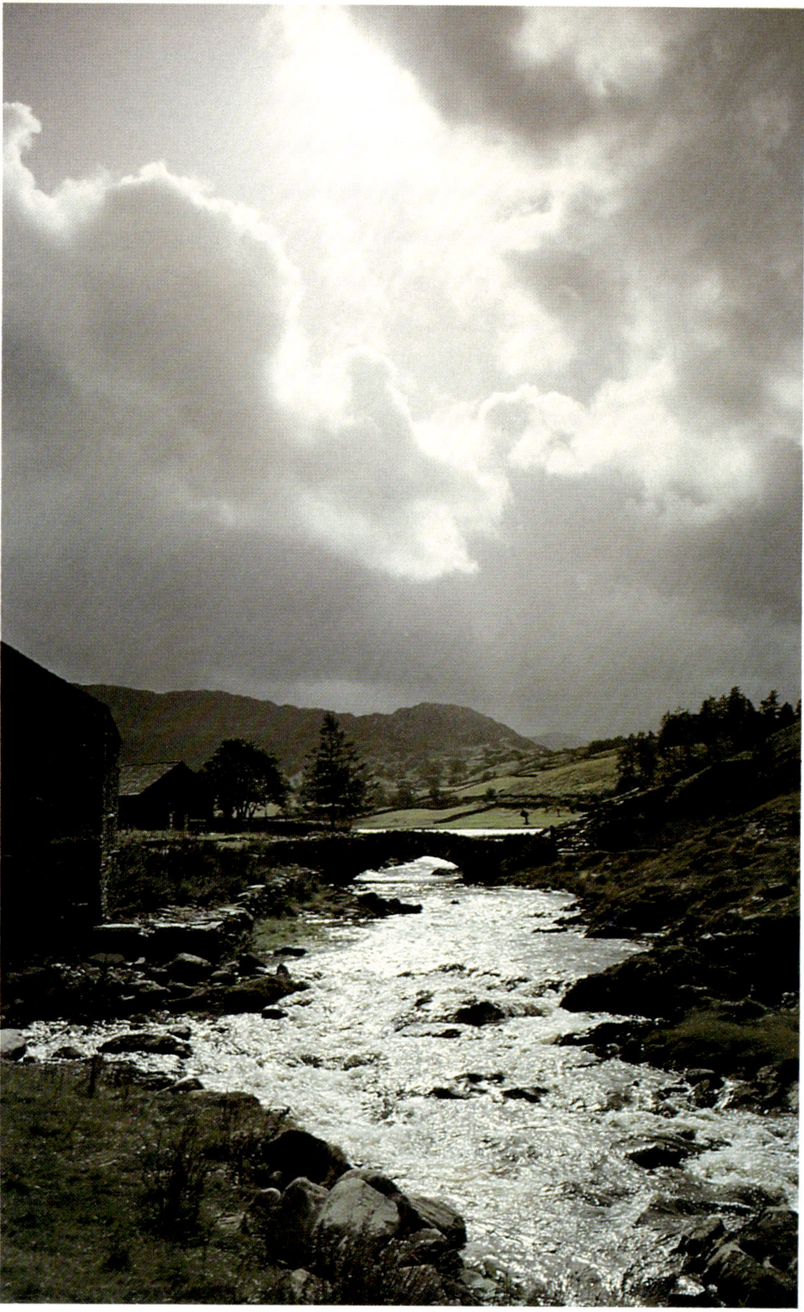

Creative decisions

When you are confronted with a scene where the contrast is high, and have no means to change this or cope with it, you have to make a creative decision about exposure. The human eye has no problems. As you look across a scene, its sensitivity changes. It 'opens up' to see into shadows and 'closes down' when confronted with glaring sun. In general terms, though, the eye adjusts to the brighter levels in a scene and ignores the shadows. Viewing a photograph, areas of solid black are acceptable as long as they do not occupy all the picture! When they do, the result looks very deliberate and graphic.

The general rule, then, is to expose for the highlights, at least to record some detail in them, even if this means total loss of detail in some shadow areas. In colour, this has the secondary effect of producing the most accurate and brilliant colours. Additional exposure, to record shadow detail at the expense of the highlights, dilutes colours and reduces saturation.

There are some cases, though, where overall brightness counts more. A backlit shot of a girl in Edwardian dress on a swing in an orchard would look most nostalgic and summery if exposed for the girl (shadow area) with the general greenery in the background allowed to become very bright and pale. An interior view with a large plate-glass window will look brighter and airier if the window shows a brilliant, overexposed outdoor scene with the interior itself normally rendered.

There may be a temptation, in monochrome photography and in video, to reduce the contrast to a level where full information is shown in shadows and highlights. At the expense of an overall greyness, detail can be made visible. The trade-off is in impact: shapes, composition and forms become less clearly distinguished. A silhouette may make a better picture than a fully detailed figure. When detail is the most important factor, record it; when it is not, think of the overall graphic force of the shot.

Exposure-measuring principles

To understand how to pitch your exposure towards the highlights or shadows, you must grasp the basic principle of exposure meters. This does not mean you have to understand their circuitry, or their scales, in detail. You have to understand their parameters.

The object of an exposure meter is to measure light levels. The perfect method is to stand in the position of the subject, holding a meter which is aimed towards the camera and fitted with a special 'incident-light' receptor. This is a plastic diffuser dome over a photosensitive cell. It receives incident light – that is, light falling on the subject from the direction of the camera. This in turn determines the light reflected back to the camera. Incident-light measuring is very accurate, and it means that the subject records faithfully in tone. If it is a black cloak, it records as black; a white sheet appears white. This method is normally used in the studio where flash is used and the subject is close to the camera. It is also used outdoors when taking portraits, or working with static subjects in a small area.

For many pictures, there is no opportunity to walk up to the subject position and take a reading. Nor is it possible to build a camera with automatic exposure able to take an incident-light reading from the subject position! Built-in exposure meters therefore use the 'reflected-light' principle. Reflected-light metering allows the meter cell, no longer fitted with a light-receiving dome, to be aimed directly at the subject. In popular cameras, it may take its reading through the lens or viewfinder of the camera. Hand-held meters have to be aimed at the subject separately.

A reflected-light meter has to be calibrated. Two different scenes may vary greatly in the amount of light they reflect; a sandy desert reflects more light than a pine forest. A reading taken from a black cloak will be much lower than a reading from a white sheet. The standard calibration of reflected-light meters, video cameras, SLR cameras and any other exposure system is to match 18 per cent reflectance. The meter is set up to expose as if the scene reflects 18 per cent of all light falling on it. This is the rough percentage from a typical sunlit landscape.

You *must* bear this in mind whenever using a camera with a built-in meter. If the subject varies greatly from the 18 per cent norm, the exposure will be wrong. Typical errors include metering when the scene has a white, plain sky and the camera is aimed upwards to include a building, or has a wide-angle lens which includes more sky than normal; the extra light makes the meter reduce the exposure, and the result is a dark subject against a glowering sky. Very dark subjects, particularly when seen with a telephoto lens so that there is no sky content, will suffer from the reverse, as the meter tells the camera to give extra exposure. There are various ways round this problem, but the most important one is thinking. Look at the scene metered: is it darker or lighter than a typical scene? If darker, the meter may be indicating too much exposure; if lighter, too little.

Selective exposure reading is one answer, with non-automatic systems. You take the reading from a suitable average area. Some exposure meters have the inside of their case lid lined with fabric which reflects 18 per cent of incident light, a built-in average subject. Selective readings can be taken by using a telephoto or zooming in to a suitable tone in a distant scene, or using a small area close-up.

Manual adjustment calls for mental assessment of how much the scene varies from the standard. After taking your reading, judge whether the correct exposure should be more or less, and by how much, and reset the camera controls. This is something

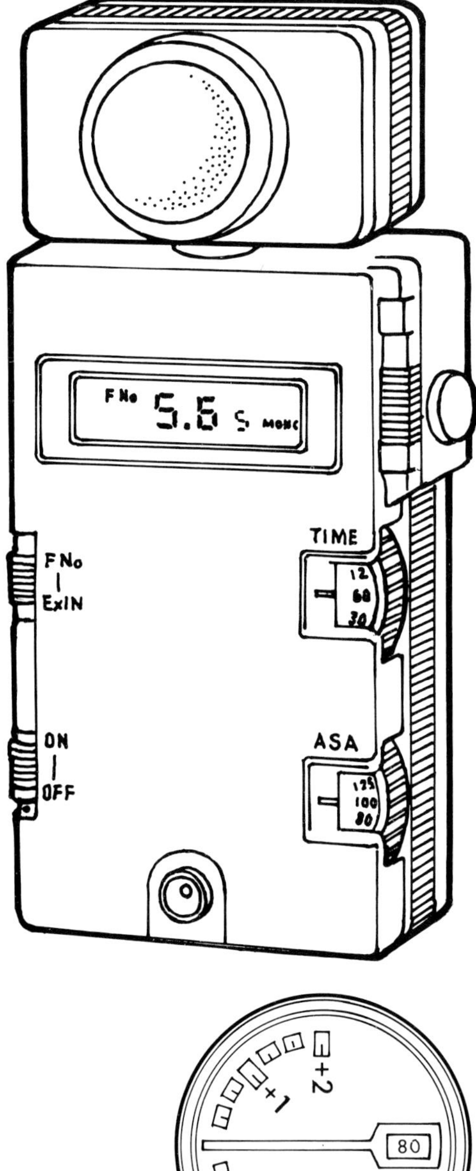

A typical advanced exposure meter will take readings from the light source via a diffusing dome, rather than just from the subject.

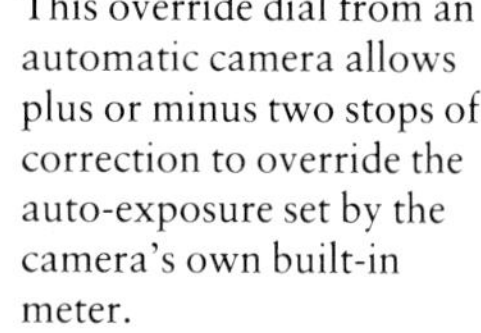

This override dial from an automatic camera allows plus or minus two stops of correction to override the auto-exposure set by the camera's own built-in meter.

you are unlikely to do until you have some experience of seeing results.

Override controls are fitted to some automatic cameras which allow the user to program a manual adjustment, so that it affects all automatic settings until cancelled. These are normally marked in steps of -1, -2, 0, $+1$ and $+2$. The camera is left set on 0 for routine exposures; minus settings reduce exposure (to compensate for dark subjects which would otherwise be rendered too light) and plus settings increase exposure (to compensate for light subjects). As one of the common faults is underexposure caused by backlight or bright skies, other makes have a 'backlight button' which, when pressed, increases exposure by 1½ steps. Other automatic makes have a memory-hold button which allows the user to take a selective reading, then hold this for the final exposure after re-framing.

The use of all these controls, and similar devices when fitted to video cameras, is explained fully in the instruction books normally supplied. It is also dealt with more thoroughly in books dealing specifically with exposure. There are some lighting conditions which you should learn to recognise, because they make exposure metering difficult. You may devise studio lighting which is similar to them, and you need to work out the exposure.

Backlight leaves the side of the subject facing the camera in shadow, but any flat surfaces such as the ground or walls of buildings may be almost fully lit. The sky may also be very bright. The exposure decision is whether to accept a silhouetted subject and normal background scene, or expose for the shadows facing the camera with a bright background. The extra over a direct meter reading is normally one or two steps.

Spotlight picks out a subject brightly against a solid black background, as in a stage production. The correct exposure can either be read from the subject position by incident light, or using a selective reading. With any built-in meter, less exposure will be needed than indicated, but as the degree depends entirely on the relative area of picture occupied by the spotlit subject, no rules are possible.

Reflective backlight usually comes from a large light source above the subject or scene, and slightly to the back of it, as when a bright overcast sky lights a wet beach or a field of corn.

Outdoors, the main problem is inclusion of the bright sky in the metering area, and the answer lies in aiming the meter downwards to the ground for a selective reading. In the studio, this type of light is now used very widely on all kinds of shot, and will be discussed in full in the chapter on light-control technology. The problem is a simple one: even an incident-light reading will not give a true exposure when a light source has been positioned to create a sheen over the surface of the subject. A reflected-light reading is recommended, with a one-step increase in exposure if the shot is intended to look reasonably light and bright rather than intense.

There are some obvious subject problems, as well as lighting problems. It does not take a great deal of thought to realise that an expanse of white snow will influence a meter drastically and close-up readings are essential. Sand and sea can have the same effect. Ground-to-air pictures of aircraft, balloons or parachutists will always be over-influenced by the inclusion of sky unless it is deep blue. Experience is the ultimate key to recognising lighting conditions which need exposure correction or contrast control, and call for creative decisions. The only way to gain experience is to produce pictures frequently, and in conditions other than those you consider to be ideal.

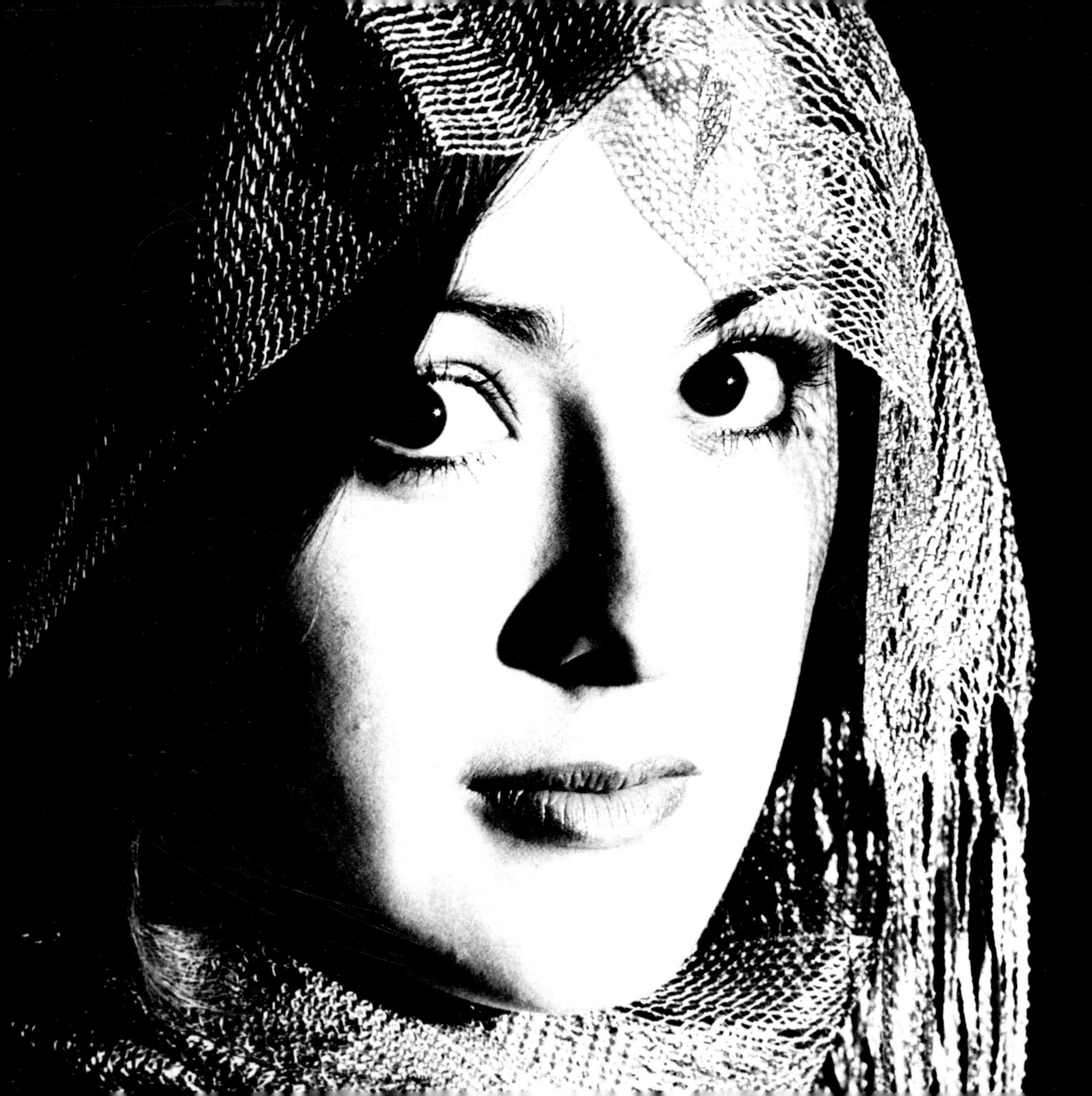

Controlling light

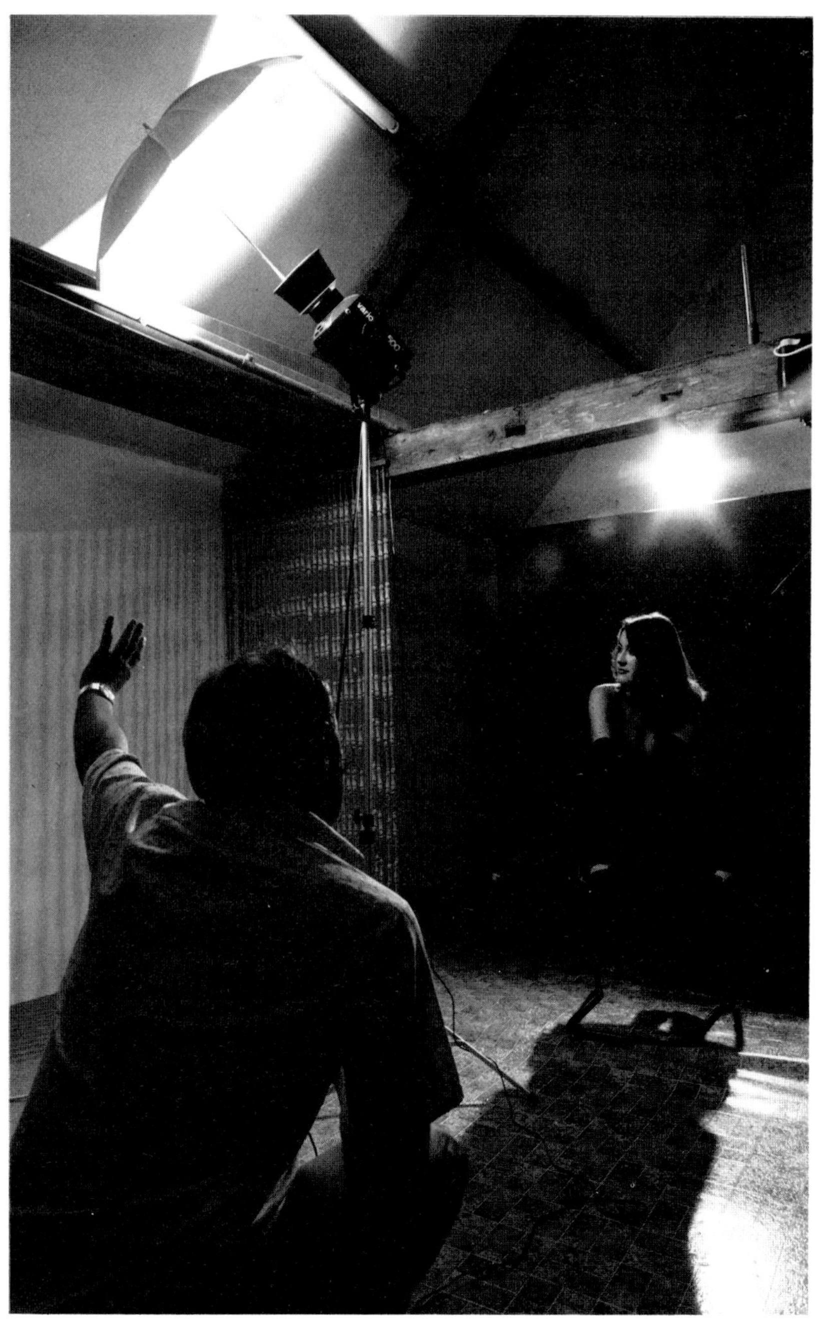

Artists with pens or brushes have the ability to make changes to their subjects regardless of the scale involved. Camera operators can change a few specific things, but total control is impossible when the subject is large and outdoors. To light a small field evenly, a light source needs to be 100 metres in the air, and remarkably powerful. Only at night can artificial light be used to create new scenes outdoors.

In a small area, great control can be exercised. It does not matter much whether this area is outdoors or in, but the size you can successfully handle depends on being able to block out other influences. A specimen plant can be photographed enclosed by a special tent with electronic flash and freedom from disturbing breezes. People can be photographed outdoors using a set of large portable reflectors and black panels with rigid stands. A large truck, on the other hand, calls for a studio of warehouse proportions rather than an outdoor location.

The means at your disposal for changing or creating lighting are simple. You can adjust existing light and use this alone, supply your own light and eliminate existing light, or mix the two in a suitable combination. At this stage we will look only at controlling or supplementing existing outdoor light, as a decision to work entirely with artificial light means (in effect) creating studio conditions either at night, or by blocking out all daylight.

Reflectors
The most basic piece of outdoor light-control equipment is the reflector. This can consist of a plain sheet of white artist's board or mounting card, or part of a roll of used background paper. A white ski jacket or an old sheet will do. When working on location, anything from a newspaper to

a wall can be pressed into service, although working with fixed reflector surfaces means moving the subject.

The best reflector colour is a clean, pure white. Higher efficiency may be achieved by a silvered or aluminium surface, but the reflected light can be patchy or too strong. Where localised fill-in in bright sunlight is needed, the lid of a silver-coloured metal camera case can be positioned to throw back light into a small shadow area. Portable reflector sheets are made, white one side and silver the other, which pack into a small pouch. Aluminium-coated plastic arctic-survival blankets can be used the same way.

A large reflector with a matt surface gives even, natural fill-in to shadow areas. There may be problems with wind and stability. For portraits, a neat solution lies in asking the model to hold the reflector; reading a magazine, or making up with a small mirror compact throwing light in a neat patch back to the eyes. To position the reflector, place it on the shadow side of the subject aiming back towards both the main light direction and the subject itself. It does not look particularly natural if the fill-in always comes from a low level in a sunlit shot. Often this effect can be dramatic, but at other times, the reflector is best positioned at eye-level.

An efficient reflector, such as one of the portable pack types held on a temporary frame or by an assistant, can be used to throw light into a shaded spot and form the main light source. Most of the light in a shaded area on a clear day is very blue, but if the reflector is held in full sunlight it will shine much more neutral, warm colours into the subject. Coloured reflectors can be used for effect. The most popular type, warming up colours to a sunset effect, is coated with gold rather than silver. Gold reflectors are flattering to skin tones. Other colours of card or painted surface you may want to try include yellow, pink, red and orange. On the whole green and blue will give unpleasant effects.

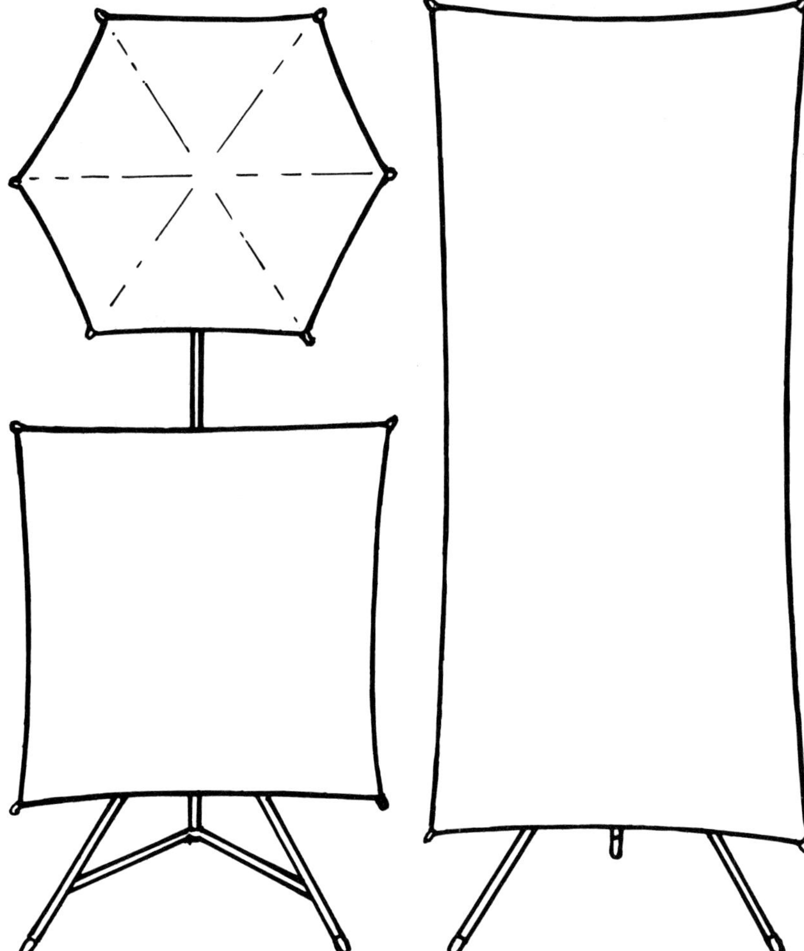

Page 50: extremely high contrast, hard lighting given by an optical projection spotlight in the studio.

Page 51: umbrellas, spotlights and reflectors play an important part in studio work. Courtesy the Minolta Club, *Adrian Bassett*.

Typical light reflectors designed for use on stands in or out of the studio.

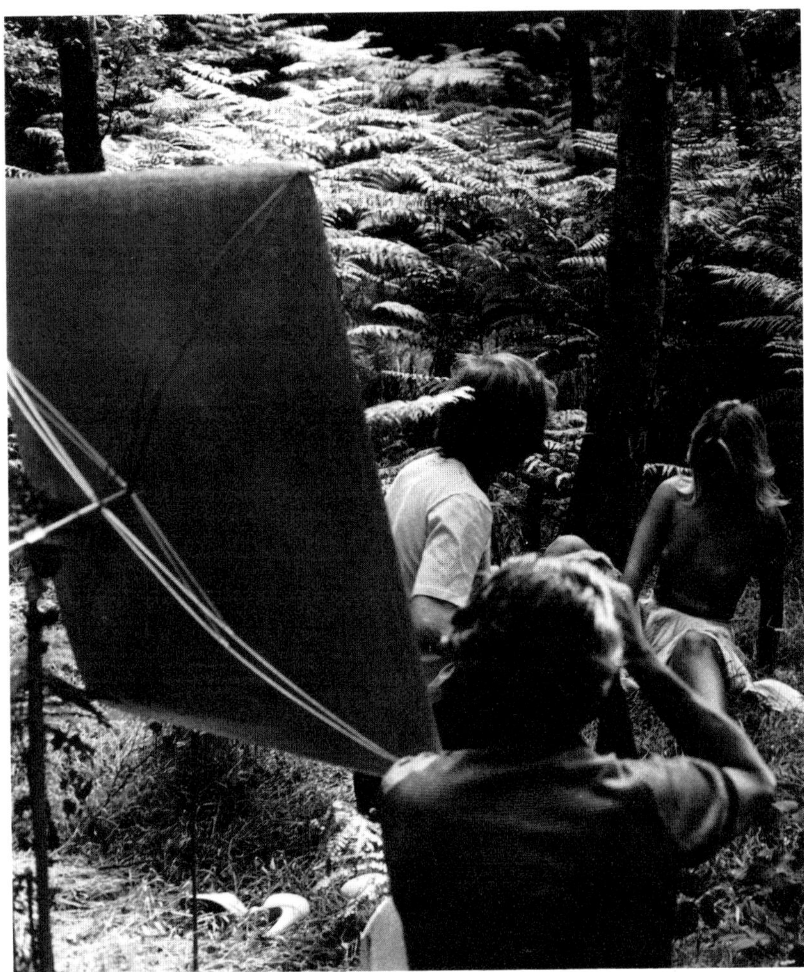

In an outdoor location, a reflector is positioned to reduce contrast under trees. Courtesy the Minolta Club, *Adrian Bassett*.

There are several natural situations where existing surfaces reflect in a characteristic way, and the lighting provides important clues to the situation as a result. A portrait subject sitting in the shade at an alfresco table, with the table itself in full sun, is lit mainly by light reflecting off the table. Someone standing by a swimming pool may be strongly underlit by a changing pattern of reflected sunlight off the water. Look for this kind of lighting, and see how it alters the mood of the picture. Very often it can be simulated artificially, or produced deliberately by picking the location.

Remember that the effect of a reflector depends on its distance from the subject. In the case of natural reflectors you may be able to include them in the shot, the reverse (shadow) side of the reflecting object showing to the camera. Other reflectors, particularly your own card or sheets, should be positioned out of shot.

Absorbing panels

'Black reflectors' have become popular in still and everyday video photography. In the movie industry they have been used for many years, and are called 'French flags'. They shouldn't be confused with 'gobos', which are similar black sheets used to go between the light sources and the camera lens and prevent any accidental lens flare.

Absorbing panels are positioned just like reflectors, but have exactly the opposite effect. The best materials are black twill cloth, black velvet, and black short-pile fur fabric. Matt black boards or cards reflect far more light than you would imagine. Some black panels are reversible and have a white, reflecting side. Used on the highlight side of a subject, black panels have little effect unless they conceal important reflecting surfaces. On the shadow side, they deepen the shadows. They are much harder to position than white reflectors as the effect is less easily judged by eye. The principles are the same, and the absorbing effect is just as dependent on distance.

There are one or two examples of standard uses for
black panels. The simplest is on a dull day, with a
plain white sky, taking an outdoor portrait. A black
panel is placed to one side of the subject's face, out
of shot, and a second panel above the top of his or
her head. The side panel creates a lighting bias
otherwise absent, giving some directional
character. The top panel eliminates the ugly
top-light effect, which overlights hair and bald
heads in particular and creates deep eye shadows.

A second use is when photographing a full-length
fashion shot, with an emphasis either on a very long
slim dress or on legs. The model is asked to stand
between two 2 × 1 metre vertical black panels, out
of shot, positioned slightly to the rear side rather
than the camera side, aimed surfaces in to the
model. This creates shade lines down the side of the
body, face and legs which have a narrowing and
shape-emphasising effect.

Finally, an outdoor still-life or food shot can be
helped along, whether in sunlight or on a dull day,
by suspending a black panel above it so that no
direct sky or sun light reaches it. The difference in
reduced sheen and top-light is considerable. Light
direction can be created, as with a portrait, by using
a side panel.

These basic set-ups can also include reflectors,
generally near the camera position, to help
overcome the loss of other light. By careful
positioning of light and dark panels, entirely new
light qualities can be made from an overcast day.

Natural surroundings can be used in the same way.
Wedding photographers have known for years that
positioning the bride and groom just inside the
church porch, through the open door, produces
flattering light even on a rainy day. The dark sides
and roof of the porch act like three black panels,
and the pair are lit (in effect) by a light source
formed by the door. It is frontal, and tends to slim.
There is no point in detailing every possible

54

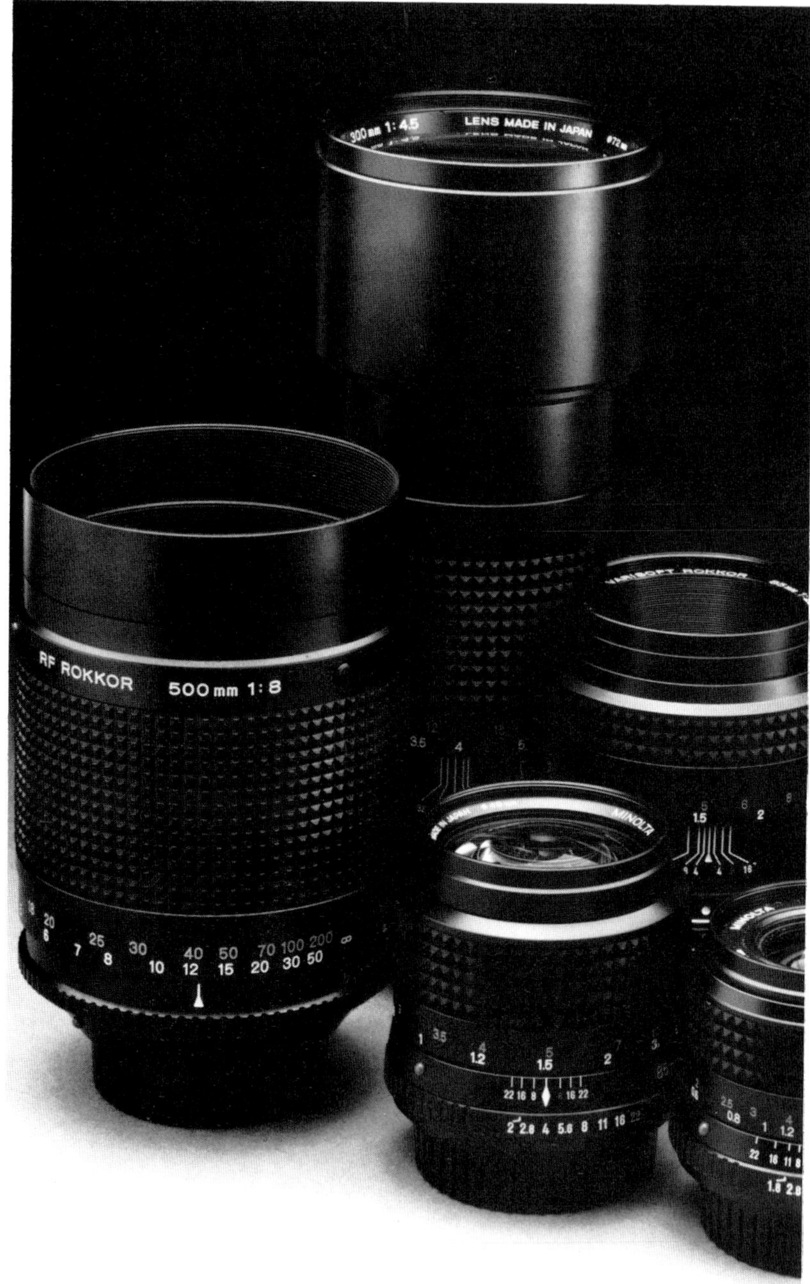

situation. If you devote some time to experimenting
with some black cards (preferably covered in velvet
for efficiency), you will begin to see how much
difference this negative lighting method makes.

Diffusers

Because they have to be positioned between light
source and subject, diffusers are less popular for
outdoor work than for studio shots. Outdoor
subjects are often bigger, the light source is
normally the sky or sun, and stands for holding the
diffusing material are not to hand. There is no point
in using a diffuser when the light is already
thoroughly diffuse. They are mainly of use in direct
sunlight, to cut out harshness. The effect of a
diffuser depends on four factors: its size, its
diffusing power, its distance from the light source
and distance from the subject. Size is naturally
limited by practical considerations, and the biggest
popular purpose-made diffusers are 1 × 2m.
Diffusing power depends on thickness and type of

material, and on the whole the greater the
diffusion, the less the light transmission.

The most effective total diffuser is opal white
perspex. This cuts the light down to about a quarter
of its original level. The least effective you are likely
to use is dressmaker's gauze or tulle in a single
layer, which has hardly any effect on either the light
quality or level.

Portable diffusers or 'sails' are made using a plastic
material called 'scrim' which is heat-proof, very
tough, and fairly expensive. Tissue scrim, a
non-woven fabric similar to interfacing material or
fibreglass mat, is cheaper. The best portable
diffusers use one or two layers of a closely-woven
white acrylic fabric. You can, of course, buy your
own fabrics and make simple frames and stands.

Colour transmission is important. A fabric or
plastic may seem white to you, but when tested
white perspex is found to change the colour

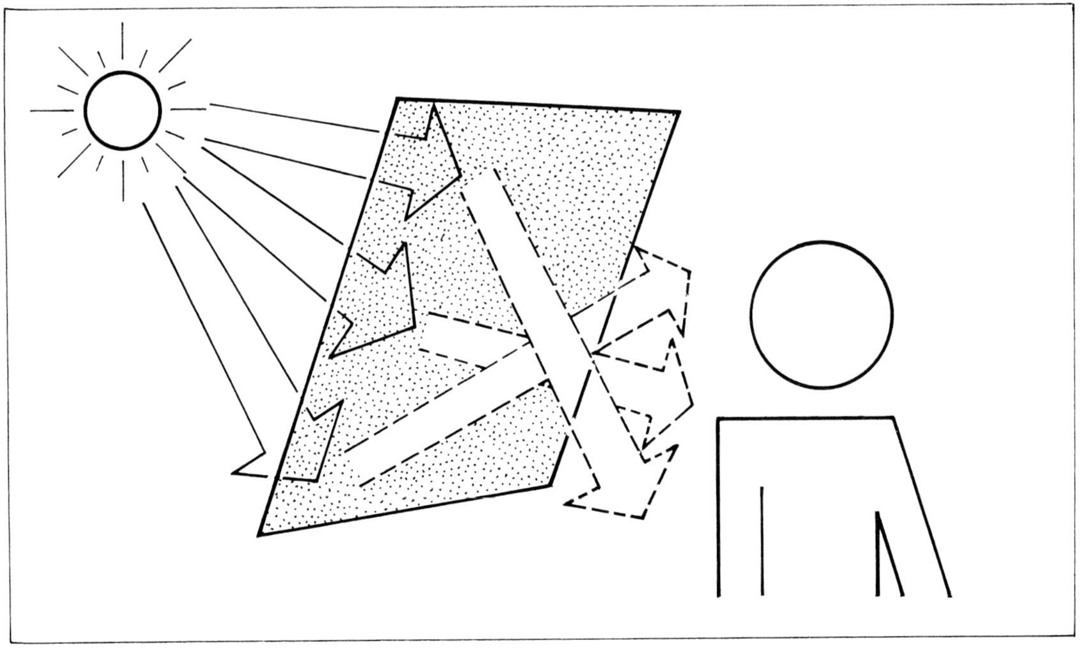

A diffusing screen passes
light, but alters its
directional character to
prevent hard shadows.

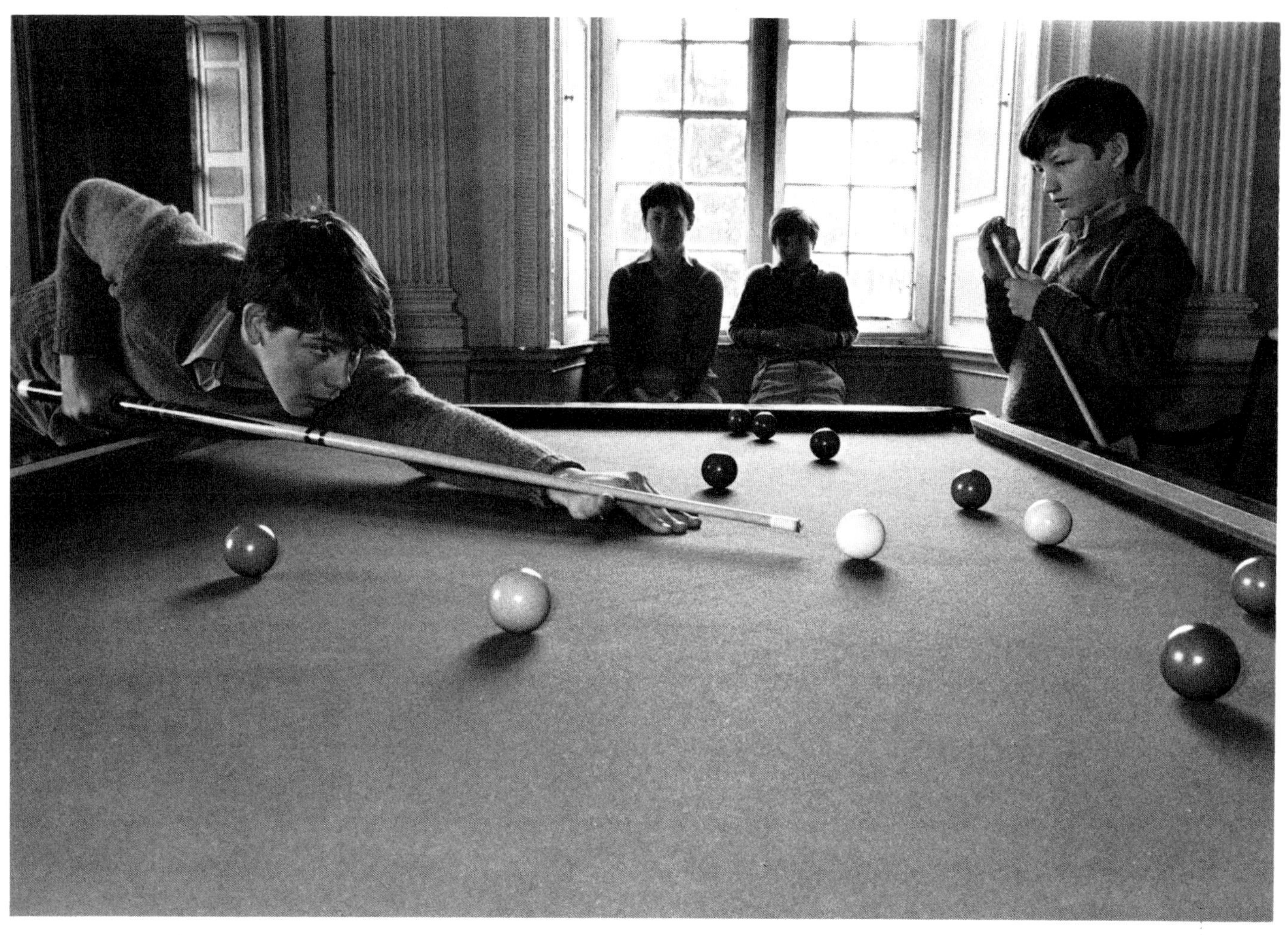

Fill-in flash can be used indoors as well as out to balance existing light, especially when the light is strongly towards the camera. In this case a shutter speed of 1/30 second was used with weak electronic flash on the camera. Courtesy Howsham Hall School, *David Kilpatrick*.

temperature of light at 5600K (daylight) to 5000K (warm daylight). Double-layer fabric panels change it by about half this.

Outdoors, the question of distance from the light source is irrelevant, but size of panel and distance from the subject both count. A large panel very close to the subject gives maximum diffusion. Reduce size or increase distance and other available light will have proportionally more effect. Where the diffuser is used over a window or opening for indoor natural light shots, then light-to-diffuser distance does become variable. The further from the light source, the greater the diffusion.

Supplementary lighting
When reflectors, black panels and diffusers can not produce the effect you need or are too difficult to position, supplementary artificial lighting is the final solution. Continuous light has the advantage that it can be used for either still or video work, and its effect can be assessed accurately. The problems to be overcome are colour balance and intensity; most artificial light sources are warmer in colour temperature than daylight, and very much dimmer than sunlight at normal working distances.

The answers are first to filter the light so that it matches the prevailing light in colour, and secondly to use enough power, close enough to the subject, to have a discernable effect. A tungsten-halogen light requires a blue filter called an 80B to be fitted over it when mixed with daylight. As only tungsten or tungsten-halogen lights are likely to be powerful enough and portable enough to use, what remains is wattage. A pair of 2000W floods will be adequate for most shots of small settings or people, but large locations may call for 10 000 watts. Small ciné lights, of 1000W each, can be used for portraiture and wedding photographs as fill-in for shadows in anything but full sun. These can be run from 12 or 24V accumulators or vehicle batteries, a big advantage 'in the field'.

By using tungsten light unfiltered, warm colours can be produced which make it clear that the light is artificial. Beware the mistake of using tungsten movielight fill-in with Super 8mm ciné camera in daylight, because on these cameras the light (when fitted) automatically adjusts the camera to match the film to the light colour via a filter. The background daylight then seems too blue.

For still shots only, flash can be combined with daylight. The disadvantage is that the effect can not be judged, even when mains-powered flash with modelling lights is used. The modelling lights are too dim to have any relative visible effect. The only reliable way of checking elaborate daylight plus flash set-ups is to shoot an instant-print test shot.

The conventional method for working out combined flash and daylight is to take exposure readings, work out the necessary f-stop, and position the flash so that on its own it would need a slightly wider f-stop (greater light transmission through the lens). As the daylight and flash will be added together, the f-stop is in fact cut down slightly. Exposures are made at different apertures, perhaps changing the shutter speed as well, or the flash power. Normally more bracketed shots must be taken to obtain precisely the correct result. Synchro sun, or fill-in flash, is simpler. The flash remains on the camera, and the method is used only for backlit subjects, with the sun facing the lens and the shadow side of the subject in full view.

The crudest method is to set the camera on automatic and switch the flash on, firing without any calculations or thought. Because the flash units built-in to many 35mm and pocket cameras are low in power, this works for all shots beyond 1.5 metres or so. However, it does not work with SLR cameras, which have a focal-plane shutter. These cameras have a maximum shutter speed for flash; it may be 1/60, 1/90, 1/125, or even 1/200. Rollfilm SLRs may have a synchronisation speed as slow as 1/30. For fill-in flash; the shutter must be set to the correct synchronisation or slower. This will dictate the aperture *f*-stop.

If a manual flashgun is owned, the calculator dial is set to the film speed in use, and the *f*-stop for correct exposure at the synch speed is located on the dial. The distance corresponding to this *f*-stop is the closest possible camera-to-subject distance for fill-in flash work. Ideally, the camera-to-subject distance should be adjusted (using an appropriate lens to include the right amount of subject) so that the flash calculator dial reads off one *f*-stop wider than the actual *f*-stop needed for correct metered exposure. The flash will thus contribute an extra 50 per cent of light to the shadow area, and brighten it. For a more controlled effect, the flash should add just 25 per cent extra (a two *f*-stop difference). If the camera needs *f*/8, work at a distance where the flash would normally need *f*/5.6 or *f*/4. Too much flash (e.g. if *f*/8 were calculated to be an adequate aperture for the flash alone, without daylight) gives an unnatural effect.

A more advanced method involves changing the shutter speed, if necessary, from the synchronisation speed to a longer time. This changes the aperture for normal exposure to a smaller one, and allows flash at a closer distance. Most popular 35mm SLRs allow a choice between 1/30, 1/60 and 1/125 for flash synchronisation. With variable-power manual flash, far more choice can be exercised. Some portable units have full, half, quarter, 1/8 and 1/16th powers. This will allow synchro-sun at all useful distances for the portrait and full-length or group shots on which the technique is most often needed.

With automatic computer exposure flash units, a choice of operating apertures may be given; sometimes two, sometimes three, and sometimes a whole range of settings. With a typical unit, the choices at ISO 100/21° film speed will be *f*/4, *f*/8 and *f*/16. The flash computer will work just as well in daylight as it does indoors, as it is not sensitive to any light apart from its own flash output. For quick and easy synchro-sun at any distance, the aperture is set to two stops wider than the lens setting. As synchro-sun is always used in backlighting, remember that it is not necessary to give the extra exposure for shadow detail mentioned earlier. The flash handles this correction for you. If extra exposure is also given, the picture will be overexposed.

Mirrors

A lighting method often neglected because of impracticality is rapidly becoming possible now that plastic mirrors which are lightweight and safe to handle can be obtained. Working in direct sun, mirror panels can be positioned to aim sunlight back to the subject, which may be in shadow or need strong shadow fill-in. The bright sun directed from a mirror can be diffused or reflected to make it more suitable.

Diffusers, reflectors and lights

All the comments on reflecting and diffusing daylight also apply to supplementary light sources used outdoors. Although power and judgment may be problems, flash can provide much better fill-in if bounced from a portable card reflector or through a diffuser panel. Tungsten lights are usually not powerful enough to allow any further dilution. Simple accessories are made for popular flashguns to clip on and provide reflected or diffused light.

Outdoor light control sometimes exists naturally, as in this snapshot where a dark rain cover on a pushchair created lighting conditions of its own.

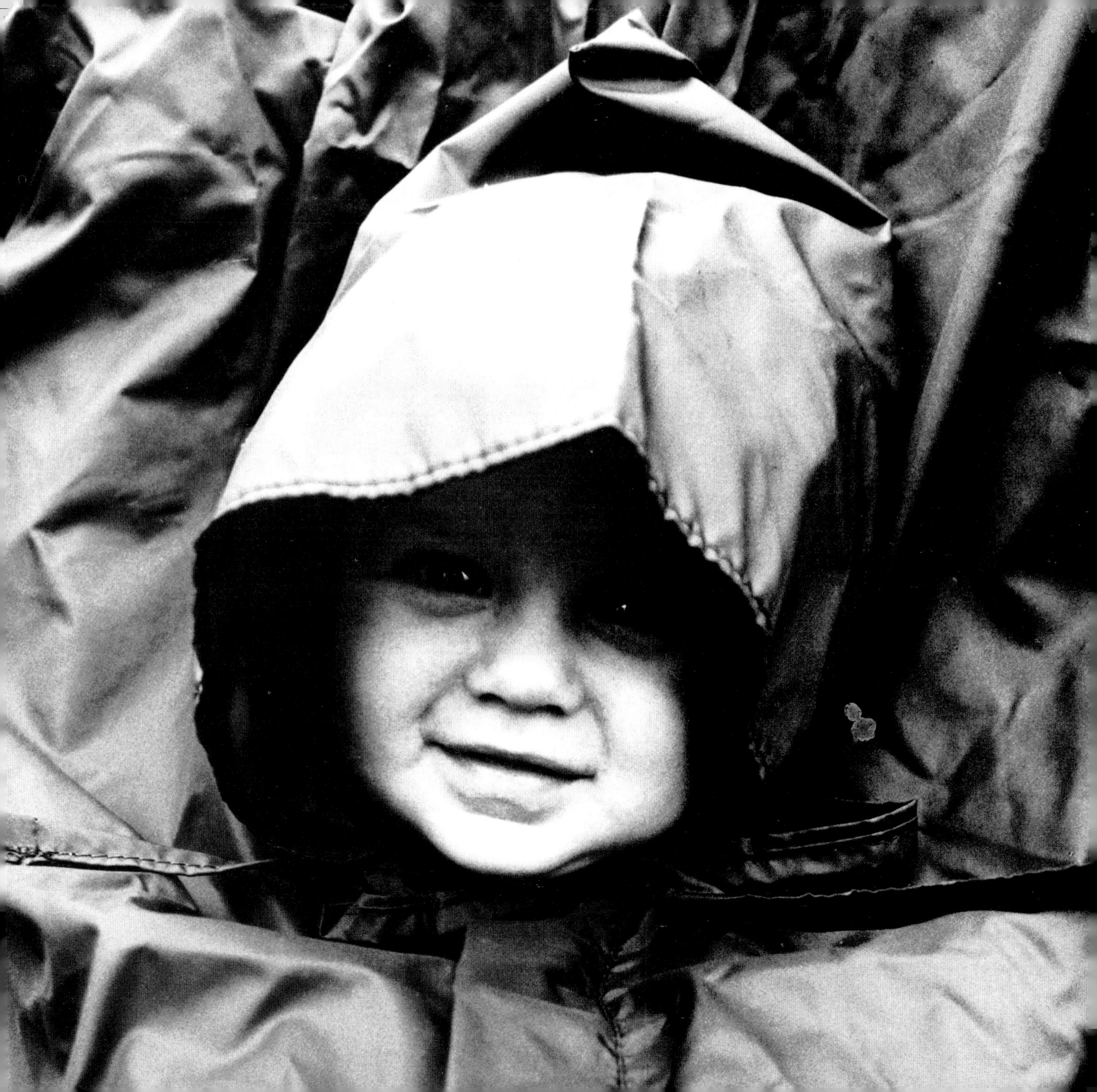

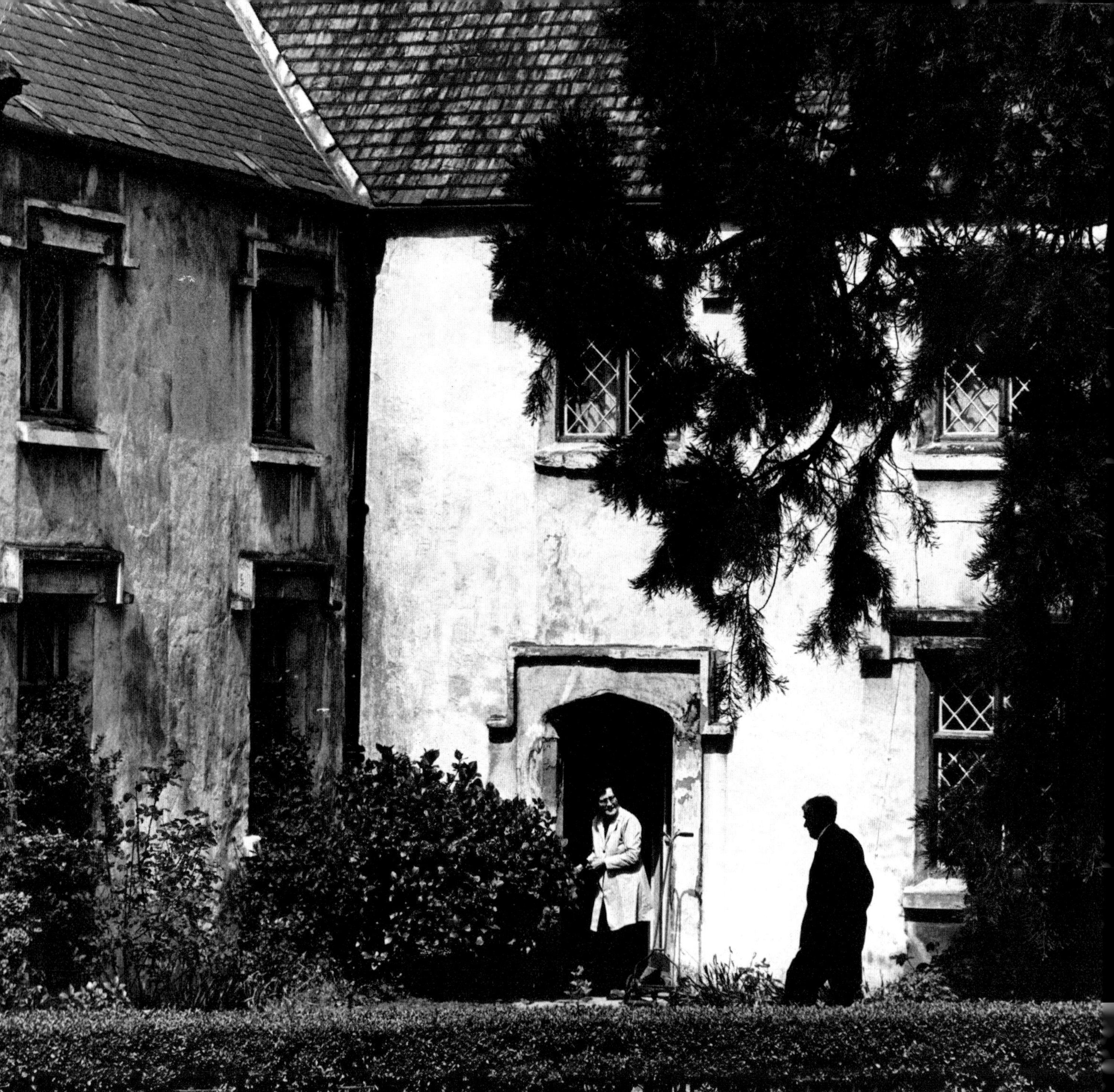

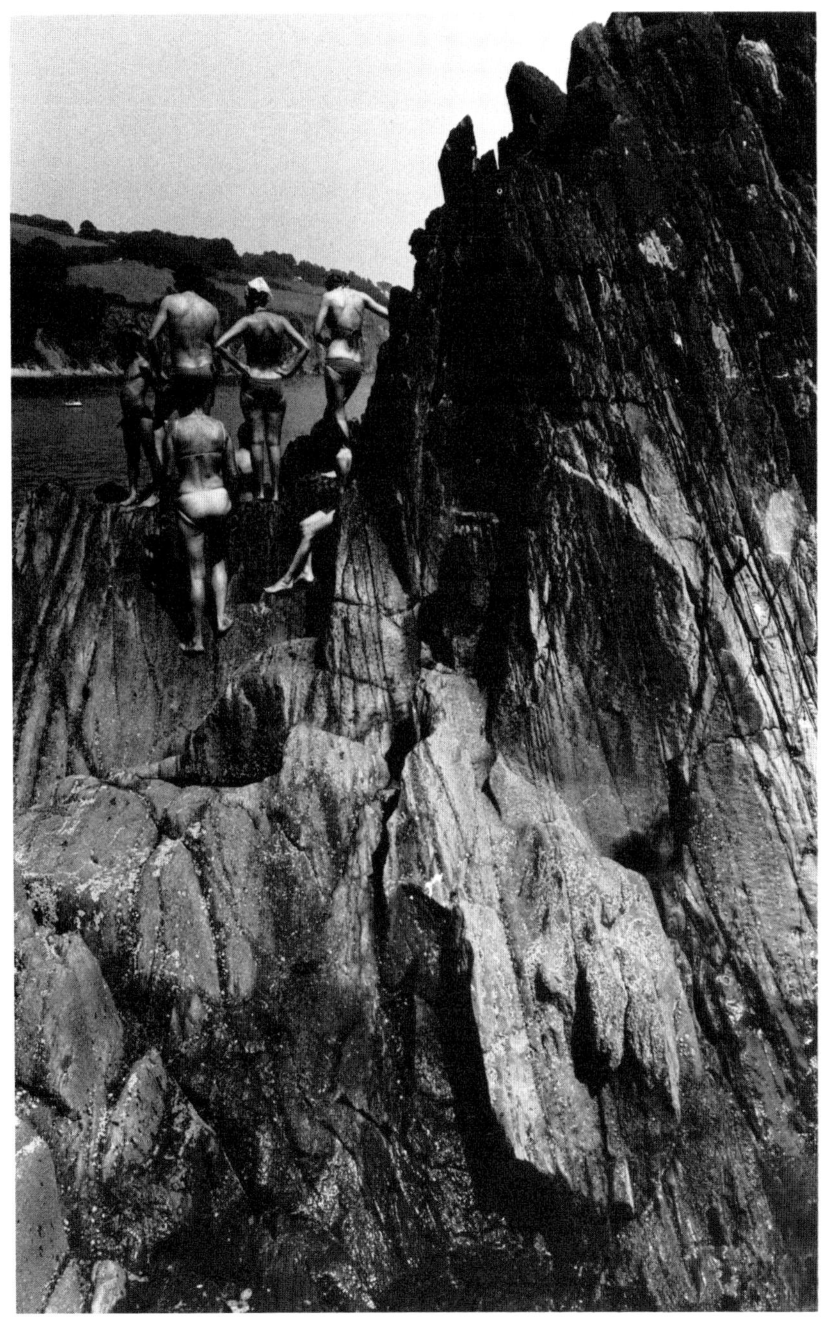

Form, texture, shape and modelling in daylight

A skilled camera operator will be able to handle the problems presented by almost any quality of available light. This is largely a matter of choice of viewpoint, composition and exposure. There are some conditions which naturally produce better pictures than others, and comments like 'the light's terrible' can be justified.

Some of the best pictures are made by the lighting conditions alone. The subject may be mundane, but unusual or dramatic light (in terms of contrast, concentration or colour) creates a picture on its own. As this kind of shot can never be predicted or set up outdoors, you have to rely on luck and your ability to recognise a picture. The craft of photography, whatever the precise medium used, lies in learning to identify and tackle everyday lighting conditions successfully.

Overcast light

Confronted with an overcast day, it may be hard to tell by eye whether the light is directional or not. Sometimes it is obvious, because one half of the sky is steely grey and the other fairly bright. When visual judgment fails it does not mean that the light is bound to be totally even. To check, use an exposure meter.

Holding the meter level, aiming at the horizon, take a series of readings at 90° intervals (north, south, east, west) and note the level of light recorded each time. Although you are in effect taking an incident-light reading, this can be done with a reflected-light meter just as accurately. With a camera, take each reading with the horizon positioned midway in the viewfinder. The object is not to measure light, but to compare relative brightness. By keeping the horizon level, you take into account physical obstructions like houses, woods or hills. These have an effect of making daylight more directional and certain where any solid object is concerned. They have little effect on flat objects, photographed on the ground, which receive most of their light from directly above.

You will quickly establish by this method where the brightest sky area is. For maximum diffused light, the subject should face the brighter part of the sky. This normally results in frontal lighting of a very even quality, slightly flat in modelling effects. The dimensional qualities and roundedness or depth of subjects will not be brought out, and the main clues to shape and form will be colour and subject recognition (the viewer knows a face is not flat, and therefore sees it with depth).

Often the sky behind a subject lit this way will be marginally darker than a white part of the subject. This can help distinguish between light detail and sky, when on overcast days generally there is a danger of the two blending together. Exposure is important in this respect, since slight overexposure may wipe out any trace of sky tone, and merge subject whites into the sky.

Overcast sidelight, when the subject is turned so that the most directional light falls across it, produces excellent modelling and shape. It is better to have the light direction slightly to the front of the subject rather than a perfect 90° to one side, but the diffused nature of overcast light means positioning is hardly critical. There will be an identifiable highlight and shadow side, particularly to solid subjects like buildings. Faces photograph particularly well, and so does fashion. The only problem with overcast sidelight is that one half of the sky, when included, will tend to be brighter; a graduated darkening of the sky from one side of the picture to the other can make the production of an even sky-tone hard. This does not always matter, but as a rule the appearance of a slight tone in the sky towards one side of a picture only is detrimental.

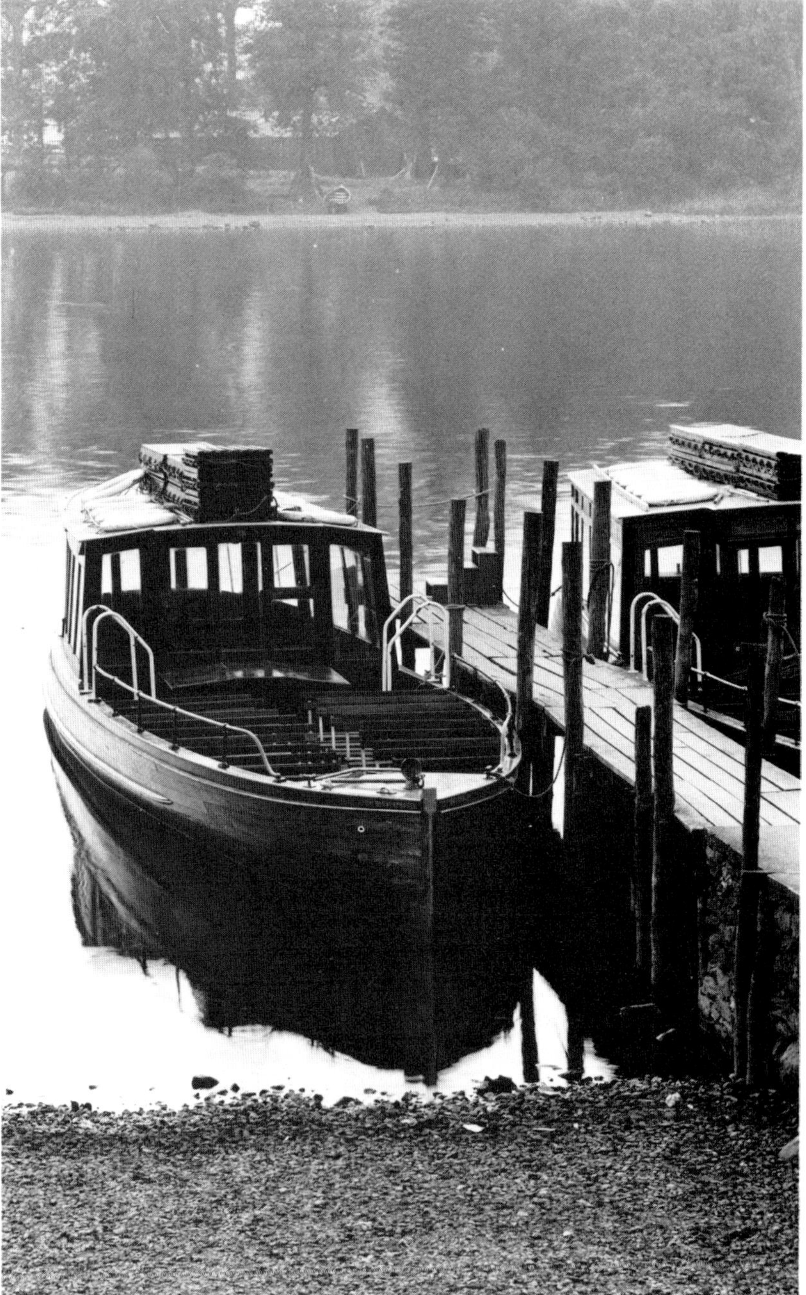

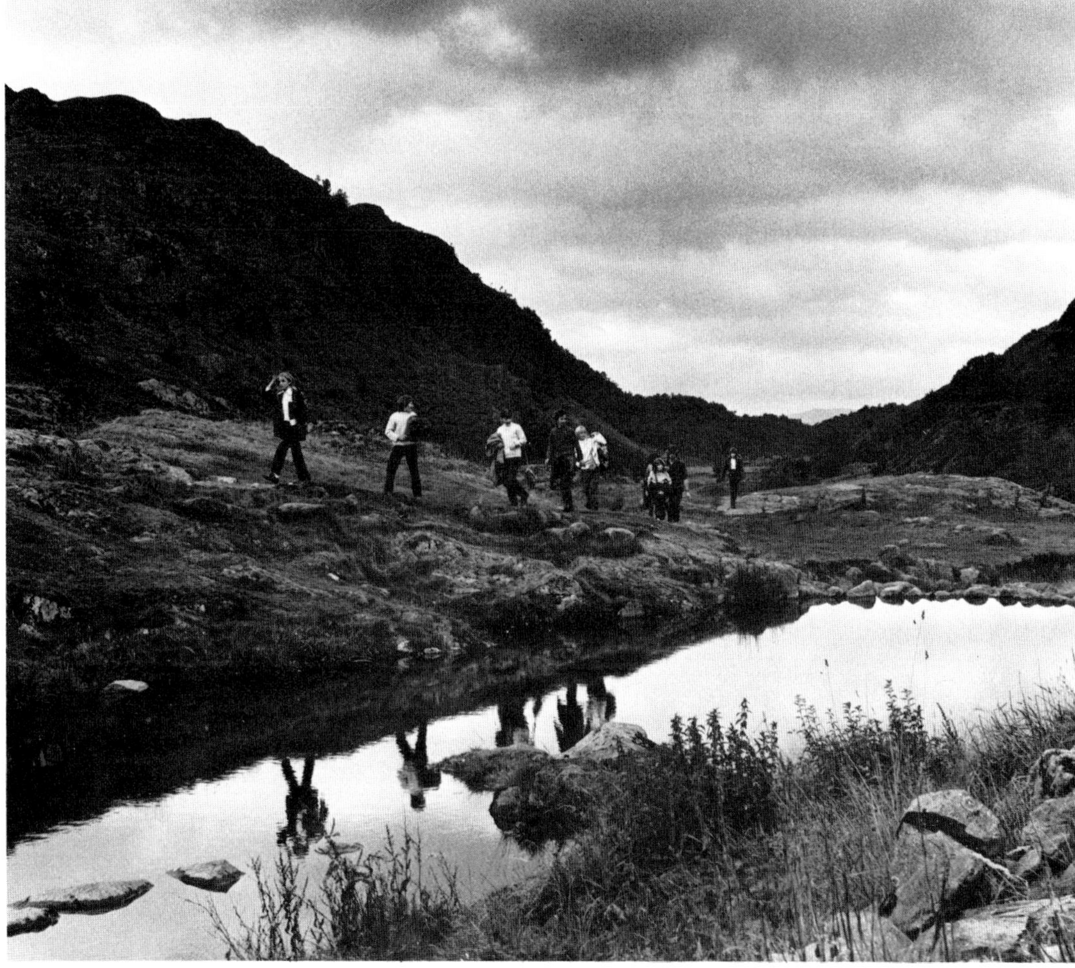

By varying the exposure, the mood of overcast sidelight can be changed. More exposure may even create a sunny effect, particularly if a warm-up filter (giving a marginal pink or yellow tint) is put over the lens. Less exposure can make the picture sombre or threatening. In black-and-white, the use of high-contrast printing with this type of light can make graphic images. High-contrast printing can rarely be used on sunlit subjects, as the result then becomes harsh rather than powerful. In frontal overcast lighting, high contrast is often necessary to make any kind of impact in monochrome, because the flattened tonal range needs expanding just to look normal.

Overcast backlight, with the brightest region of sky behind the subject, gives an entirely different effect. If the exposure is read correctly, taken from the subject rather than from the scene as an average, the sky will be bright and probably appear pure white. Surfaces like grass, streets, rooftops or water will pick up a strong reflected sheen. Translucent

63

details like leaves may appear brighter. Contrast in the overall scene is likely to be higher than normal, with fairly dense shadows facing the camera. This depends on the ratio between light and dark sides of the sky.

Lighting on surfaces facing the camera, although in shade, will be even. Given the correct degree of extra exposure, the effect will be one of luminosity. All rim and edge surfaces, particularly fur, hair and foliage, will pick up the backlight. Shiny subjects like cars look glossy when photographed in this light, as the bright sky is reflected in the paintwork.

Overcast backlight can, therefore, produce some of the most attractive outdoor pictures. Against this, problems have to be considered. Most are caused by the existence of a large, diffused light source partially included in the picture. To begin with, the picture may not call for a total tonal wipe-out of the sky. Given correct subject exposure, some edge details like twigs on trees may be lost entirely due to light spread, especially when differential focus is used. Automatic exposure, with video systems, may be upset to the extent that as the camera is panned across to follow a subject passing from the front-lit area to the backlit area on a dull day, the whole scene darkens.

A solution, though makeshift and partial, is to use a graduated filter. This has its bottom half clear, with a soft-edged transition to grey or a suitable colour (like sky blue) in the top half. The idea is to compose the shot so that the ground area is seen through the clear half, and the coloured half covers the sky. The smooth graduation, achieved by dipping the filter in its dye-bath with controlled movement, avoids any sharp change. The artificial blue sky produced sometimes looks realistic. When conditions mean that it will look false, some photographers prefer to use a brown or sepia filter, which gives a glowering impression. Graduated filters are made in various strengths and almost every colour for creative effects.

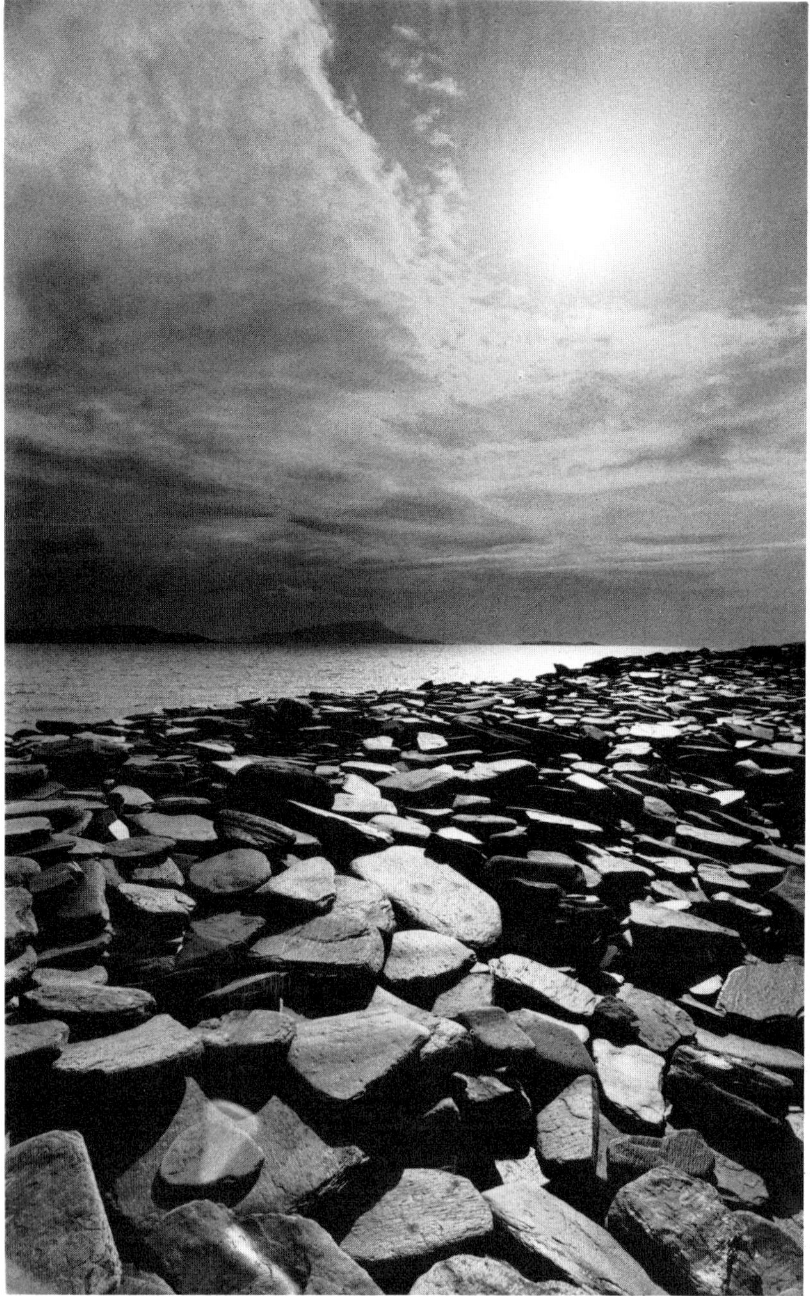

Modelling, surface texture and plasticity in overcast shots depend to a great extent on the quality of the film and lenses used. Video images in general show very little roundedness or tactile quality, because of the coarse resolution called for. Large-format camera lenses and film (5×4 in or over) do the reverse, and convert overcast light into a medium for displaying incredible surface detail and dimensional depth. In 35mm and rollfilm, better lenses and slower films will always beat cheap lenses and fast film.

Unfortunately, one of the worst effects of strong backlight from a large expanse of bright sky is to degrade image detail. Stray light, reflected within the optical system of the camera, produces flare. This is not immediately visible; unlike flare from a single bright light source, which may form strings or patches of coloured light, flare from a bright sky is scattered over the whole picture area. This lowers contrast, veils the finest highlight details, and flattens the picture. To avoid flare, use a deep lenshood matched to the lens, and avoid including large area of sky. Pick a high viewpoint, so that you look slightly down on to the subject, and limit the sky to a quarter of the frame area. A graduated filter naturally helps reduce flare by cutting down the level of the stray light, but what flare there is also induces a slight colour-cast if the filter is anything but grey itself.

Clear sunlight

To some extent, it is easier to recognise typical lighting conditions in sunshine. There is no real doubt about the directional quality of the light. The typical light conditions – front, side, back, rim and low cross-light – are well-enough known to be identified and used for their equally well-known qualities. The only type of sunlight which is not encountered in temperate latitudes is direct overhead sun. This produces harsh, unpleasantly top-lit shots and is particularly unflattering to faces.

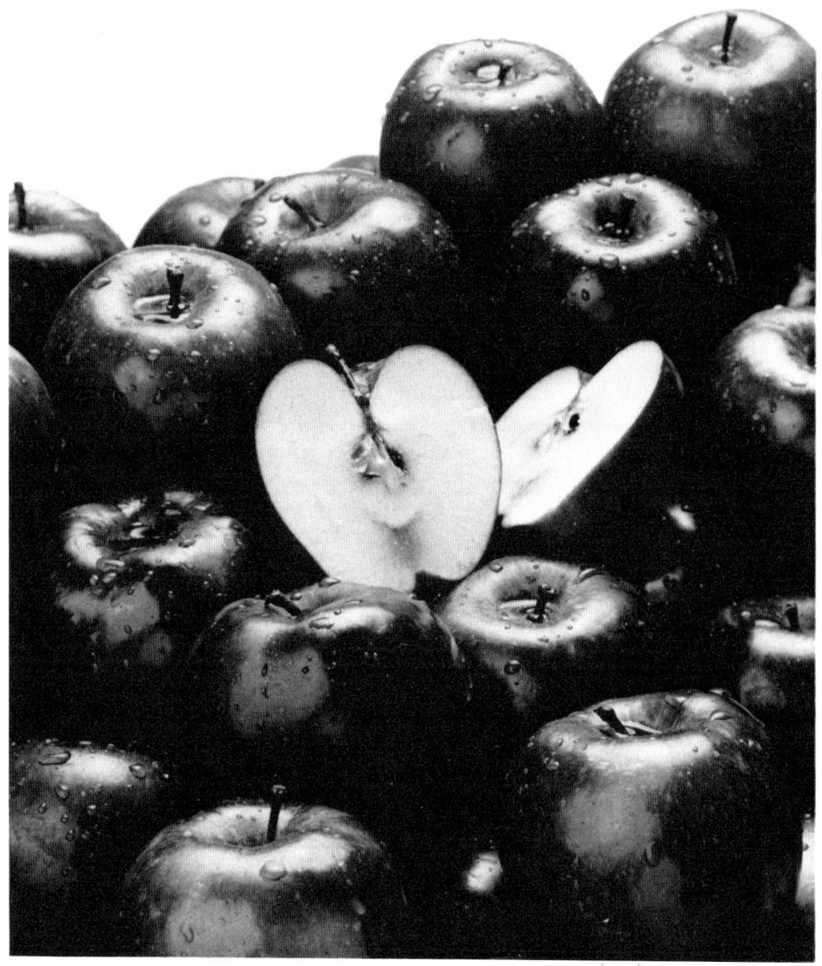

Left: diffused sunlight directly into the lens gives a strong surface sheen to flat slates on Seil Island, Western Scotland. A 20 mm lens permits the close viewpoint and wide expanse of sky.

Above: diffused backlight outdoors is an ideal condition for environmental food photography, often used by magazine photojournalists.

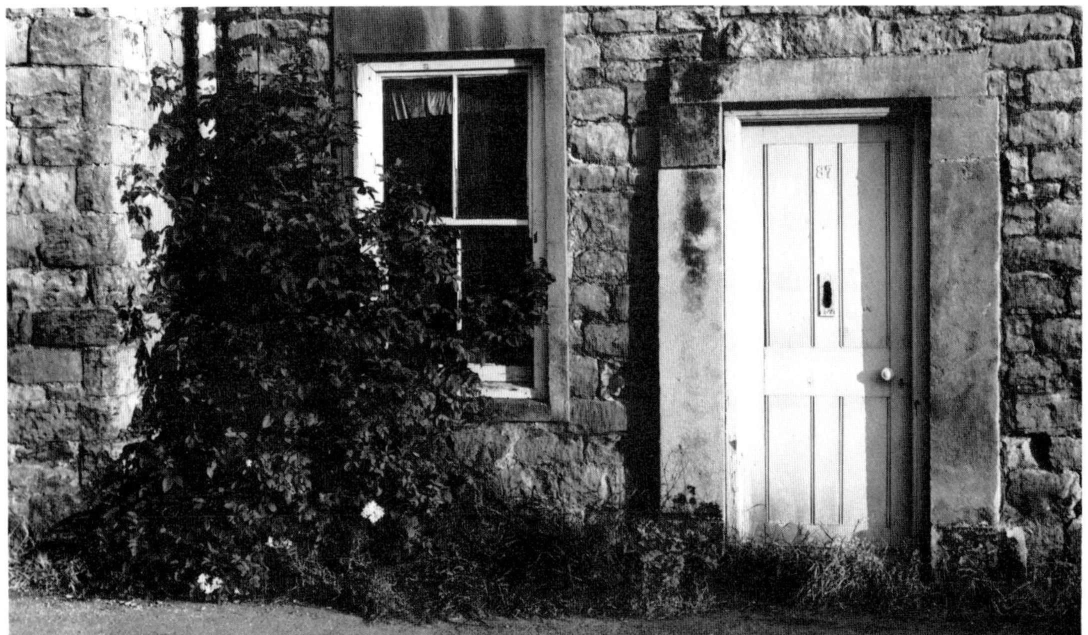

Direct sun with a slight degree of sidelight kills texture and creates strongly blocked-up shadows.

In subtropical and tropical countries, camera units normally pack in for the four hours round noon, and only shoot early or late in the day. This gives rise to a myth that noon is to be avoided at all costs regardless of location, which is untrue. Low winter noon sunlight at 45° latitude resembles late evening light in the tropics and is ideal for photography.

Frontal sunlight causes problems. When the sun is high enough, the modelling becomes very flat, and any aerial haze or dust is emphasised (much in the same way that firing a flashgun through a smoke-filled room picks up the smoke unexpectedly well!). When the sun is low enough for reflections to be produced in vertical glass surfaces, or sharp shadows to be cast behind the subject (both interesting effects to use), the photographer's own shadow tends to be cast into the scene.

So do the shadows of other people and buildings. A strong black line from a telegraph pole or a large blob from a tree may spoil otherwise well-lit ground detail. The solution of moving closing, with a wide-angle lens, does no good; the wide-angle includes the user's shadow even more effectively. In practice a telephoto often has to be used. High frontal sunlight produces much the same ugly eye-shadows and chin-shadows as overhead sun. Fill-in flash is of little practical use, but a reflector can be an advantage. It is better to avoid over-your-shoulder lighting.

Sidelight, which may be from 45° to 90° across the subject, can be found when the sun is fairly high as well as when it is low. As one side of the subject is fully lit and the other falls into shadow, with a gradual terminator line on all three-dimensional rounded subjects, modelling of form and depth is greatly improved.

Natural reflectors come into their own, with buildings casting strong fill light when the sun strikes them full-on. Different orientations of parts of the subject pick up different light qualities,

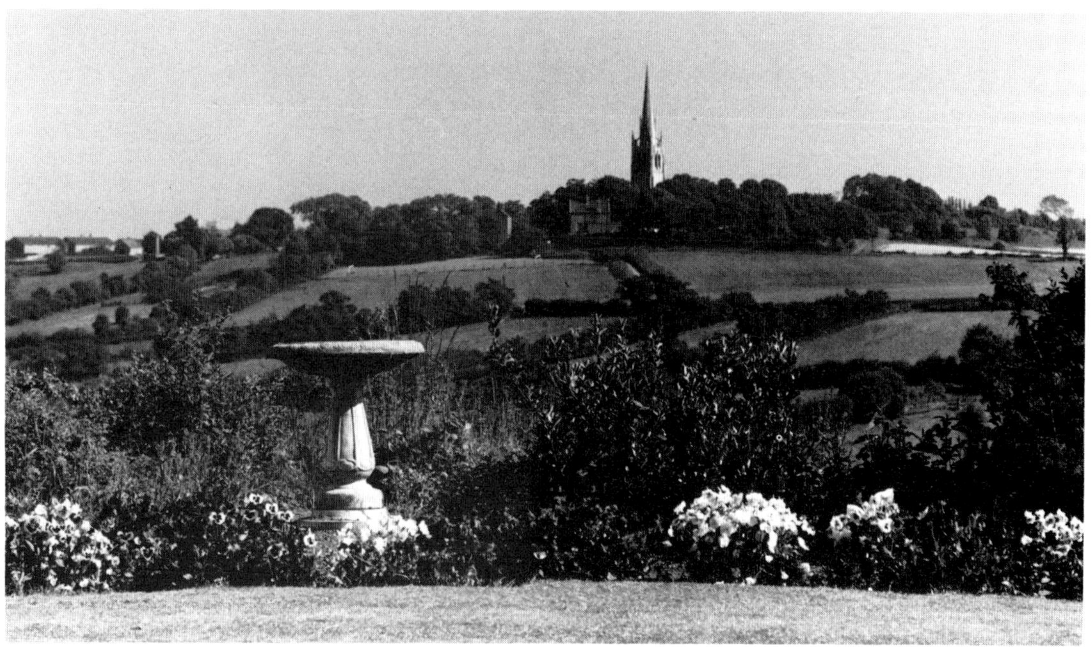

which is not the case in frontal lighting. A wall facing the sun is fully lit; one just skimmed by the sun will show texture and detail as well as being darker; one that is turned away from the sun will be in shadow.

Cast shadows, from the photographer or other obstructions, fall across the picture and generally look less obvious. If one does fall very close to the camera, a move of a few metres may be enough to avoid it. Sidelight also allows the cameraman himself to move into shade when there is some risk of lens flare with very wide-angle lenses, and the sun may almost be included in the shot.

In general terms, sidelighting is recommended for all outdoor scenic photography regardless of the medium. The sky is likely to be a pleasant blue behind a sidelit scene, especially if the sun is at 45° between subject and camera. The balance of light and shade is likely to be optimum, and exposure readings are straightforward.

Crosslighting is a variation on sidelight, when the sun is very low. It will normally be from around 90° but may be slightly in front or behind this angle. Crosslight only exists in relation to a subject with one main orientation, like the facade of a building. The characteristic result is heavily textural, with long sharp cast shadows. In the studio, this kind of lighting would be referred to as 'skim' lighting. A whole landscape can be crosslit shortly before sunset, and hillsides or other inclined surfaces may be crosslit (in contrast to the rest of the scene) when the sun is higher.

Direct backlight, in bright sun, can produce anything from a light and airy portrait to a powerful silhouette. The exposure determines the result. If it is based on the overall scene, expect strong contrast and dense shadows. If it is taken from the shadow side of the subject selectively, then the background will be bright and the shadows should have normal tones.

The use of both reflectors and fill-in flash has
already been discussed when tackling backlight. As
for the form and dimensional qualities of the
picture, strong sunny backlight tends to reduce
every element to a flat cut-out positioned in a
strong aerial perspective. Distant parts of the scene
will probably have haze veiling them, closer detail
will be clear. The impression of depth is given
without any appreciable recording of dimensional
shapes, roundedness, or textures (except in walls or
the ground catching the sun obliquely).

Simple logic will tell you that backlight is most
likely to be found morning and evening, as it can
not exist when the sun is more or less overhead, and
during autumn, winter and spring. As a result,
viewers tend to associate backlight with summer
evenings, early morning, springtime, autumn and
sunny days in winter. All these associations are
pleasant, often nostalgic. Backlight is therefore
used in advertising images to create atmosphere.

The simplification of shapes and loss of detail,
particularly when there is strong aerial perspective,
add to this.

Rim light is backlight taken to an extreme, when no
sky is included. The subject is normally seen against
a dark background – buildings, trees, or perhaps
the ground from a higher than normal viewpoint.
Backlit sun strikes from slightly to one side, and
lights only a narrow rim defining the edge or shape
of the subject. The exposure is kept to a minimum if
the object is to produce a bright rim shape against
solid black. Rim light produces no form, texture or
modelling whatsoever; just shapes, outlines. It is a
highly graphic lighting condition.

In direct sunny conditions, whenever backlight is
encountered, a good lens hood is essential. Unlike
the overall flare given by large bright areas in a
scene, flare from direct sun may combine general

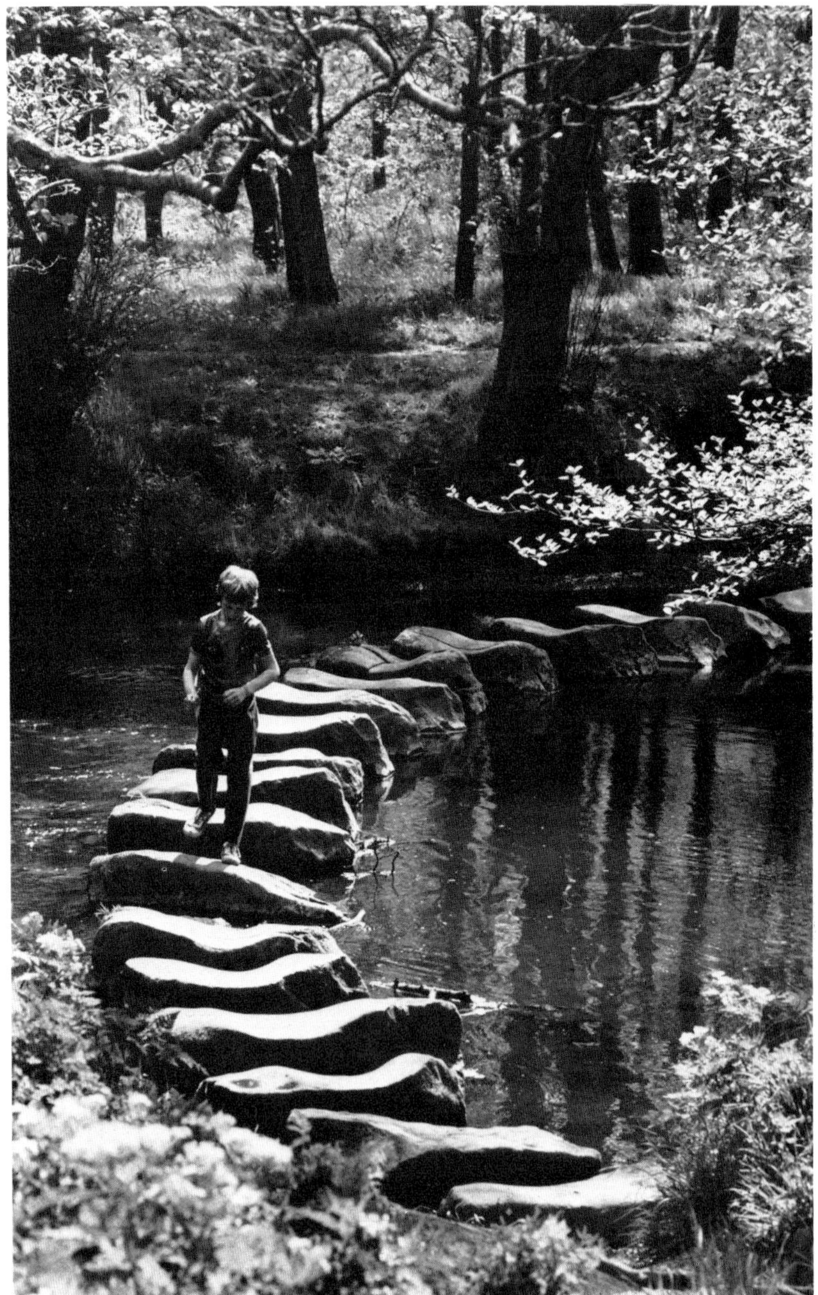

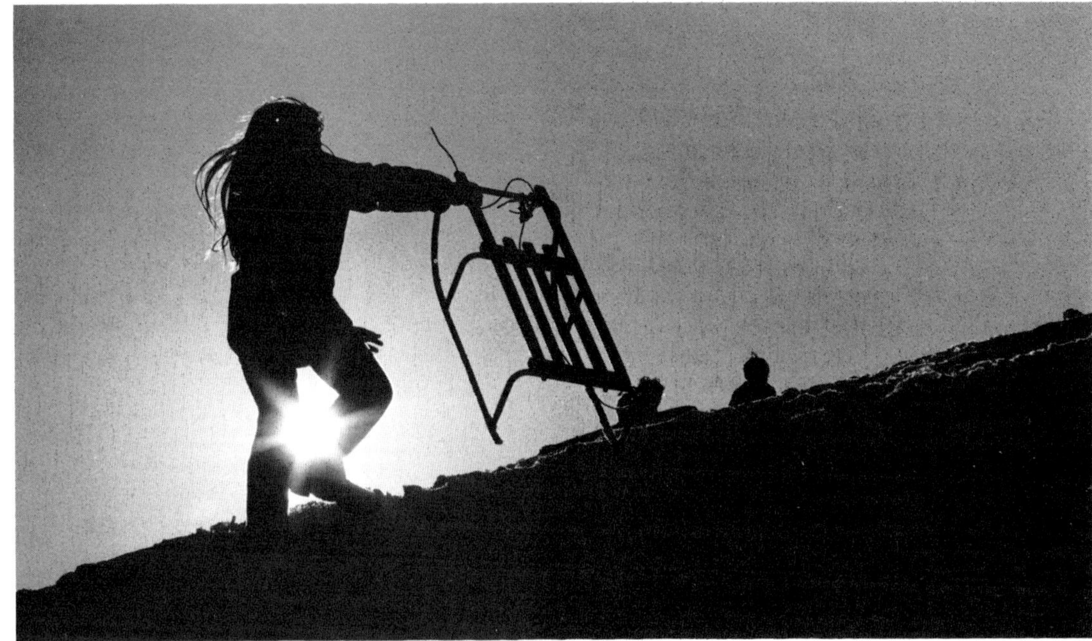

degradation with bright patches of light. These are
impossible to remove from the picture later. To
ensure they do not appear, the scene must be
viewed with the camera's lens set to its final
working aperture, not at full lens aperture, as flare
often appears on stopping down. The most
annoying kind of flare is created by the shape of the
lens aperture being reproduced as a series of
coloured polygons. Good lens design has helped to
eliminate this in many modern optics but some
zooms and wide-angles remain prone to it.

Lens flare and aperture 'ghosts' are acceptable
when the sun itself is included in the picture. To do
this, manual exposure setting is essential. The
exposure must be based on whatever is correct for
the scene in general, without including the sun. This
applies whether the sun is behind an obstruction, or
clearly visible. Generally it is safer to compose the
shot with the sun neatly obscured behind a branch,
or perhaps behind the subject's head so that the
hair is dramatically halo-lit.

Portraits

Outdoor portraits are best taken in overcast
sidelight, overcast backlight, sidelight (for effect) or
sunny backlight. Avoid frontal overcast or frontal
sun. Use fill-in synchro sun flash, or reflectors, to
lighten shadows. There is a basic rule in portraiture
which says that both eyes should be evenly or
equally lit. When overcast or sunny sidelight is
used, the face should be turned three-quarters into
the direction of the light so that the shadow-side
eye does not fall into shade itself. The shading
should start on the cheekbone, beyond the eye. A
deliberate decision to place one half of the face in
shadow in direct sunlight can work well with some
subjects (no rules are absolute!).

If you are obliged to photograph your subject in
overhead sun, find a spot in the shade and get out
of the open daylight. On a totally even overcast
day, with a strong top-light bias, ask the subject to
sit down, but remain standing yourself, so that the
sitter has to face upwards to the camera. This

69

avoids the heavy under-eye shadow normally
produced.

Buildings

Good architectural shots are taken with planning,
working out the best time of year and time of day
for the sun. Buildings look their worst in direct
backlight, and an overcast day is preferable (when
clouds are available, wait for the sun to go in).
Frontal sun rarely produces the best results, unless
there are problems with the standard of finish. Side
or cross lighting, which reveals the texture and
shape of architecture, also picks out uneven
brickwork or surface finishes. To conceal faults,
use frontal light or a dull day.

Scenics

Pictorial views often depend on the quality of light,
state of the subject and weather conditions for their
impact. There can be no hard-and-fast rules. In
general, sunlit conditions produce pictures
preferred by most viewers. For very detailed work,
particularly in close-up, overcast light may be
better. Mood is vital; a windswept heath looks at
its best stormy and windswept, a botanical garden
looks best in full bloom in sunshine.

Shadows

In lighting practice, there is a difference between
shade and shadow. One side of a subject may be
fully lit, and the other will then be in shadow. The
shadow cast by the subject is a different thing, as it
contains no clues to modelling and shape. It is not
important to include a subject's cast shadow in a
picture unless it adds to the composition or
information. Shadows on the subject itself,
revealing its contours, are the most important
results of good lighting. Shade is produced by cast
shadows, and is a lighting condition. A subject
placed in shade may still display directional
lighting, with its own soft shadows. Open shade is
any small area of shade lit by reflected or sky light;
deep shade does not really exist, as it becomes
identical in effect to natural light indoors.

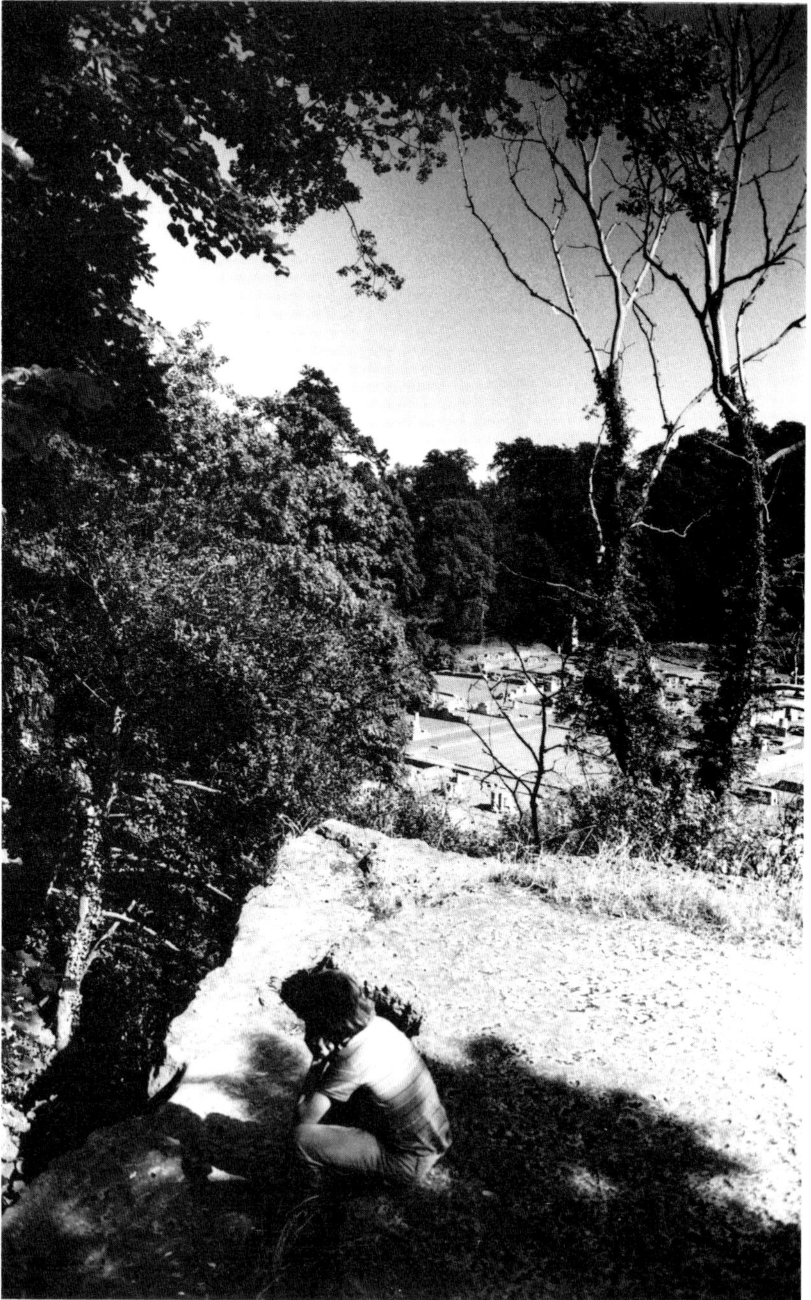

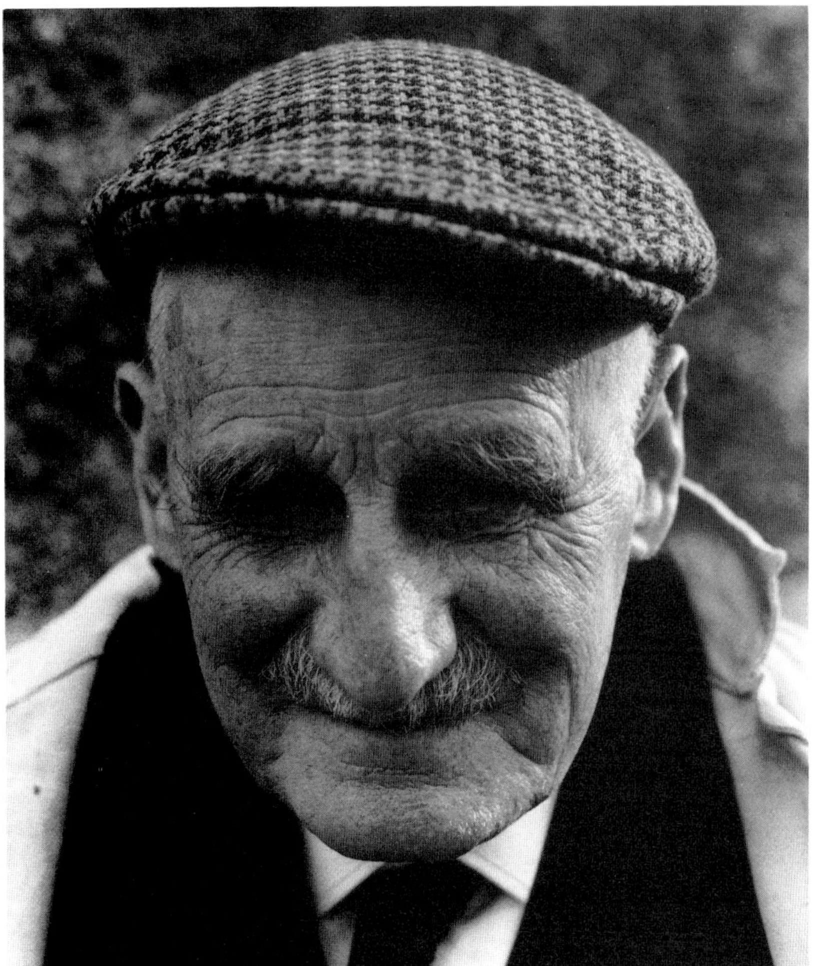

Left: shadows can contribute to a photograph if they fall in a planned, carefully composed way. A 20 mm lens allowed this viewpoint. *Richard Bradbury.*

Above: in this outdoor portrait, the face is in shadow, but a medium-toned background means the overall range is suitable for printing.

Late and early light

Dawn, sunset and dusk are of special interest photographically. The change in light colour compared to midday is considerable, ranging from a golden hue to vivid pink. The principal area of sky light is likely to be a narrow strip along the horizon, of one colour, augmented by a wide expanse of overhead sky with a different colour. At sunset very warm, strong sun is contrasted with cool blue skylight from above. This combination alone guarantees exciting results. The effect is similar to that of light and shadow in shape and dimensional modelling. A colour shift delineates contours and roundness. Reflective sheen takes on a colour, as when a setting sun is reflected off wet streets.

After sunset (or before dawn) there may be a condition where the sky is 30 per cent pink, gradually changing to white or blue, and then to deep grey opposite the sun. Without any direct light, this vast graduated light source offers subtle and beautiful effects. When clouds are present, sometimes catching the rays of the sun to show brilliant red against blue, the complexity of the light is increased. Large bodies of water (lakes or sea) enhance things further.

Under conditions like this, the most attractive shots of vehicles can be taken. This is only because they have reflective, polished paintwork with complex curved surfaces able to reflect the colours of the sky. Any reflective subject, placed with a sunset or dawn background, will be reflecting back to the camera the sky opposite the background, which is normally very different in colour. The contrast makes the picture. Where vehicles look best against the sunset, reflecting the cool sky, fashion and portrait shots look best facing the sunset with the bluer sky tones behind. The warm light is flattering to skin where blue skylight is not.

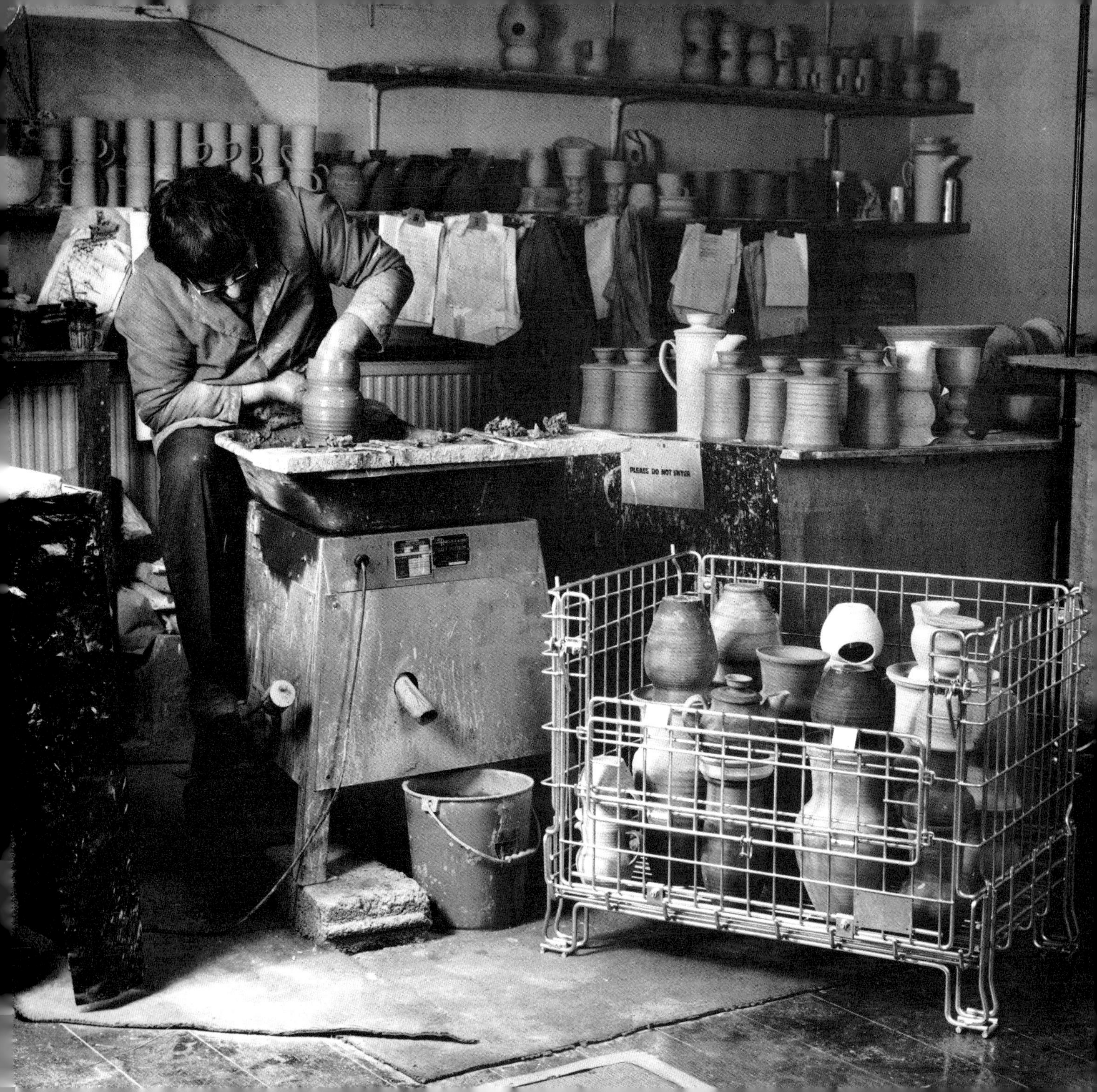
PLEASE DO NOT ENTER

Artificial lighting

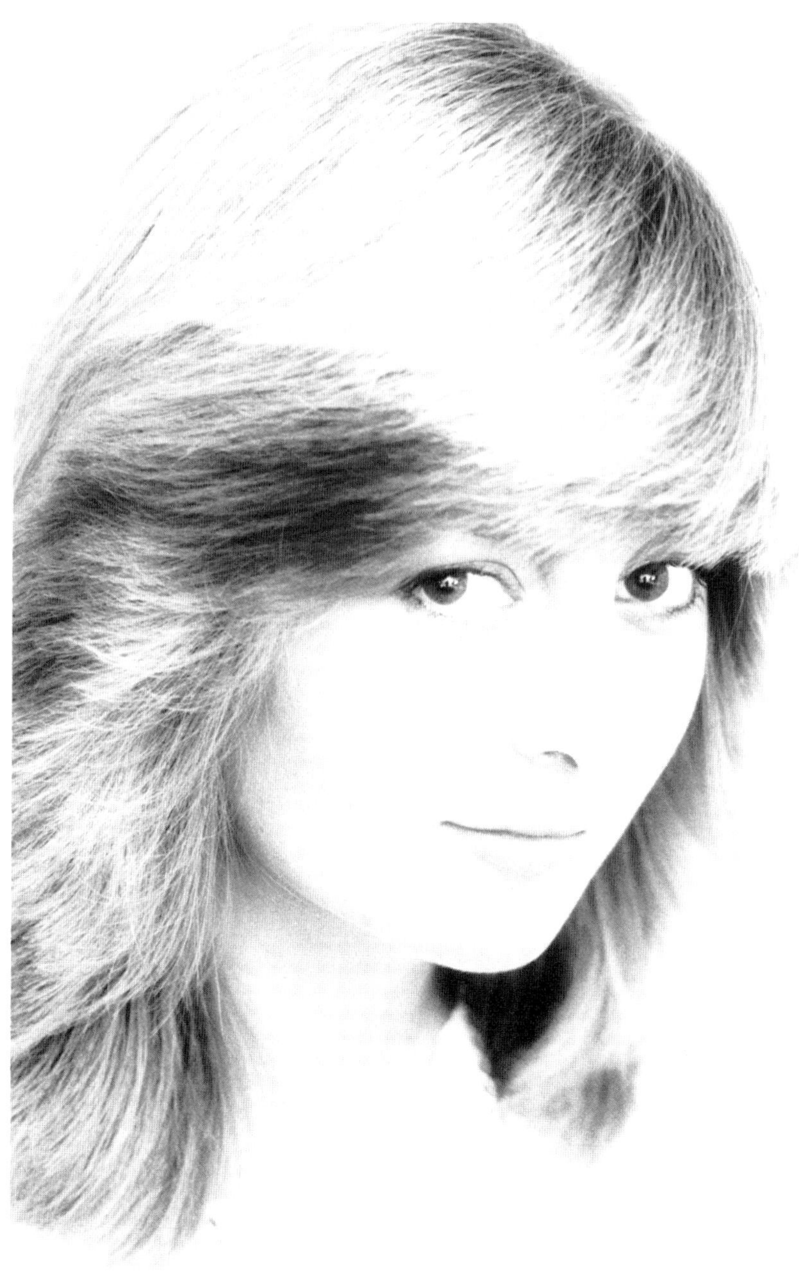

Most pictures of products and people taken for commercial purposes, whether as advertising material at one end of the scale or family portraits at the other, rely on the studio. A studio is a workroom where all unwanted light is excluded and only controllable light is used. As an incidental benefit, there is a relative control over backgrounds, accessories, and environmental conditions. Because the subject must come to the studio, cameras too bulky or complex to be portable can be used. Time may also be saved because everything may be set up ready for the next picture, as in the portrait studio.

The lighting in a studio may include daylight, admitted through ceiling lights with diffused glass and individually operated blinds. Very few studios have this advantage; it must be built-in deliberately, and the rooflights must face north to avoid any possibility of unwanted direct sun. Most studios are equipped with electric systems. For ciné and video, as well as still photography when preferred by the operator, continuous tungsten or tungsten-halogen light sources are used. When black-and-white was universal, mercury vapour, carbon arc and fluorescent lighting was also used. Because these sources give unacceptable colour rendering, they are now obsolete for general studio lighting. All continuous-light systems require a mains circuit able to handle a heavy continuous load.

Still studios are able to use electronic flash, mains operated but requiring far less current. An ordinary domestic mains circuit is able to run a comparatively large professional studio flash system. The mains flash units do have tungsten lights built-in, but these are of low power (typically 100 to 600W compared with the 1000 to 5000W of tungsten lighting units). The modelling lights are

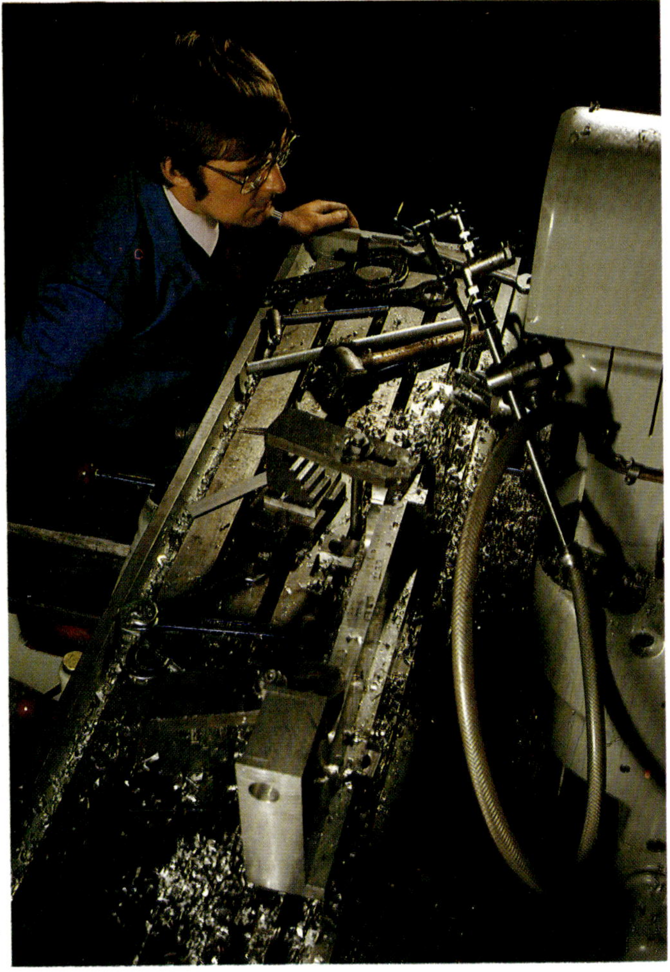

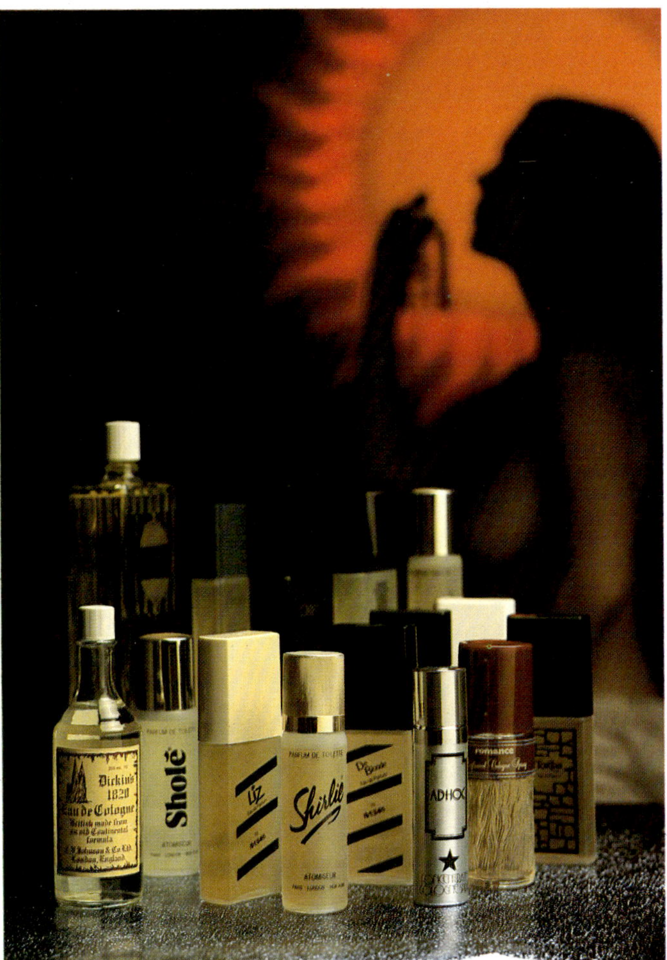

Page 72: the studio can be taken on location using portable flash units. Two umbrella-bounced mains flash units were used to photograph this potter in his studio. Courtesy TWIL Group.

All photographs on pages 72–75 by *David Kilpatrick/A1 studios*

Page 73: controlling the light in a studio using white panels can create very high-key effects.

Left: two flash units lit a small area in a large factory with undiffused reflectors. Courtesy Pandrol Ltd.

Above: in the studio a windowlight picks out products, and a spotlight flash the background. Courtesy Azure Perfumes Ltd.

The headlight from two
cars were 'feathered' using
cards for this tungsten film
shot taken outdoors at
night. Courtesy Kirkby
Central Ltd.

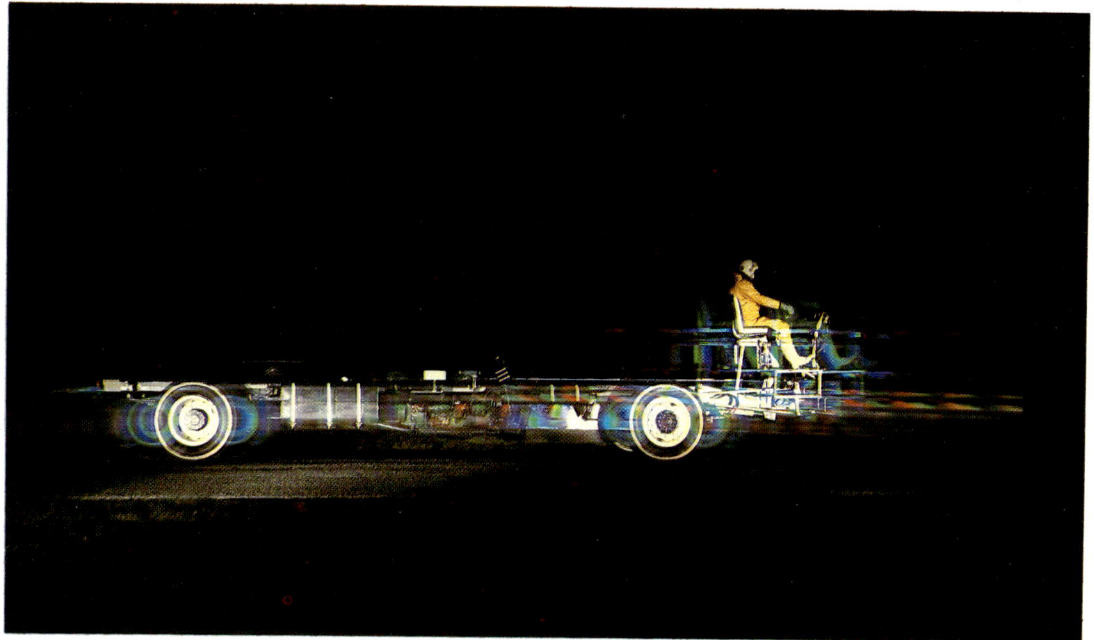

Near right: a glass table,
windowlight and a flash
spot on a reflective
background gave this result.
Courtesy Steadfast Tools
Ltd.

Far right: main lighting
from a diffuse umbrella
with a separate background
light and side backlight.
Courtesy Sandra Williams
Publications Ltd.

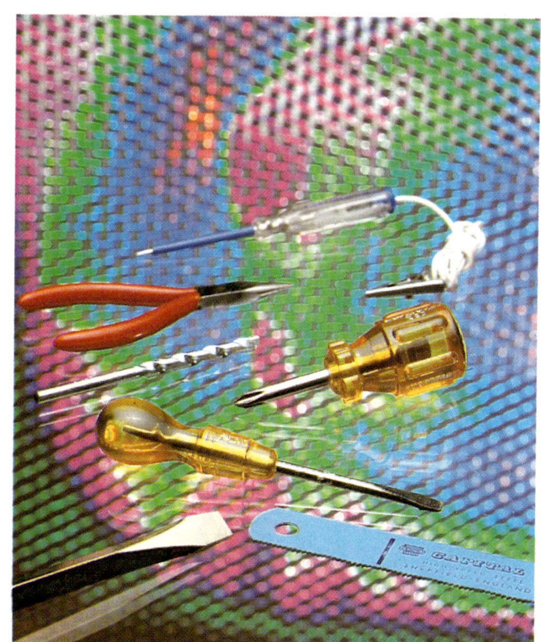

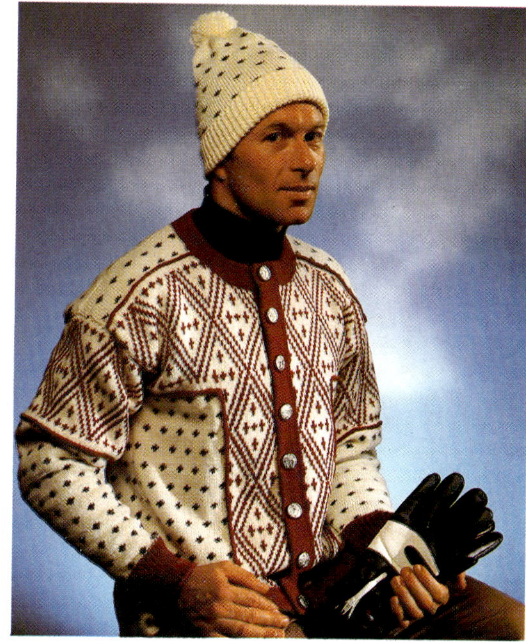

adjacent to the flash discharge tube, and may be linked to the power control so that they can be dimmed in ratio to changes in the flash output. They are used to preview the lighting effect, view and focus the picture.

Studio decor remains a point of argument. A studio must have total blackout, with no daylight admitted, to allow precise lighting evaluation. Some photographers like a completely matt black studio, with no reflective surfaces. The theory behind this is that total absence of reflected stray light puts the operator in full control of the result. Reflectors, when needed, can be positioned round the subject.

Other photographers like to work in a completely white studio. The theory here is that the entire studio, walls and ceiling, can be recruited to act as reflector. Stray light is eliminated at source. Any small amount which does bounce off the subject area, to the walls and ceiling and then back, remains neutral in colour and has little effect other than a marginal fill-in to shadows, which is desirable with colour materials to bring overall contrast within the recording range of the material.

Personal choice depends on style and subject-matter. Black studios tend to produce the highest colour saturation and purest black shadows. White studios often yield greater detail and a lighter, cleaner effect. Those who can afford it maintain a studio with white and black areas, large rolls of black polythene sheet, special curved walls which join the floor and ceiling with no visible corners, and a store of emulsion paint to change the entire colour on demand.

One thing is firmly agreed by all: a studio should be large enough to allow the lighting to be positioned freely. Because of the inverse square law, which states that illumination is quartered in intensity for a doubling in distance, you can not light a tall or deep subject with a light which is very close. A more powerful light at a distance or a very large diffused light will be needed to give even illumination from head to foot or front to back. A small photographic studio needs to be at least 5×8 metres with a 4-metre ceiling height. A commercial studio should be twice this size with a 5-metre ceiling. Industrial warehouses are often used as large advertising studios. A modern television studio, constructed on traditional lines, will have a 15-metre roof height.

When space is limited, controllability of individual lighting units is even more important. The ability to change output power to $\frac{1}{2}$, $\frac{1}{4}$ or less increases the 'size' of the studio; if all lights work at full power only, distance is the only way of altering illumination while retaining original light-source quality. With tungsten lighting, the output can only be altered by fitting neutral-density filters (grey plastic sheets) or using a lower-wattage lighting head. Studio flash can be controlled by either of these means when fixed power heads are employed, but most models have a switch for full and half power or other ratios.

Simple artificial light
The simplest forms of lighting in both still and video media are used on-camera, or on a bracket attached to the camera. They provide direct, undiffused lighting from the camera position. As such, they should not be considered creative lighting aids; their sole purpose is to ensure adequate exposure when it would otherwise be impossible. Harsh shadows, flat frontal light, red or glinting eyes are a few of the problems given by on-camera flash or lights.

To reduce the harshness of light quality, and add some directional interest, an on-camera lighting unit can be aimed at the ceiling or a wall to give 'bounce' light. The bounce surface chosen must be white, and the room must not be too large for the diluted light to have any effect. Exposure metering (including flash metering when flash is involved) is

Near right: two flashguns can be aimed into a single umbrella attachment to give maximum output with portable equipment.

Far right: a typical press-type flash unit has a head which can be tilted and swivelled to allow bounce flash operation.

Near right: a mains studio flash unit may have a control panel which allows continuously variable dimming of both the flash and modelling light.

Still cameras can have their own small built-in flash units.

Far right: video and ciné cameras can be fitted with lights, normally for direct use, but in this case able to be tilted to allow bounce lighting.

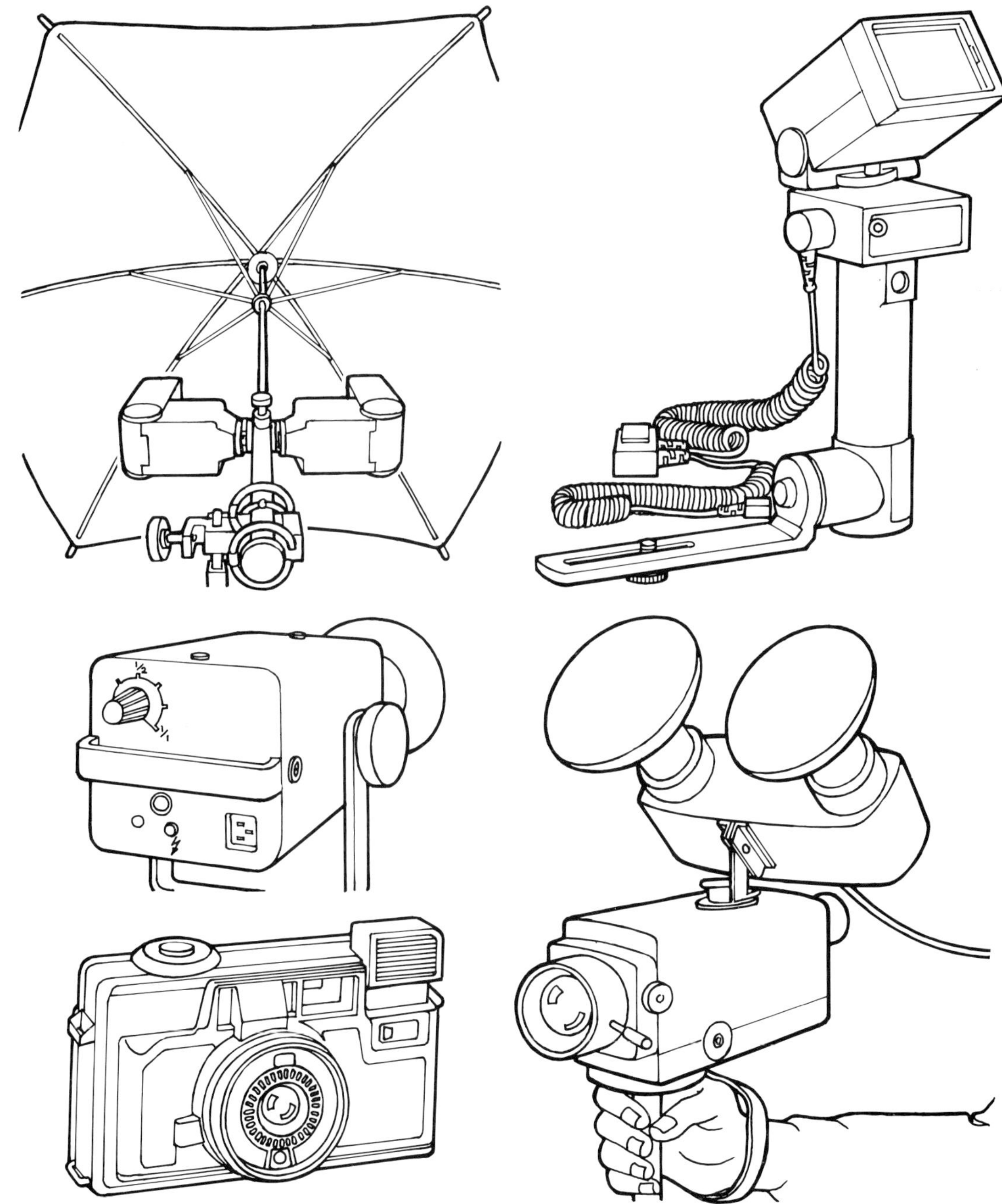

the only accurate way to judge the result of
bouncing light. Bounce from the ceiling is often
used with flashguns without modelling lamps. The
shadows and light direction are both so diffused
that there is little need to preview the result.

A second point about on-camera artificial light is
that this is the light you use outside the studio, on
location. It is taken along with the camera. It is
used to augment existing light or improve it. The
on-camera light can fill in backlight (synchro-sun)
and also add small reflected highlights, called
catchlights, to the eyes of portrait subjects. A
catchlight in the eye adds life and sparkle to a shot.

Portable on-camera lighting may be the only
solution with highly mobile and unpredictable
subjects like children or personalities in the news.
There may also be situations where no other kind
of light can be allowed; a sealed and tested flashgun
may be allowed down a colliery, or a video light
with battery accumulator belt pack used by a
pot-holer filming caves. In the absence of mains
power, flashguns give hundreds of still shots from a
set of cells, and video lights can often be run from a
vehicle battery.

Controlled lighting

In the studio, whether permanent or created
temporarily to suit the subject, lighting can be
controlled and taken off the camera. The lighting
heads are supported by stands which are adjustable
in height, and light enough to wheel or lift from
spot to spot. The main problem in controlling light
is control of the subject; if mobile, the light must
cover a big enough area to cope with the
movement. When the subject can be kept still (or is
inanimate), closer, more precise lighting can be
used.

Control of the subject extends to more than
keeping it stationary. In order to produce a
particular reflection or catch the light in a certain
way, a product may have to be suspended several

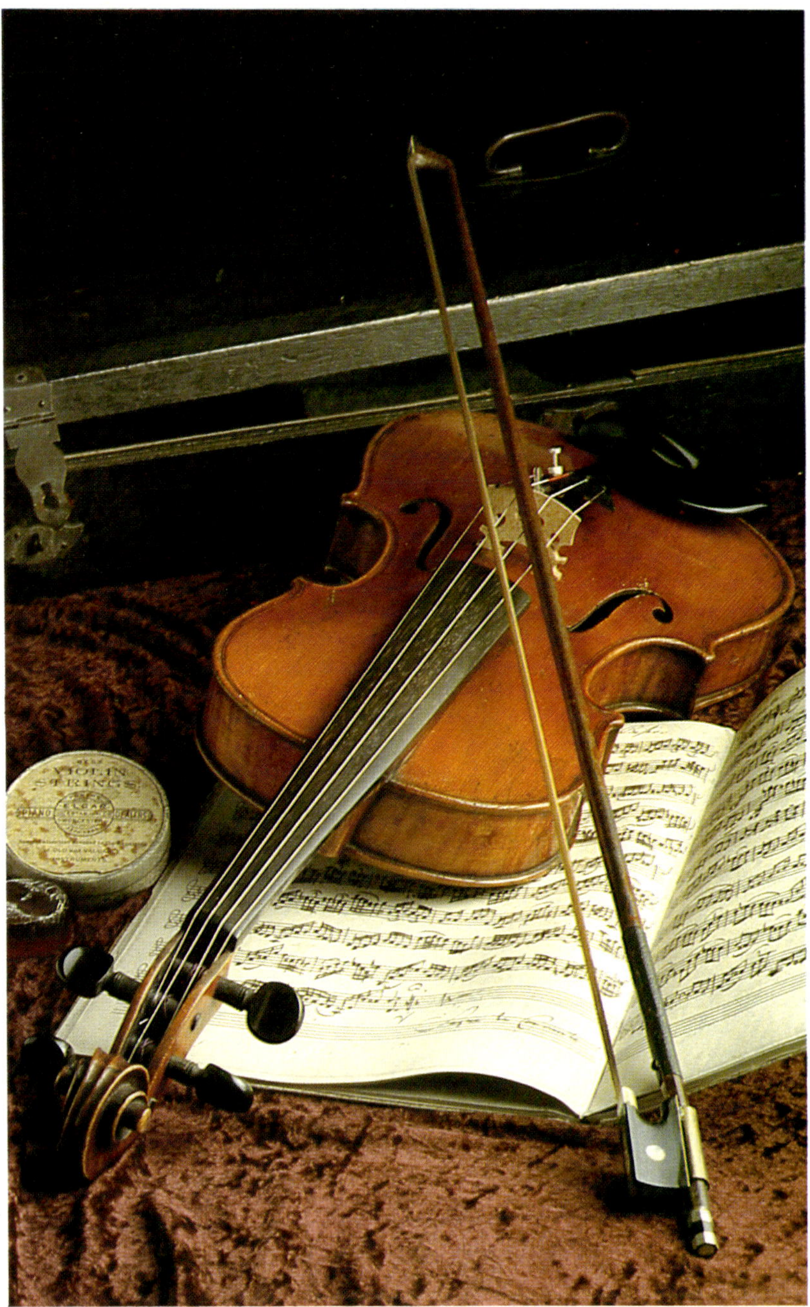

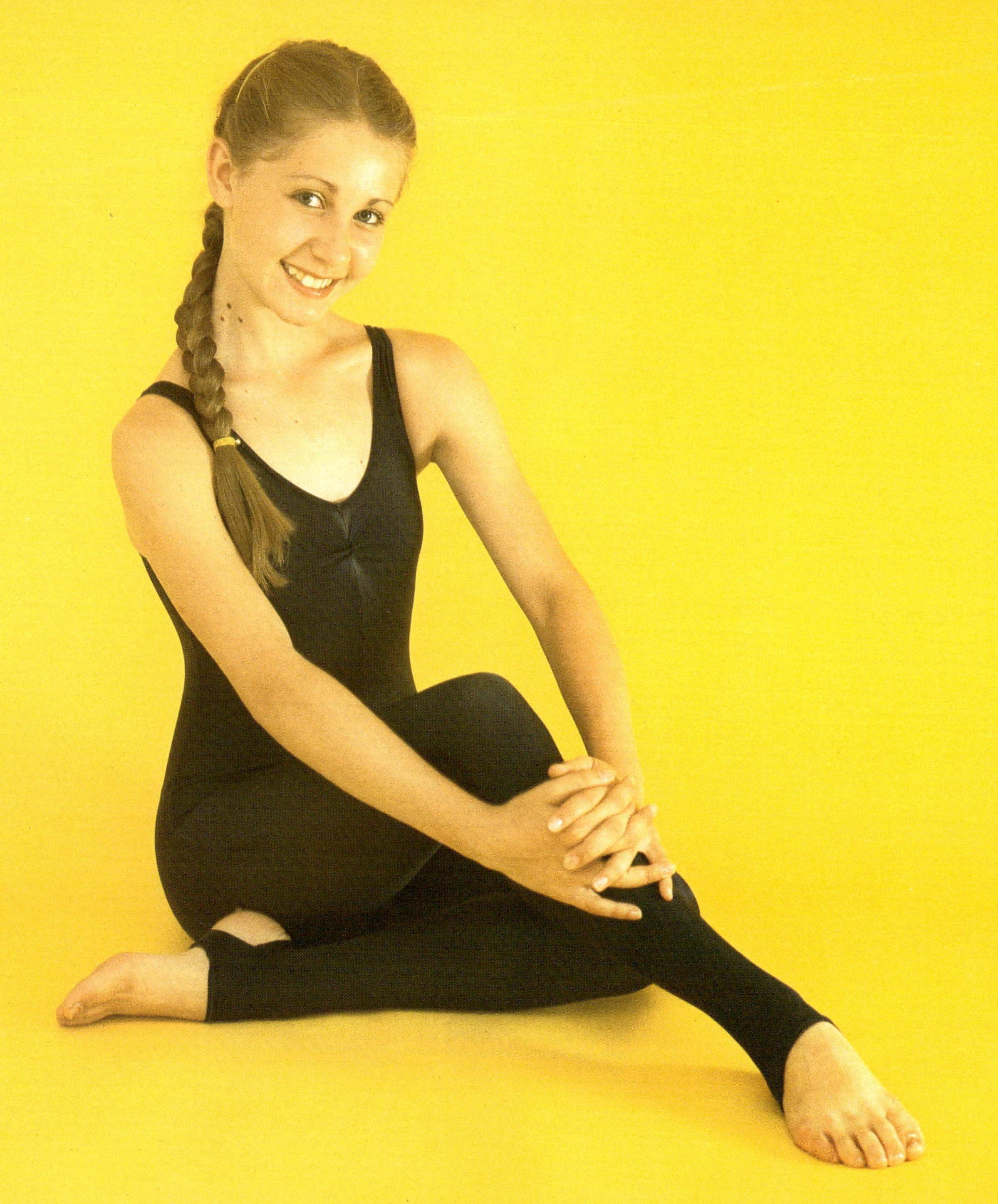

inches above the background material at a precise
angle, with reflectors or lights positioned just out of
shot. The camera may have to be at an unusual
height, and perhaps in order to achieve the right
perspective to obtain the lighting effect wanted, a
very long lens will be used from a distance.

In the studio, a whole range of accessories from
complete glass-topped tables to clamps, wire,
spikes and sticky fixing pads, and a carpenter's
workshop may be built up just for the purpose of
controlling the subject. Part of the control allows
the right backgrounds and viewpoints, but at least
half of the effort is put in just to enable good
lighting effects.

People

A studio for still photographs of people may be
converted from a normal living-room. If the
curtains can be drawn to exclude light, and there is
about three metres clearance in a straight line to
allow for a backdrop, subject and camera, portraits
will not present a problem. Full-length shots are
different. For a good rendering, the camera should
be five metres away from a full-length subject. The
main lights should be at least four metres above
ground, at the same distance as the camera or a
little closer. Very few full-length shots are taken in
ideal conditions as so few studios have them.

Three-quarter length shots, however, can be taken
in the smallest studio. The problem with full length
is that some clearance is necessary below the feet,
which should never be cut off just at the ankle or
touch the bottom edge of the picture. This doubles
the picture height, and in turn all the studio
dimensions. There are other logistical problems
involved once you exceed three-quarter length. The
best viewpoint is waist-high, for the camera, and
this means the background must extend for a metre
or more above head height to avoid the top edge
appearing in the shot. Full-length shots look
terrible on film or video because of the space
wasted on each side, and even a vertical 35mm still

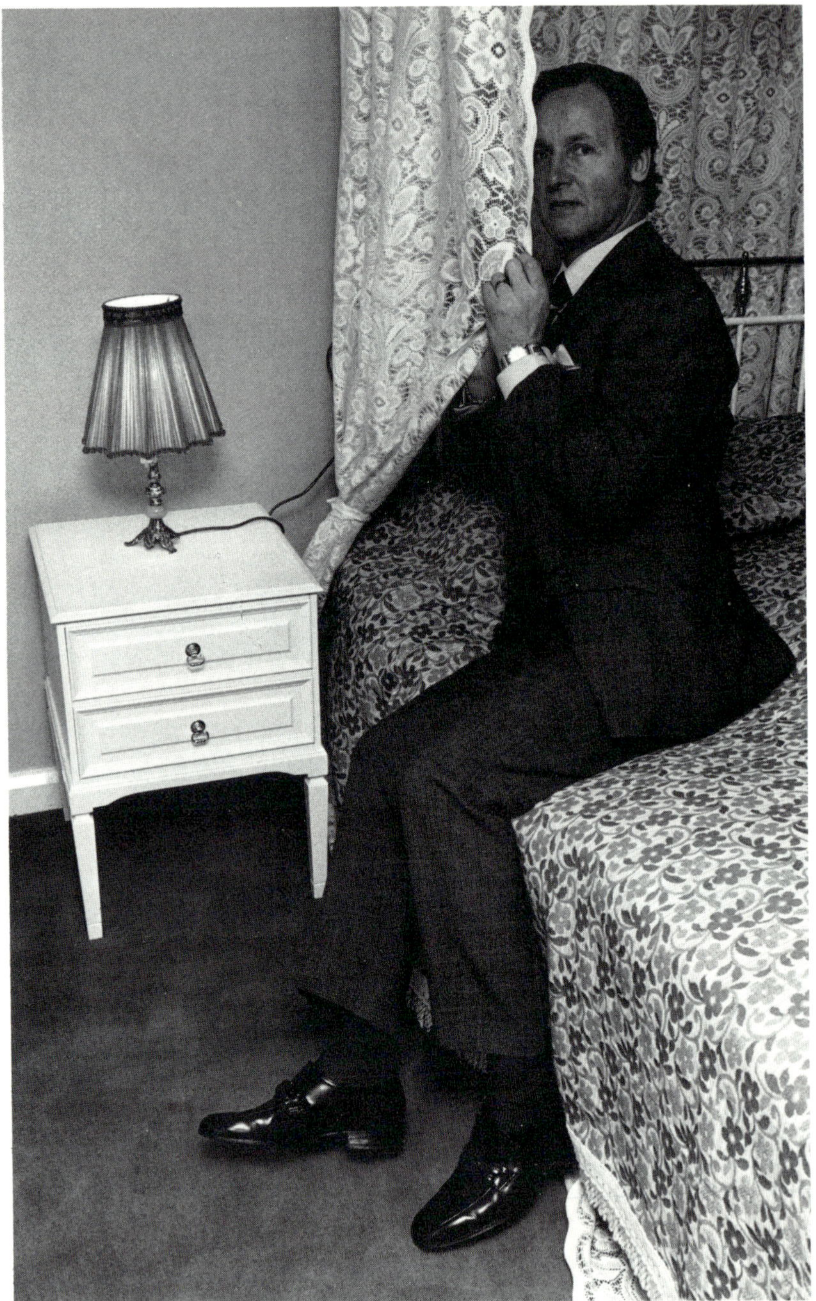

frame does not suit the standing human figure unless elaborate props or backgrounds are used to fill the space.

Because of this, studios for photographing people are rarely built to a size for full-length work. Family groups, and occasional full-length shots, may be taken using seated or half-supported poses. The lighting installed can use conventional lighting stands which extend to little more than two metres high, and judicious use of reflectors (see chapter on light-control technology) can solve the problems associated with difficult shots.

Objects

Lighting and studio facilities for objects – normally products or artefacts – depend entirely on the size of the subjects involved. Any subject brought into a studio should have at least its own dimensions to clear all round it as leeway. A free-standing machine tool, for example, should be placed on a background so that there is at least its own height to clear in front of it before the background ends, and the same in clearance above it. The background should extend for the width of the subject on either side. By the time camera viewpoint and perspective have taken their toll, reducing the apparent width of a roll of background paper which hangs down a metre or two behind the subject, this clearance will not seem as generous. There must be room to maneouvre the lighting outside this zone, and room for the camera as well! Just because you can drive a small car into a single garage does not mean that a single garage could ever serve as a studio to photograph the same car.

In practice, a conscientious photographer should turn away work when aware that the item is just too big for comfort. As a guide, the width of a standard background paper roll is just under three metres. To light an area this wide, rolled out with a two-metre high vertical drop, curving on to a two metre flat run on the floor, needs a studio 5 × 9 metres in floor area and four metres ceiling height.

The largest subject you could expect to tackle on this basis would be something like a small office desk and chair, a large lawn-mower, a small motorcycle, or a double-width kitchen unit. If this sounds a depressing analysis, remember that many photographers squeeze quarts into pint pots daily, but not without technical problems and severe restrictions on lighting and viewpoint.

Basic light systems

It is possible to start out in studio lighting with just a single light source. This should be powerful enough to be used through a diffuser or reflected, and still allow reasonable exposure settings. For video and ciné work a 2000W flood is recommended, and for still photography a mains flash unit with a power rating of 400–500 joules (or watt-seconds) should be used. The single light source should be supplemented by an efficient $1m^2$ reflector panel with adjustable stand. This serves as a fill-in, positioned to accept stray light from the main source and return it to the shadow side of the subject. A diffusing scrim or translucent nylon umbrella, to aim the light through, is also a great help.

Much more is possible with two lights. The reflector panel is still useful, and one should be kept around if possible, but a second light makes its use optional, as properly controlled shadow fill-in can be given. The second light must either have a means of power control (even a neutral density filter will do) or be roughly half the power of the first. As there are some jobs which call for two equally-balanced light sources, such as copying a document, it pays to decide on the former option. The second light may benefit from a different kind of diffuser or bounce umbrella, to give some further choice of effects.

Once you add a third lighting head, the kit is effectively complete. Very few lighting set-ups call for more than three light sources, as we shall see in the next chapter. If the reflector panel is also available, there will be no need to complain that it is impossible to light a subject properly. There may not be enough power to hand and you may not yet have the correct lighting control accessories, but three heads are enough for almost anything.

The third head can be different fromt the other two; there is less need for it to be matched. For economy, one half the power can be picked. In video and ciné this will probably be a 1000W unit, and it is likely to be much smaller and more portable than the 2000W heads. This makes it an ideal location light. At 1000W, it may also match the output of a battery-powered sun-gun, though most are dimmer to save battery time.

In still electronic flash systems, a 200 watt-second unit can be added at low cost. If the system chosen offers it, this third head may be a special type – rapid recycling for motor drive shooting, or spotlight effect for concentrated lighting. Alternatively, a larger 800–1000 joules head can be added. This step takes the basic outfit for 'portraiture and small products' into 'general commercial' as a category. The larger head will probably stay in the studio, and may be fitted on a heavy-duty stand or boom arm. The two smaller heads will double up as a location flash kit. It is important, whether the third head is more or less powerful than the main two, that its modelling light is in correct ratio so that the system can be used together with accurate assessment of lighting effects.

The ciné or video studio with little call for outside work may find a similar option in adding to the kit further 2000W heads, but not limiting the number to three. Five or six lights may be appropriate. The reason is simple; moving subjects can be lit in any one place with three lights, but not in two places. Having one 5000W light-source will do little good to a video unit when a subject may have to be tracked through an interior room-set, and need five areas of general illumination. Lights can always be

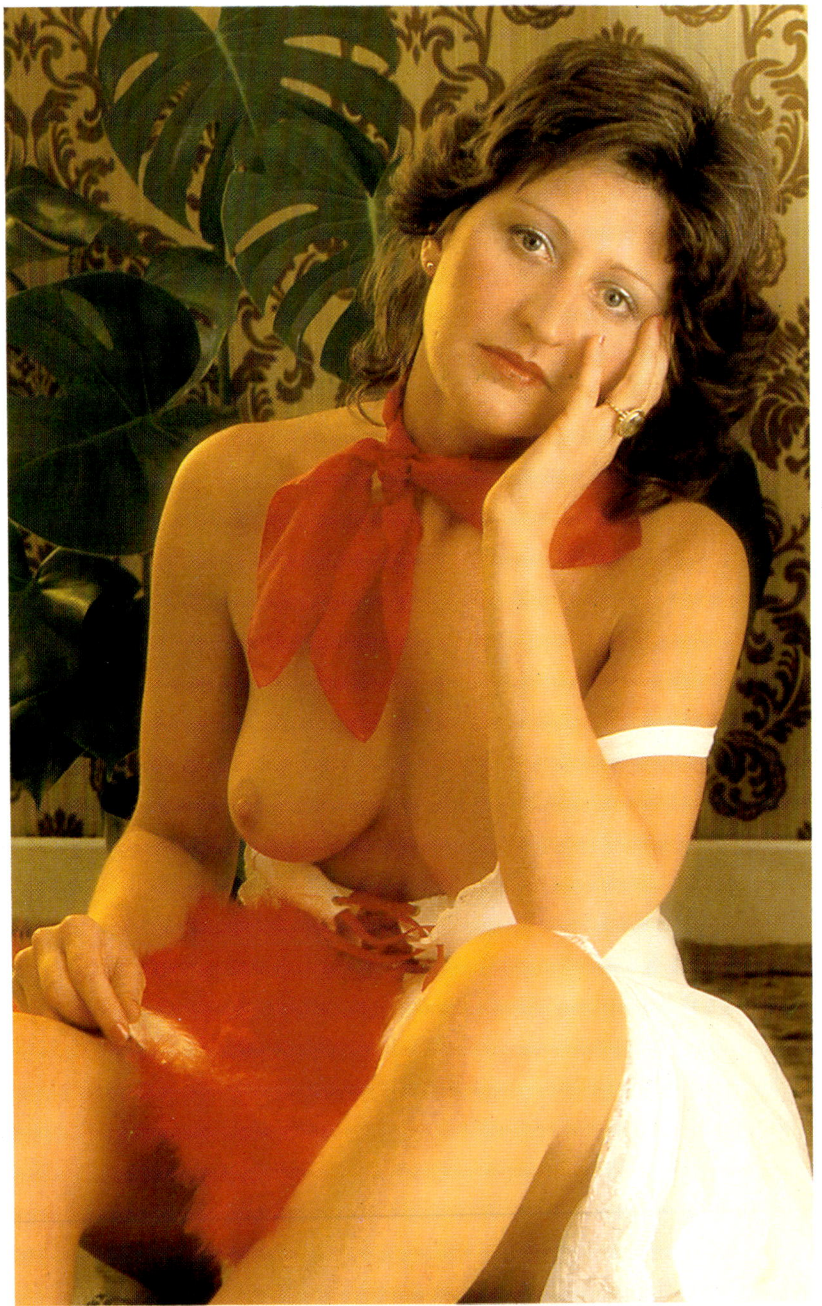

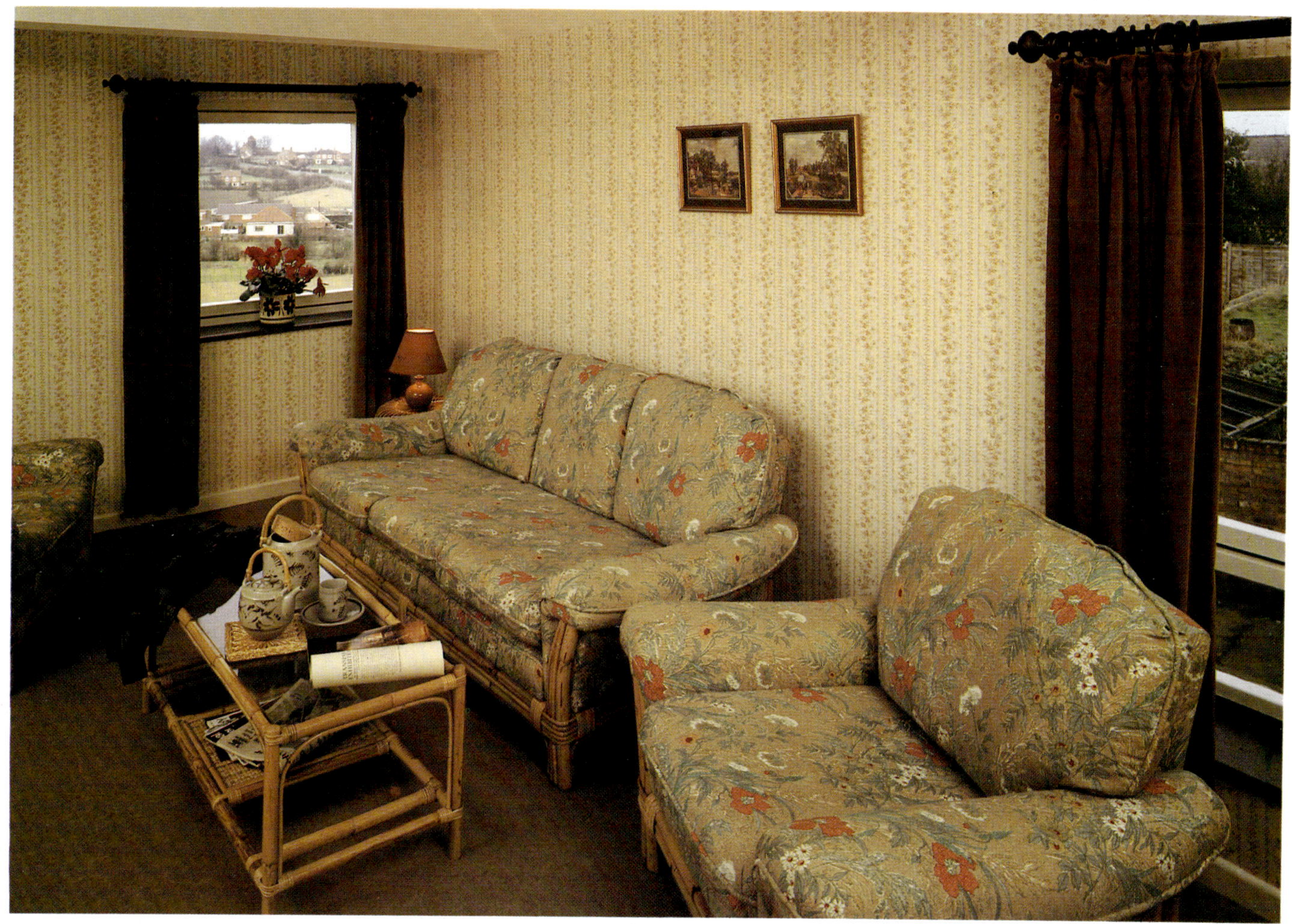

Left: two lighting heads can be enough to make fairly complex effects if they are reflected off coloured surfaces or filtered, and arranged to imitate natural light rather than to 'light the subject'.

Above: three fairly powerful lighting units were needed to balance the light in this roomset so that the window and room appeared equally bright. They were diffused by bouncing off ceiling areas behind the camera. Courtesy Worley Wallcoverings Ltd., *Andy Haslam/A1 Studios*.

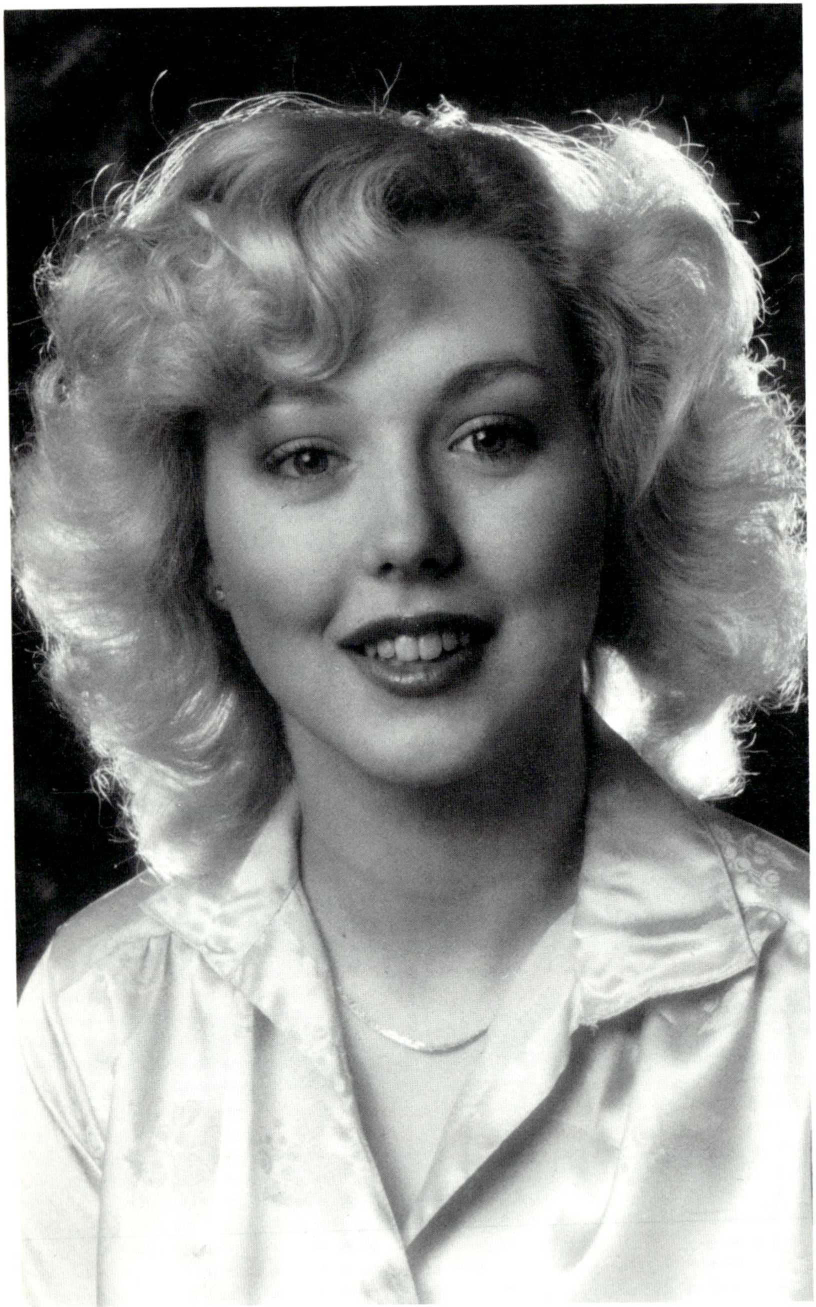

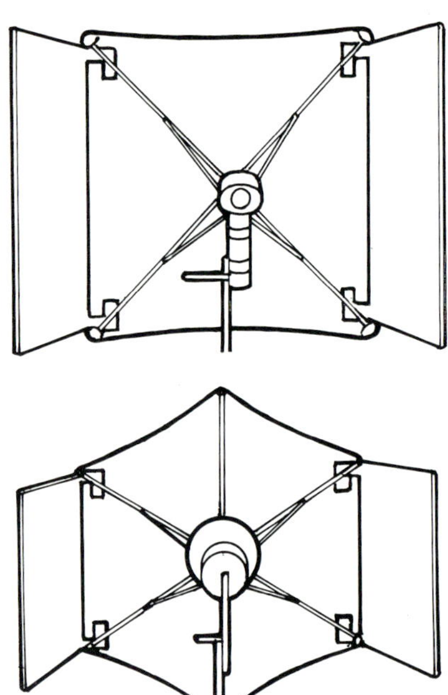

Above: bounce umbrellas can be traditional or square, and can be fitted with further control attachments such as barn doors to prevent stray light spill. Left: bounce-flash brolly lighting is ideal for portraits.

banked together or aimed off reflectors to provide large areas of even illumination.

Both tungsten-halogen and flash sytems come in kit cases, fibre boxes with stands, leads and accessories all included. The most popular kits have two lighting heads, two stands, one or two light-control attachments and a single carrying case. Larger kits may have three heads, and special compact kits will pack miniature heads tightly into pre-cut foam inserts and hold the stands separately in a shoulder quiver.

Light control
It is impossible to mention lighting kits and heads without referring to light-control devices. Tunsten lights, for video, do not usually have reflectors or bounce umbrellas included. The lighting is more often than not direct, and any loss of light level in ciné work is considered detrimental. As video cameras are now relatively sensitive, the standard light-diffusing devices sold with still photography flash outfits could usefully be included in tungsten kits.

The later chapter on light-control technology (page 105) will deal with most of the various forms of light control, but at this stage the bounce and diffusing umbrella has to be mentioned, because this is considered an integral part of electronic flash. Most mains flash units are so powerful that it would be impossible to obtain correct exposure on ISO 100/21° film in a small room with direct flash. They have to be bounced or diffused. This also greatly improves the quality of light, as direct mains flash is like a direct floodlight. Still photography is a critical medium and examines subjects with no mercy shown. Skin texture, under direct light, can be unpleasantly clear. Cast shadows, which do not matter much in moving images, occupy large static blocks of a still picture and almost seem to be joined to the subject.

A flash umbrella is just what it says: an umbrella with a stalk which fits into a socket or tube on the flash-head near the flashtube. The light is aimed into the dish of the umbrella, and bounced back to the subject with a reasonable degree of diffusion. The umbrella becomes a light source from around 75cm diameter (small types) to as large as 180cm. Translucent nylon skin umbrellas can be used between the subject and the flash, aiming through the brolly. This gives even greater diffusion, and offers an alternative arrangement as far as the height and position of the flash itself are concerned. Many kits contain one umbrella of each type. Bounce models may be lined nylon, white-coated opaque material, silvered or gold-lined for a warm colour bias.

It is a mistake to bounce light off a 'shoot thru' brolly, intended as a diffuser, because it has very low efficiency. This can be done to reduce light output deliberately. Metallised umbrella surfaces give higher output than matt white, but slightly harder light quality. To assess the softness of light from a reflector, sit in the subject position and look at the umbrella. If the reflections are even, or it seems evenly lit, then the light-source effect will be even. If there are hot spots on the silver then these are, in practice, localised light sources.

In the studio, much more sophisticated types of reflector and diffuser can be used. The brolly has the advantage of being highly portable, light, and efficient in a wide range of situations. It is particularly popular for portraiture, and the 'stalk' makes the light easy to aim – when the stalk aims at the subject's eyes, the angle is correctly set.

The cost of umbrellas and other light-control attachments varies widely from make to make. When buying flash or tungsten lights, request a full list of accessories and examine the prices. You may find that savings on the heads themselves are eaten away by higher costs of accessories (in effect, essentials) in some ranges.

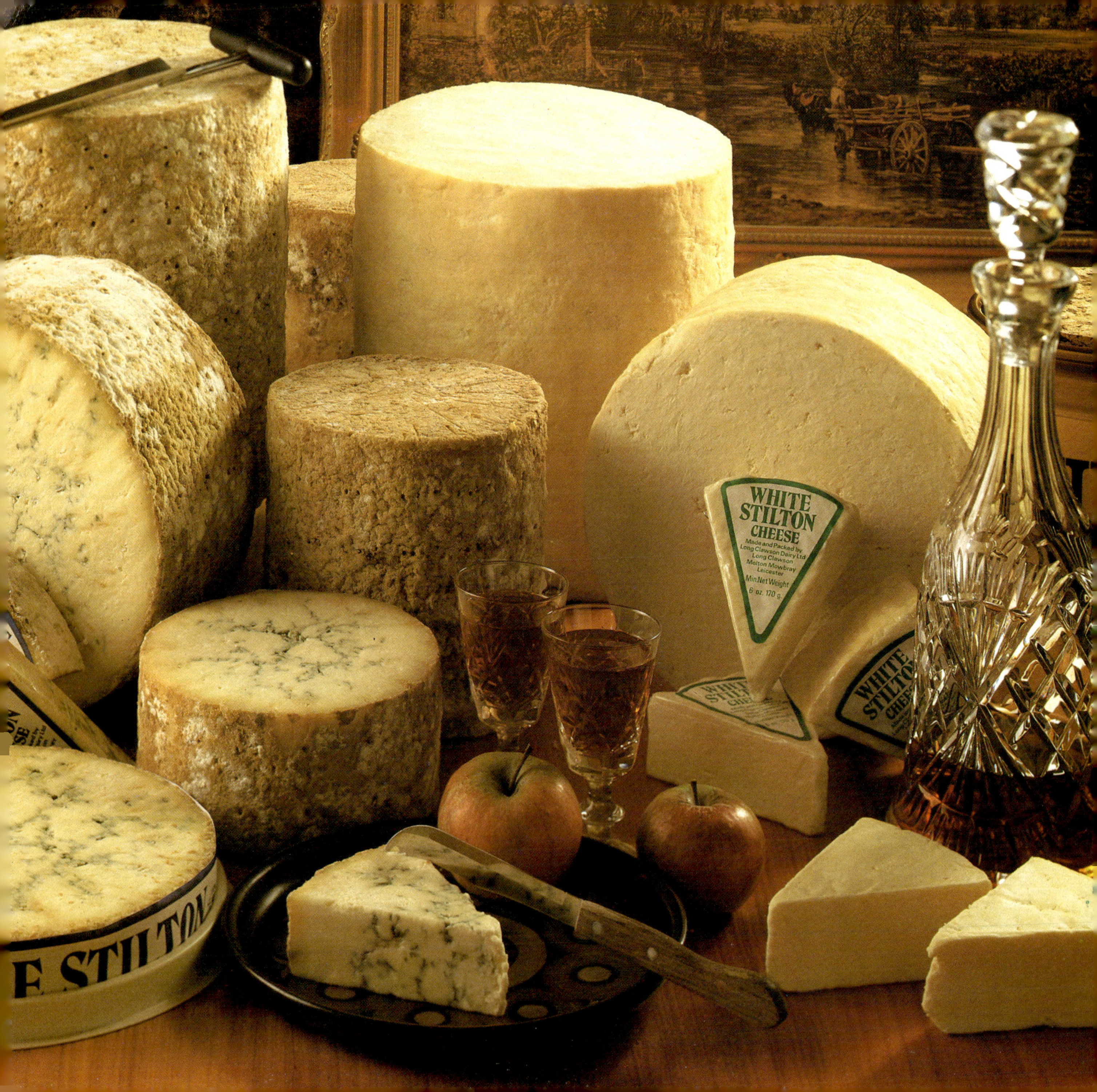

WHITE STILTON CHEESE
Made and Packed by
Long Clawson Dairy Ltd
Long Clawson
Melton Mowbray
Leicester
Min. Net Weight
6 oz. 170 g.
WHITE STILTON CHEESE
WHITE STILTON
E STILTON

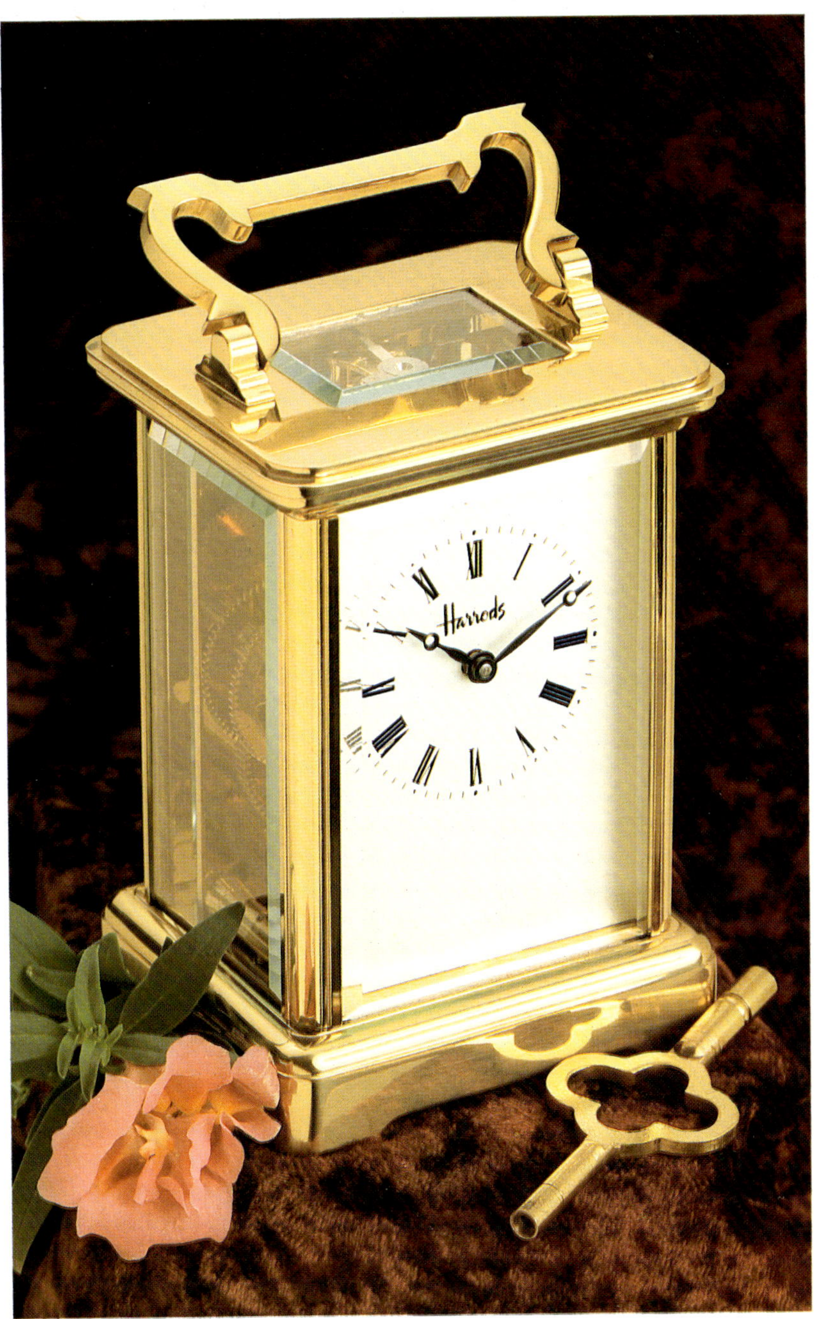

Lighting angles and set-ups

In theory, a single light source is the best way to achieve natural lighting, because the sun itself is a single source. In practice, the sun is surrounded by 180° of sky, providing a complete light tent as well as point source.

A single light in the studio produces much deeper shadows than sunlight. However small the light source the shadows will never be as sharply defined as those produced by the sun; a few centimetres from the subject, a cast shadow will have a sharp edge, but at two metres it will not only have increased in scale but also lost its sharpness. This is because a studio light is very close to the subject and relatively large. The secret of single-light work lies in controlling the shadow areas, and making the boundary between light and shade follow the right contours. As a light is moved round a face, you can see clearly how some angles show the cut of the cheekbones and jaw, others emphasise the nose, and yet others flatten all features. The apparent width of a face can be altered by moving the light a few degrees.

With products, single-light technique calls for very careful handling of shadows. Many items cast ugly, square shadows which do not enhance the picture, but some intricate subjects like jewellery cast fascinating shadows which can be included as a powerful compositional feature. In every case, the operator has a choice between hard and soft lighting by using umbrellas or diffusers. This is a basic choice, and is also one of degree; a large nylon umbrella creates far softer light than a small, parabolic silver umbrella. The kind of fine-tuning achieved by using special reflectors, strip-shaped lights and single lights within large windowlight boxes is dealt with in the next chapter.

Before launching into the individual examples of single-light effects, it is worth repeating the inverse square law again: whatever change you make in light-to-subject distance, the illumination changes by the square of that difference. Half the distance, four times the brightness; three times the distance, one-ninth of the brightness, and so on. This applies only to point-source lighting. When a diffuser is used, the law is degraded by a degree which is determined by the size of the reflector compared to the reflector-surface-to-subject distance.

There are no hard-and-fast rules, but when an umbrella is used which is roughly equal in diameter to its distance from the subject, the inverse rule becomes almost proportional: a doubling of distance halves the light, and halving distance doubles it. The valuable effect of this is to produce much more even illumination in depth, so that parts of a subject slightly closer to the light are not too badly over-lit. A very large diffuser surface is needed to produce this advantage with anything other than a small table-top still-life subject.

Page 86: diffused sidelighting from a 1 m² hazylight with fill-in from a white dish reflector created this atmospheric light in an office. Courtesy Long Clawson Dairies, *Andreas Vogt/A1 Studios.*

Page 87: lit entirely by illuminating reflective panels and sheets of perspex, to provide reflection in the brass. *Andreas Vogt/A1 Studios.*

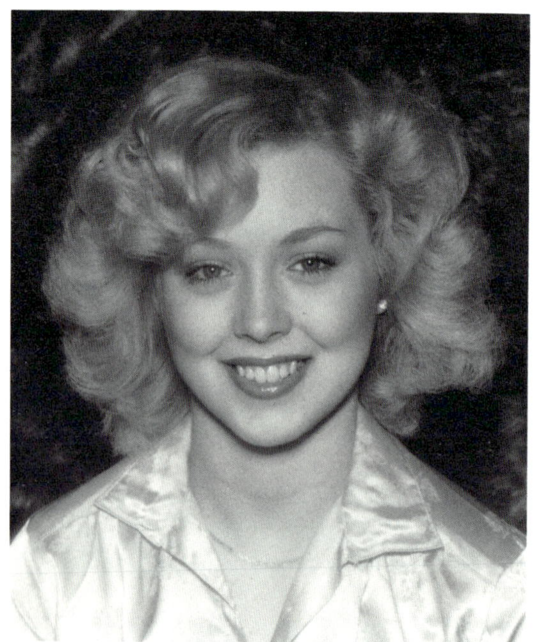

Single direct frontal light

Here the light has been positioned immediately above the camera, centred over the lens axis, and is an undiffused direct flash source in a 20cm reflector. Note the harsh shadow immediately under the chin, and on the background below the hair. The eyes are, however, well lit. The direct light gives considerable lustre to hair. There is no facial modelling, and the face looks fairly broad, with small features.

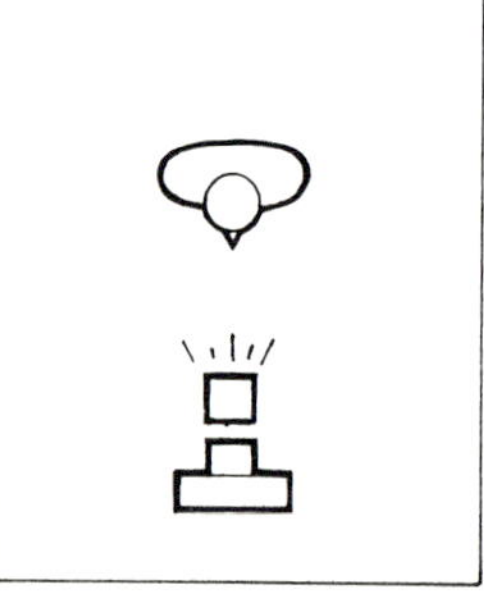

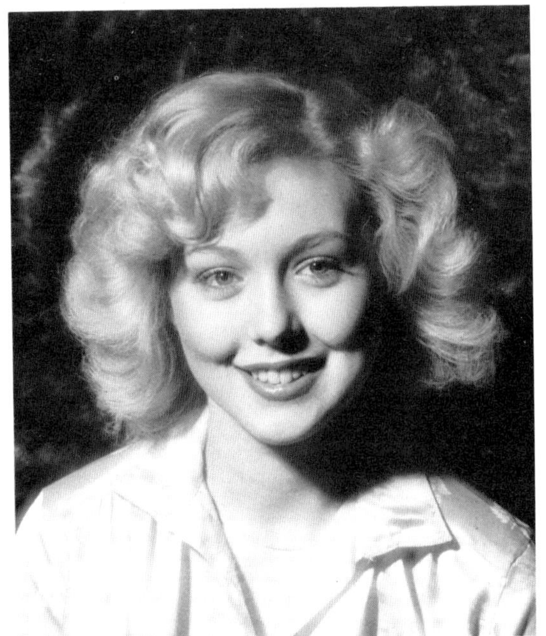

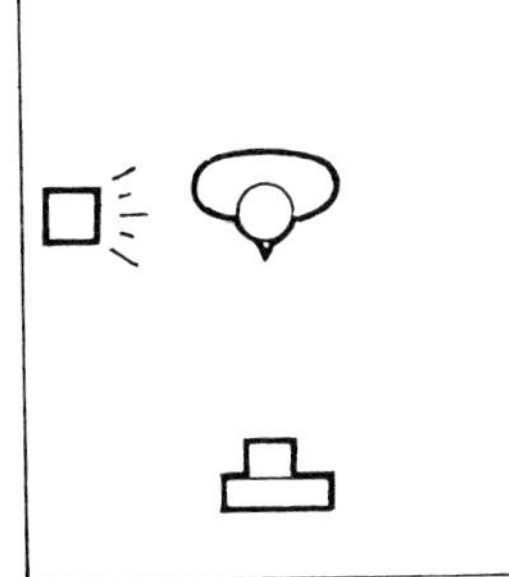

Single direct light at 45°

The light is moved to position roughly 45° to the camera's left-hand side, and 45° above the subject. The position is adjusted so that the nose shadow falls neatly within the triangle formed by the smile crease-lines and the upper lip. No shadow should be formed down the side of the nose, and both eyes are fully lit. Note the heavy side-shadow, but improved modelling on the sitter's left-hand cheek.

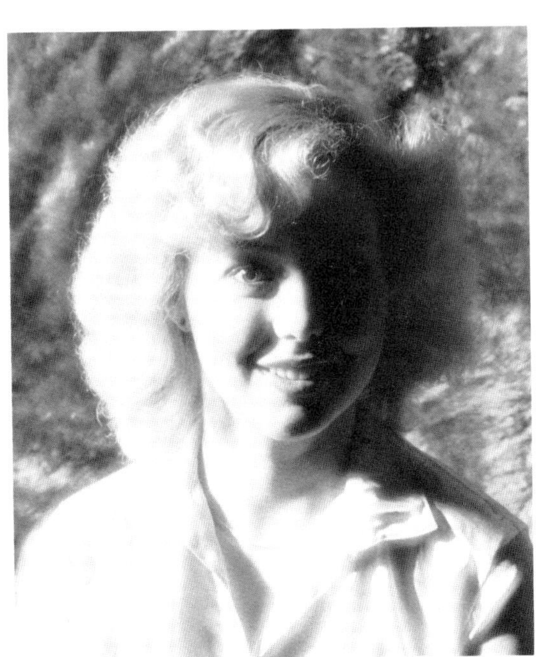

Single direct light at 90°

Pure side-lighting divides the face perfectly into a lit side and shadow side. The result slims the shot considerably, but the shadow side tends to look broader than the lit side. This can be prevented if the background is solid black as well. The lighting on the eye is poor and the nose looks longer; the hair casts a shadow on the forehead. The skin texture towards the terminator of the lit half is crosslit.

Single direct light: toplit

The light is now directly overhead, and slightly in front of the subject. The nose casts a strong shadow vertically down over the lip, and the eyes are deeply shaded by the eyebrows and forehead, which in turn is affected by a hair shadow. The cheekbones do have some modelling evident. By moving top-light gradually down until the nose shadow is above the upper lip and the eyes are lit, this light can be used with some subjects.

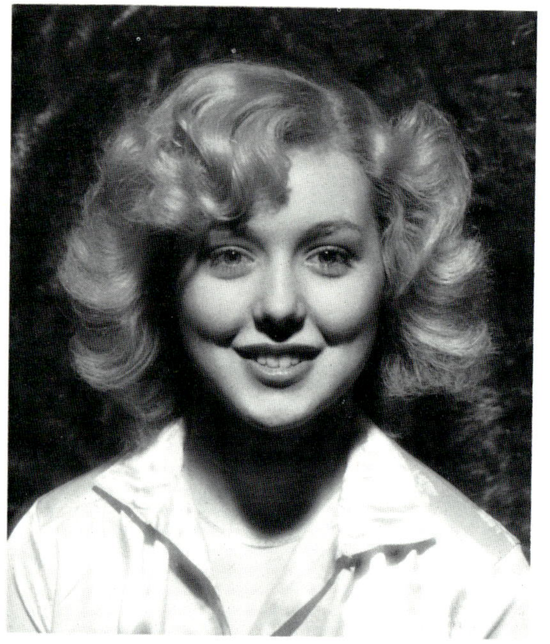

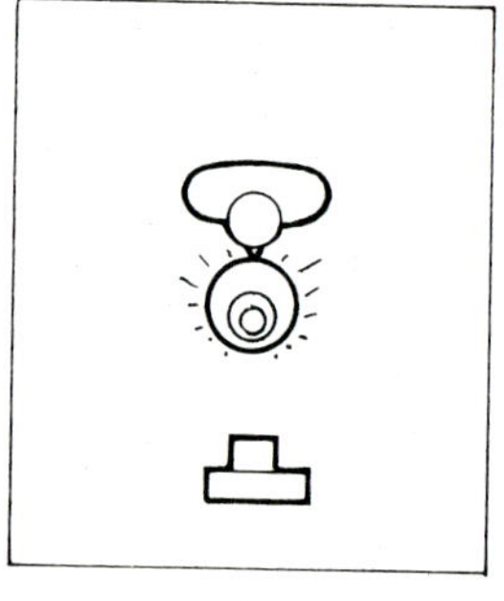

Single direct light: underlit

Footlighting or underlighting, from a light positioned at floor level in front of the sitter, produces a dramatic and ghostly impression. It is the kind of light never encountered naturally except when lying down. A delicate underlight can be used, heavily diffused, to create a glamorous image. Note how the entire shape of the face appears to change when lit this way. Theatre footlights can give the same effect.

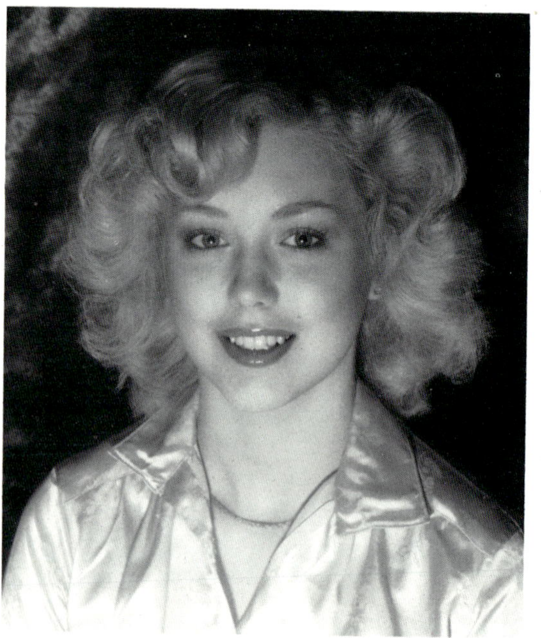

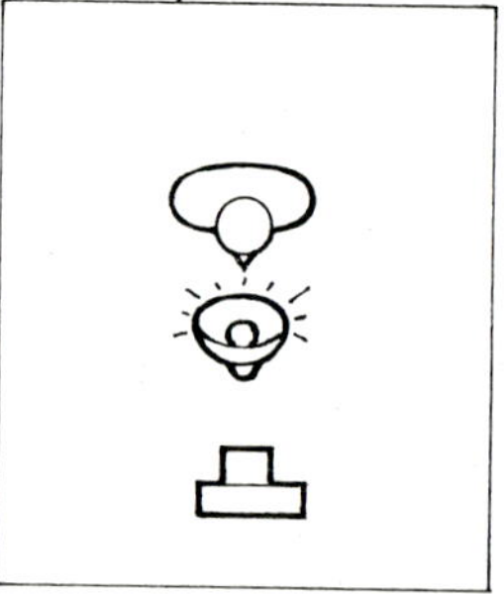

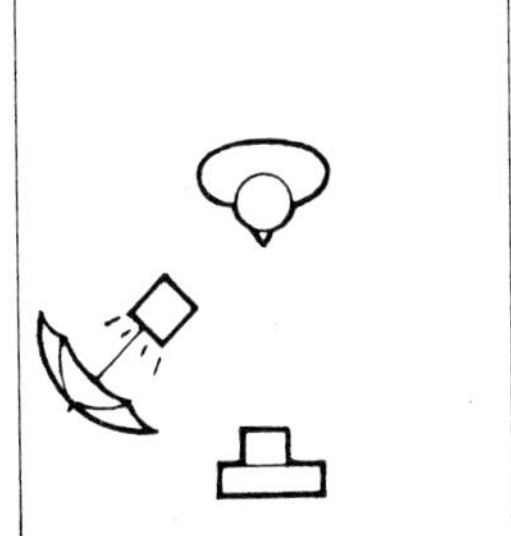

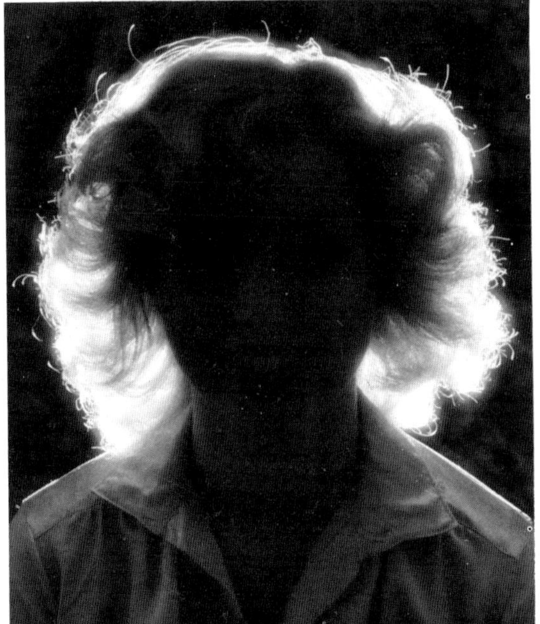

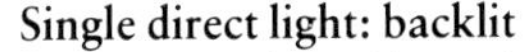

Single direct light: backlit
A silhouette has effectively been created, using a single light direct'y to the rear of the sitter and concealed by her head. The light produces a rim or halo on both hair and shoulders; the shape is unmistakably a portrait, but no detail can be seen in the face. Normally this lighting is only used in combination with other frontal lighting, to add the bright backlit effect to the picture. The light may be positioned out of shot, above the subject.

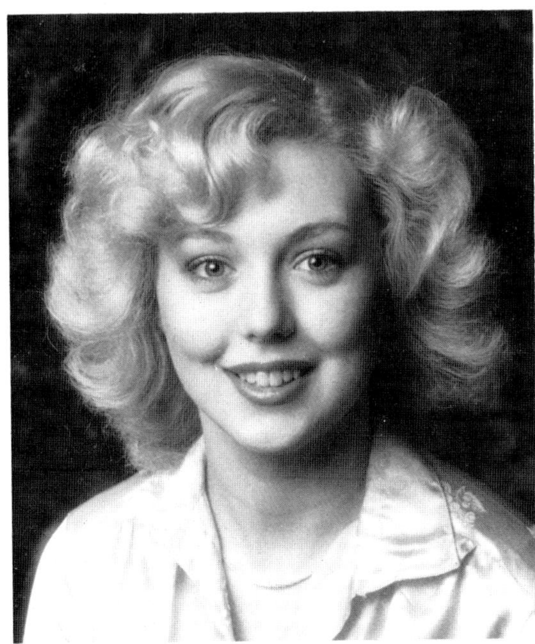

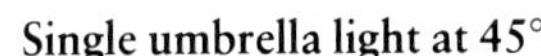

Single umbrella light at 45°
Returning to the 45° lighting angle which is generally considered best for routine portraiture, two changes have been made. The sitter has been asked to turn slightly, so that the face is no longer seen straight-on, and the light has been reflected from a 1m diameter white umbrella. The nose shadow has still been contained within the lip/crease line area. The under-chin shadow is greatly softened.

Single diffuser light at 45°
This is the same basic set-up, but instead of
reflecting the light off an umbrella, a nylon
diffusing brolly has been placed between light and
subject. The surface of this 80cm square umbrella is
1 metre from the sitter's face. The effect is softer,
because the light-emitting surface is much closer;
the white reflecting umbrella was twice this
effective distance. The chin shadow is now quite
acceptable.

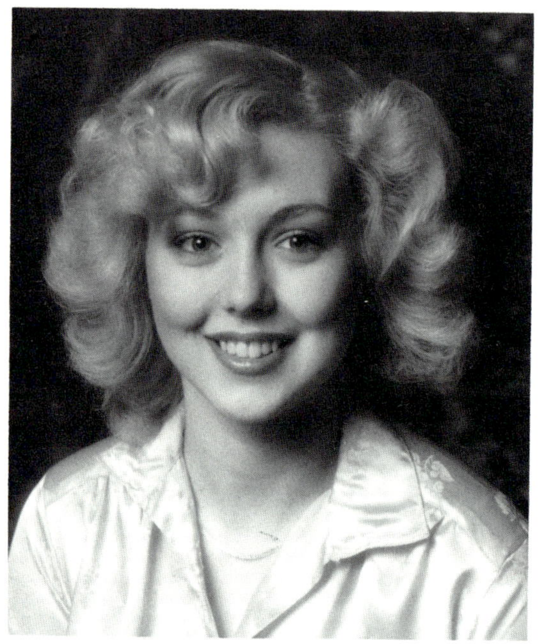

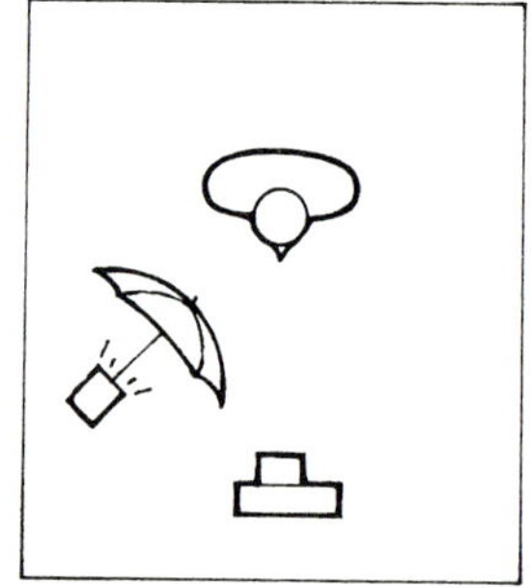

Adding a reflector panel
Level with the sitter's shoulder and just in front, to
her left side, a 1m² matt white reflector has been
positioned, angled upwards to fill in the shadows.
The effect on the underside shadows (chin, under
hair) is strong, but there is not much effect on the
nose shadow. Facial modelling remains goods. The
reflector has now completed a basic single-light
portrait set-up which takes little time, space or
outlay.

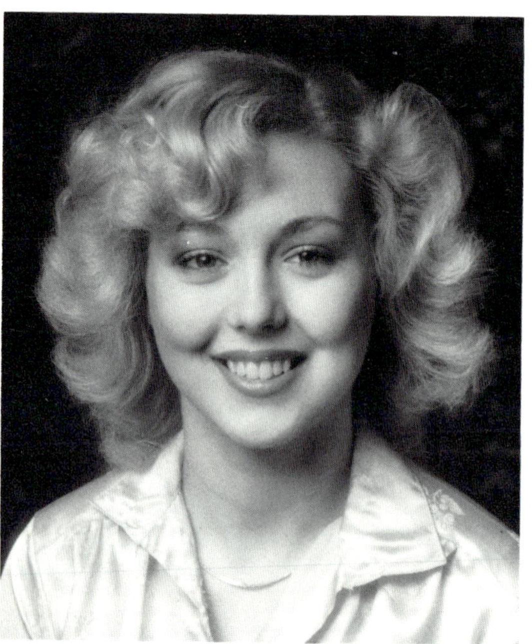

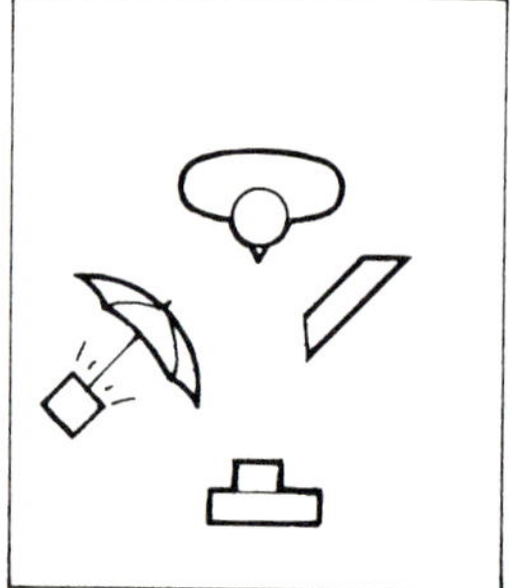

92

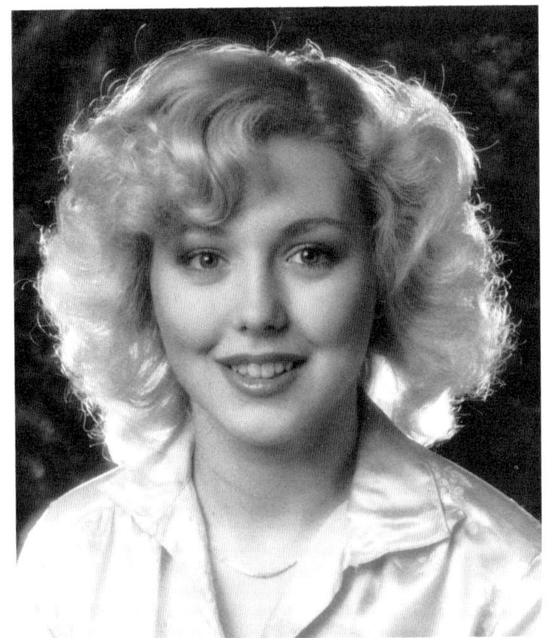

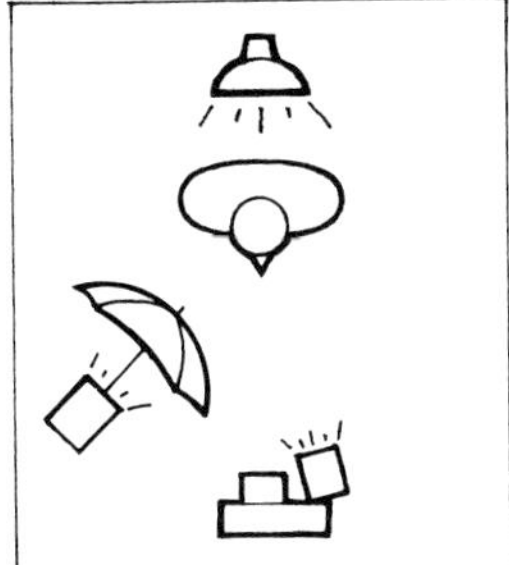

Adding a hair light

The backlighting shown on its own earlier has now been added to this shot, creating a bright halo in a normally lit picture. The power of the backlight has been carefully adjusted to avoid overexposure; as it is used direct, and is fairly close-to, a filter has been placed over it. This reduces the power sufficiently. In colour, a filter to match the sitter's hair can be used; light red for brunettes, deep yellow for blondes.

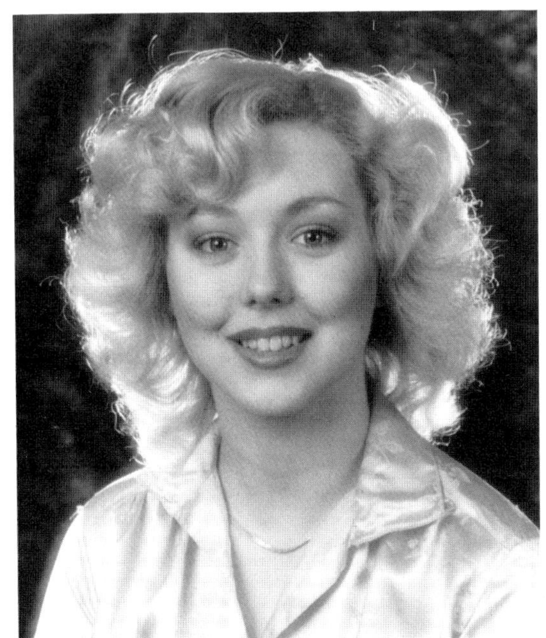

Adding a front fill light

In the very first picture, we saw how the direct frontal light above the camera produced very good rendering of eyes. The strong catchlight gives eyes sparkle which is absent in the soft catchlight produced by a diffused source at 45°. Here a small, very low-power flash has been placed on the camera. It is a fraction of the power of the mains flash units, and the only visible effect is the added catchlight.

Replacing the reflector

For this version, an umbrella-bounced flash has
been added to the sitter's left, only very slightly
above camera height (lower than the main light, but
not as low as the reflector was). On half power, it
fills in the shadows but does not need to be as close
to the sitter as a reflector. It also lights a larger area,
and does not depend for its efficiency on precise
alignment. Its power has to be low to prevent
double shadows.

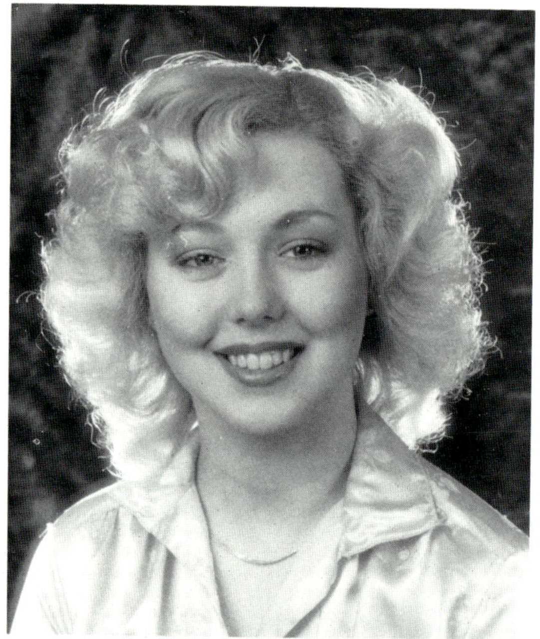

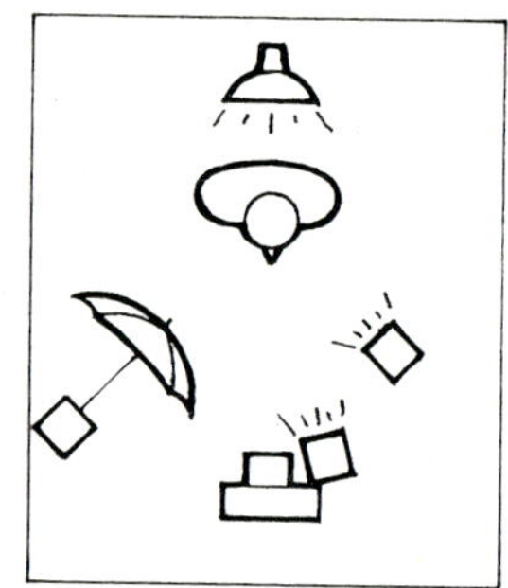

Direct flash and fill

For a male portrait, the very soft shadows of the
diffused light source do no harm, but are not
necessarily good. A strong male face can take the
hard, precise shadow of a direct light. As this is a
dense shadow, reflector fill-in may not be
satisfactory, and the same umbrella fill-in light has
been used as for the last example. It now has to be
on full power, and closer, to level up to the extra
power of the direct flash.

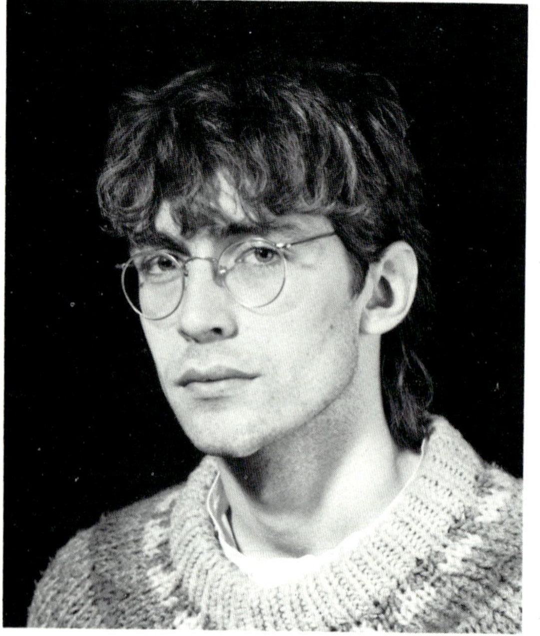

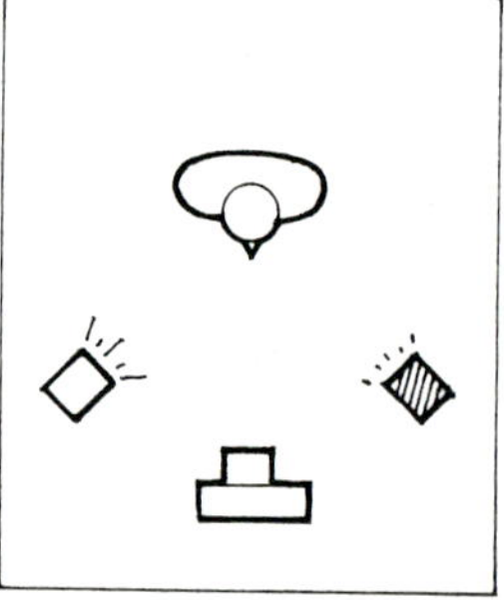

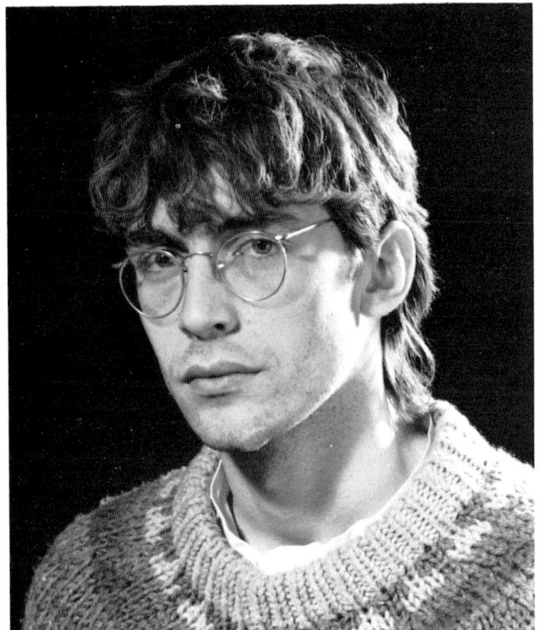

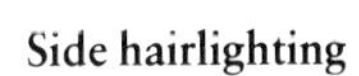

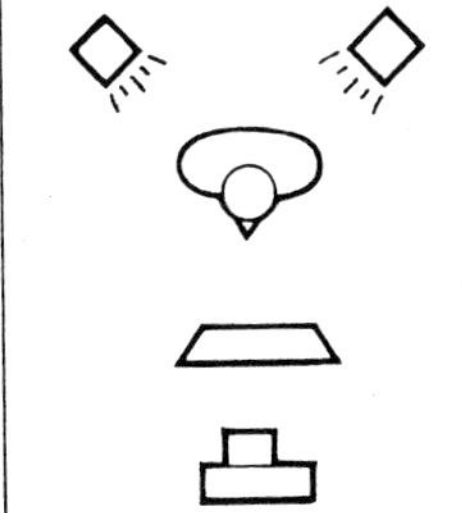

Side hairlighting

For many hairstyles, concealed rim backlighting is not appropriate. It tends to show stray hairs on very neat styles, and does not suit male sitters. A better alternative is a side hairlight, positioned out of shot to the rear, at one side, slightly above the sitter. The sheen produced is only on one side of the head. Normally the side hairlight comes from the same side as the main light to look natural.

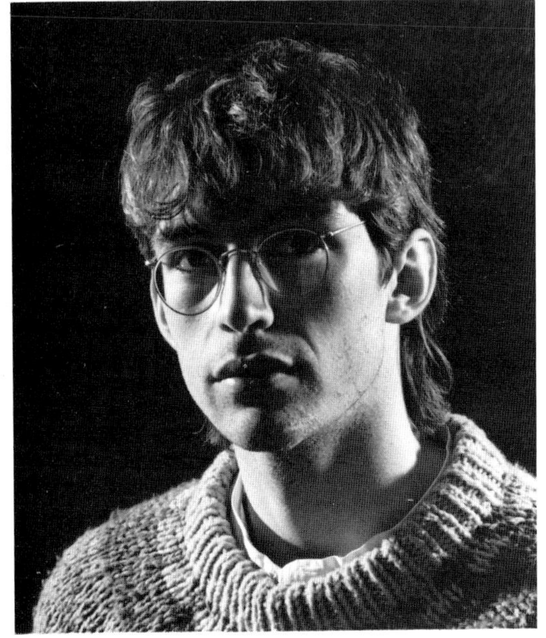

Twin direct sidelighting

A particularly strong textural lighting for male portraits can be achieved by using two direct lights, positioned at head height slightly to the rear and either side of the model. A reflector panel can be placed in front of the sitter just out of shot, or a single diffused fill light used directly over the camera. As this is effectively backlight, skin texture is revealed. It is a dramatic rather than flattering light.

Sidelit profile

True 90° sidelighting, as far as the camera is concerned, can be used for full profile. a direct or diffused source may be used, and this determines the sharpness of facial modelling. The eyes are fully illuminated. To avoid a slight nose-side shading, the light should be a little in front of the sitter (nearer the camera). A fill light or hairlight can be added to relieve the shadow at the back of the head.

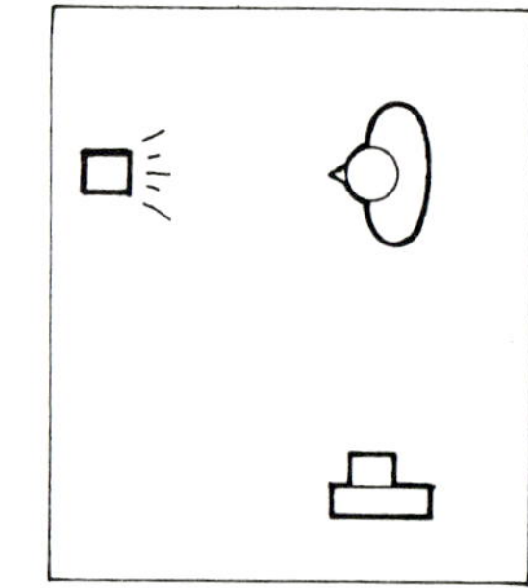

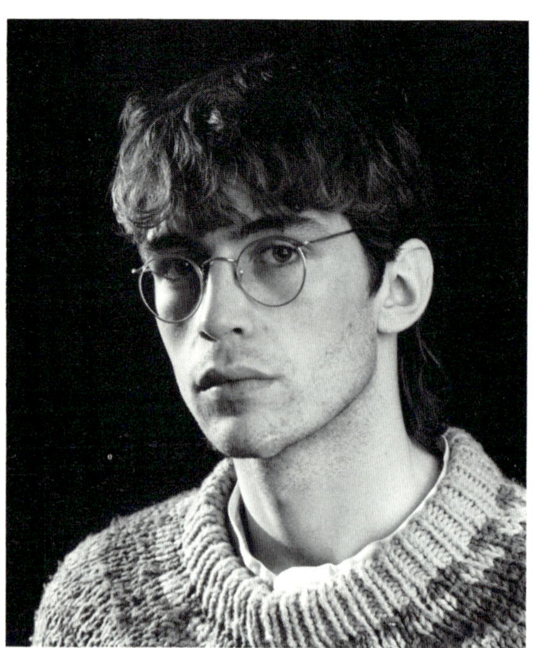

Rim lighting

Rim lighting uses a single light positioned at 45° behind the sitter, opposing the main light, which may be a much less powerful diffused source near the camera. It is used mainly with the face turned in three-quarter profile. This light picks out the hair, forehead, eye, nose, mouth and chin in a bright profile rim or line. It can be used to separate the subject from a neutral or confusing background, as in a factory.

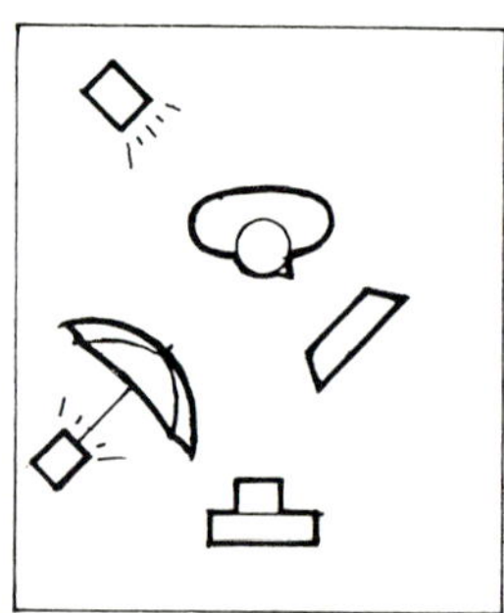

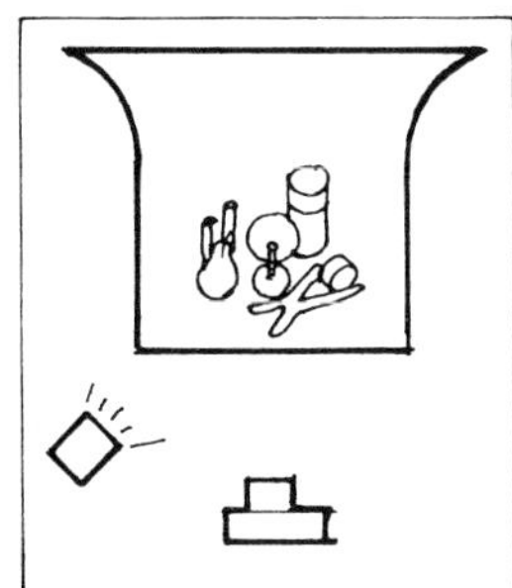

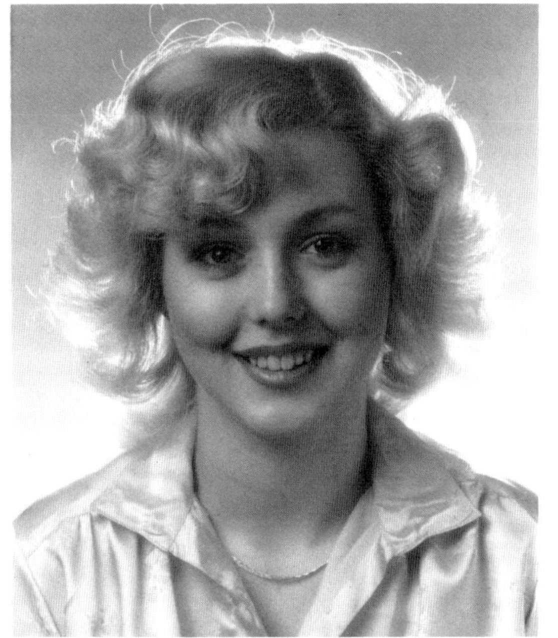
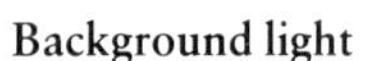

Background light

When a paper or plain wall background is used, interest can be added by a single direct low-power light at floor level, behind the sitter, producing a patch of light behind the head. This falls off gradually at the picture edges, so attention is drawn to the portrait. Coloured filters can be used to change the background colour, or boost it; red paper looks redder when lit with an additional red light.

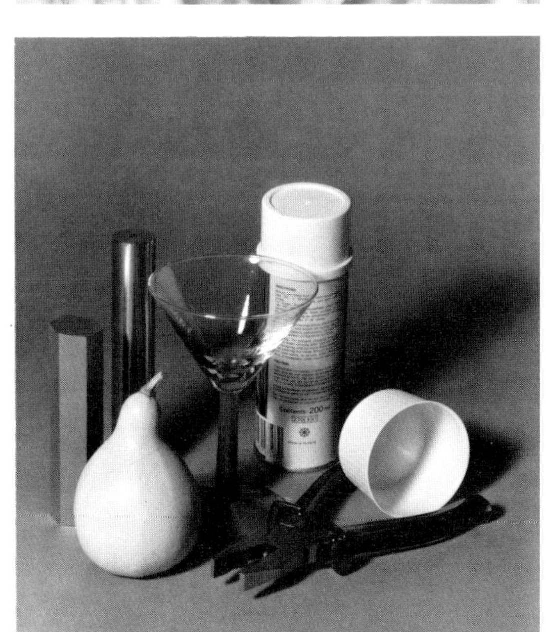
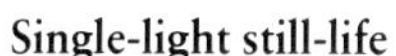

Single-light still-life

Here a single direct light has been used to photograph a small still-life. Because products and objects do not have eyes or chins, problems with these shadows do not exist. However, the strong highlight reflection can be seen in reflective surfaces, and the shadows cast by the light (positioned slightly off camera, to the left and above) are not pleasant. The background paper shows every flaw.

Single diffused light

By using a large translucent umbrella, the lighting
has been greatly improved, just as for the portrait
subject. In this case, however, a strong soft-edged
shadow is still cast, and does not enhance the feel of
the picture. The light is still at a top and side
position, as shown by the cast shadow. The
highlights on shiny surfaces are much more
diffused, and the background paper still looks
unpleasantly grey.

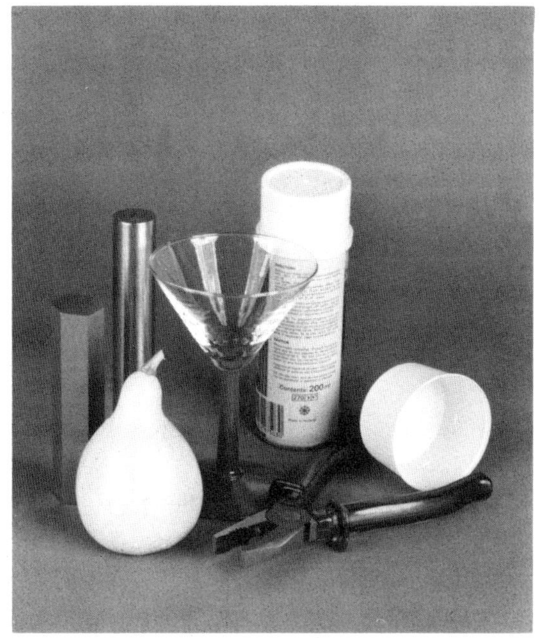

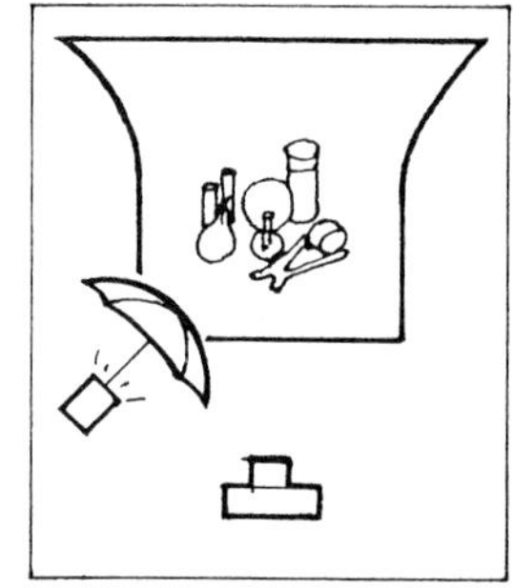

Twin umbrella light

Two matched units, each illuminating the group
from an equal 45° angle on either side, with
identical umbrellas. This is a popular quick lighting
set-up for small still-life subjects, but misconceived.
Only in the middle of the shot do the shadows
'cancel-out'; they still show at the edges, and the
three-dimensional modelling is destroyed, so that
cylindrical objects do not appear to be as solid as
they should.

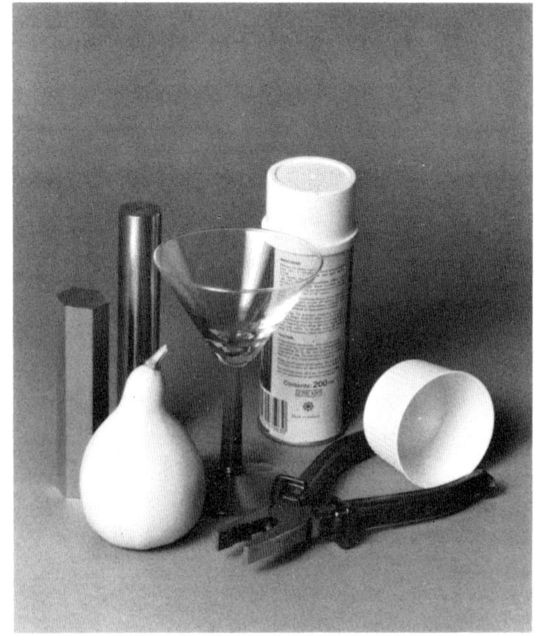

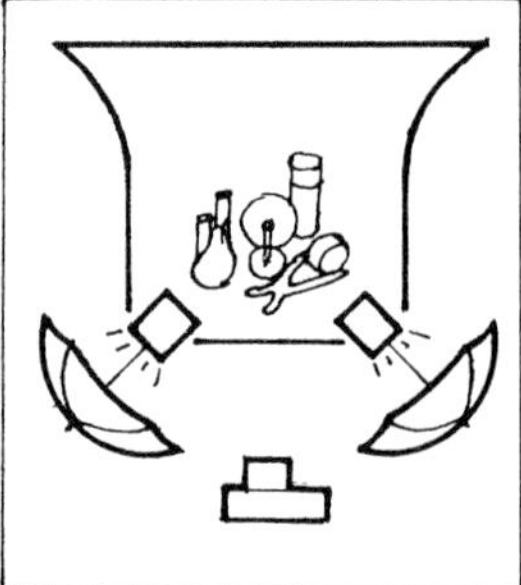

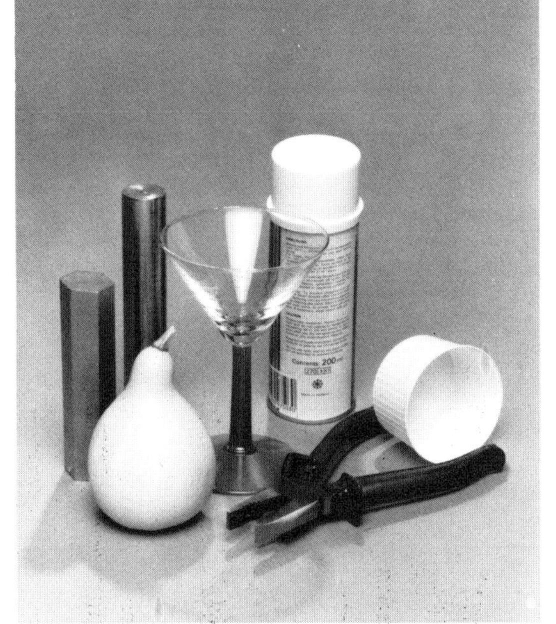

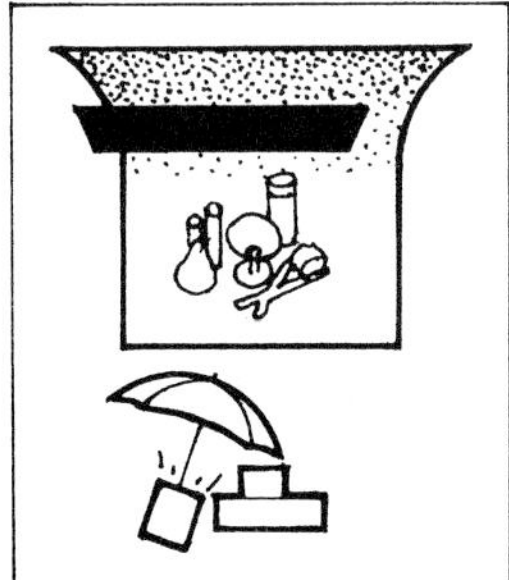

Single main light, background light

By re-positioning a single diffused light directly over the camera, the shadows are effectively lost. The modelling of dimensional shape and depth is not good, but the appearance of the shot is much cleaner. To remove the fall-off in light which made the background an uneven grey, the second light has now been positioned behind and above the subject to light the background. In the process it also top-backlights the group.

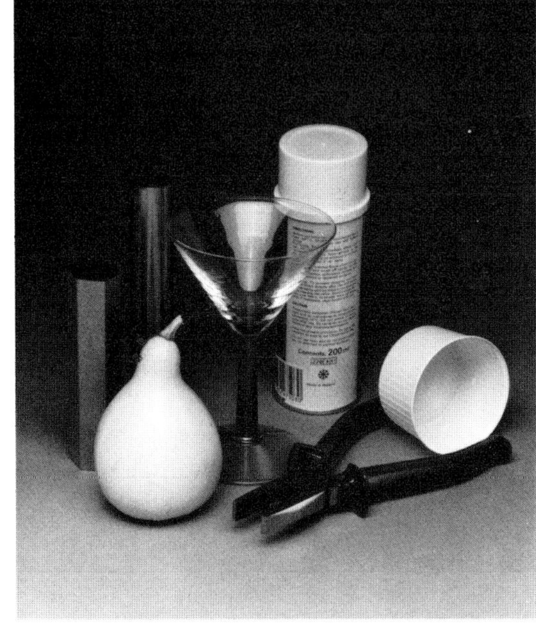

Feathering off the background

When a dark background is required instead of a light one, many photographers try to adjust the main light so that it forms a pool of light falling off just behind the subject. This rarely gives ideal main lighting. Here a simpler solution of a large sheet of black card suspended a few centimetres over the back of the subject and background paper casts a deep, soft-edged shadow to form the graded background.

Adding a modelling side-light

Without affecting overall lighting or casting new visible shadows, a small diffused light source has been placed just out of shot to the right of the product group, almost at 90° but slightly in front. It produces a highlight down the side of the products, with some shading on the opposite side, and gives them depth. The power is low; it acts in the same way that a catchlight flash does in a portrait.

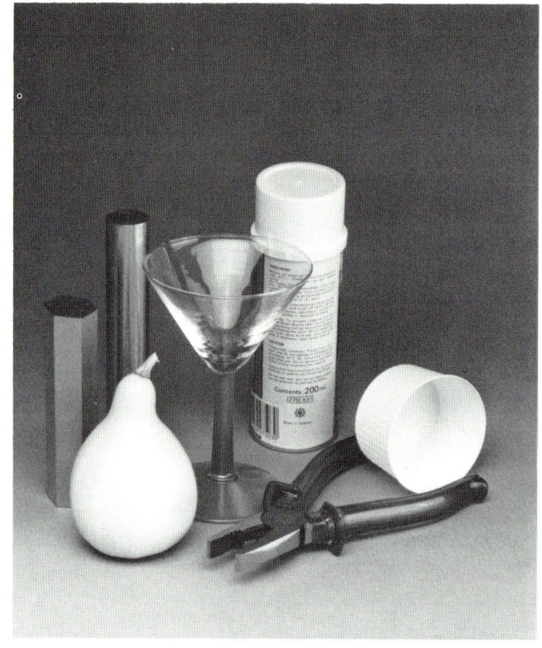

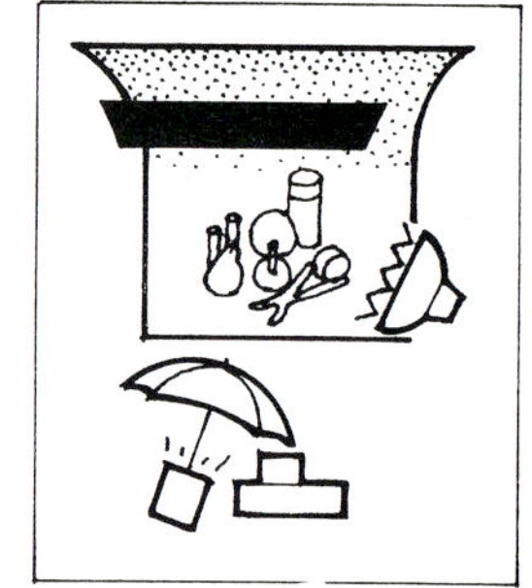

Textural crosslight

This subject has strong textural qualities, and therefore direct lighting is a better solution than diffused. The light has been positioned to skim across the surface, and is two metres away, so that there is no serious fall-off in brightness from one side of the shot to the other. With the light closer this would happen. The light is slightly to the rear of the subject, so it resembles late evening backlighting.

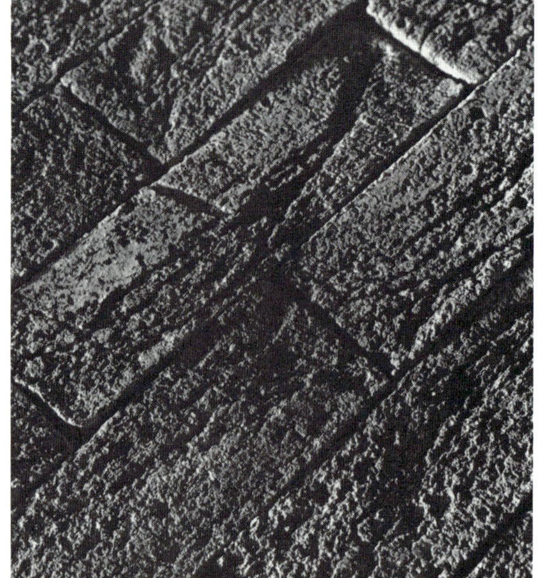

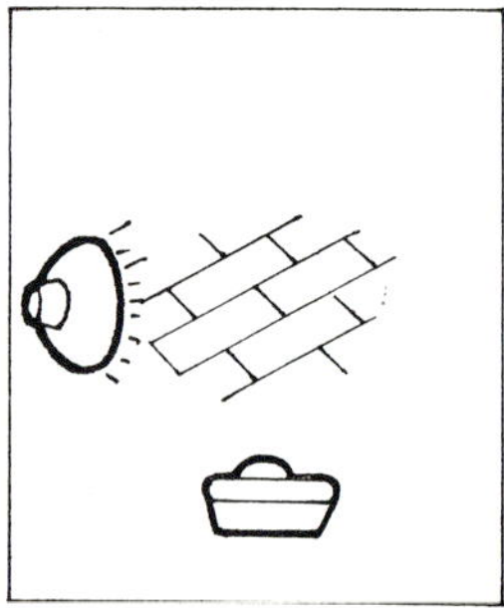

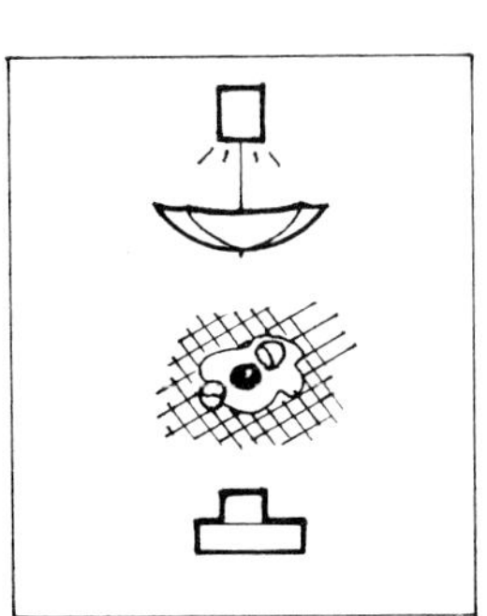

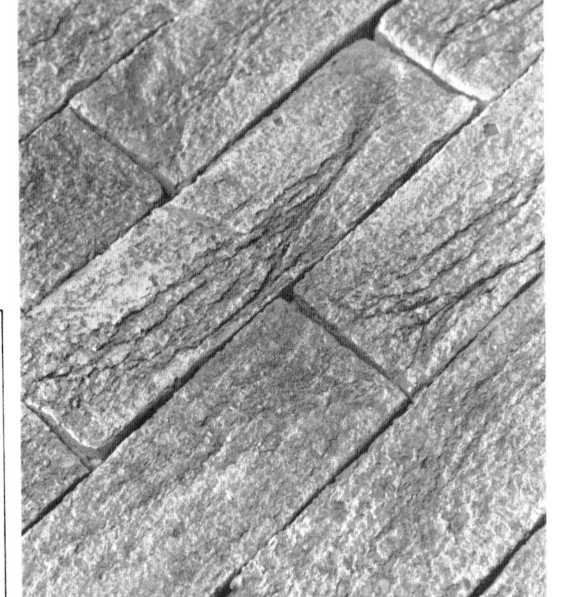

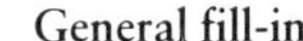

General fill-in

To reduce the density of the shadows in the textural shot, a second diffused light has been aimed at the surface from directly above it, and slightly to the opposite side from the main light. This does not destroy the shadows, which retain their sharp edge, but fills them in with extra detail. The positioning means that any slight exposure bias will tend to counteract the natural fall-off in the main light.

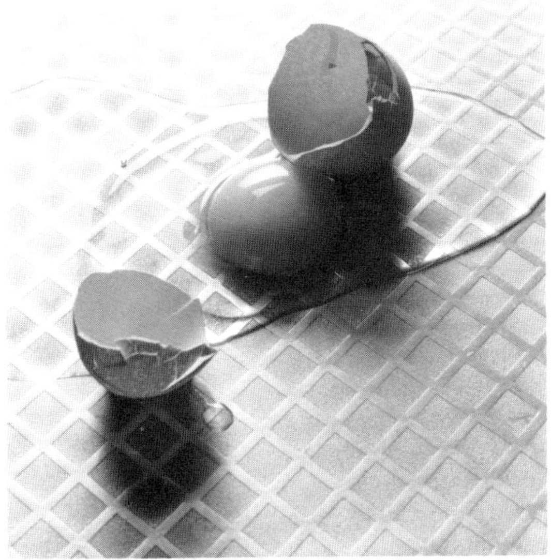

Diffused backlight

A white nylon shoot-thru umbrella has been used to the rear of this subject, positioned just out of shot, aiming down. The background paper is actually taped to the lighting stand itself. The light source is above and behind the subject. This single-source light brings out gloss, texture and translucency and is ideal for food, leather, and other reflective textured subjects. A reflector below the camera filled in shadows.

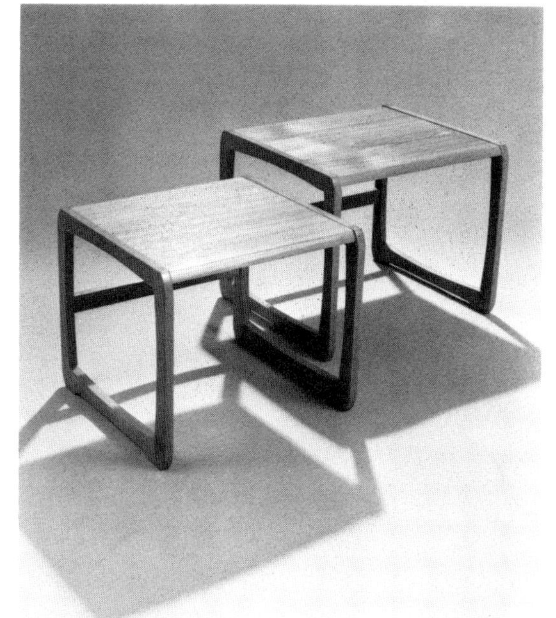

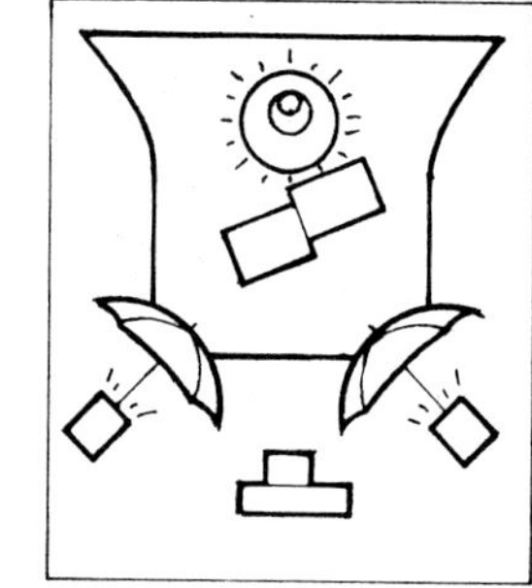

Additional backlight

A direct backlight head has been used on this shot, where it was felt that the cast shadows coming towards the camera were fully justified. Without the backlight, the grain on the wooden table-tops was not visible and there was no visual clue to their degree of polish. The main lighting is very diffused, from two large umbrella sources near the camera. The backlight also brightens the background paper colour.

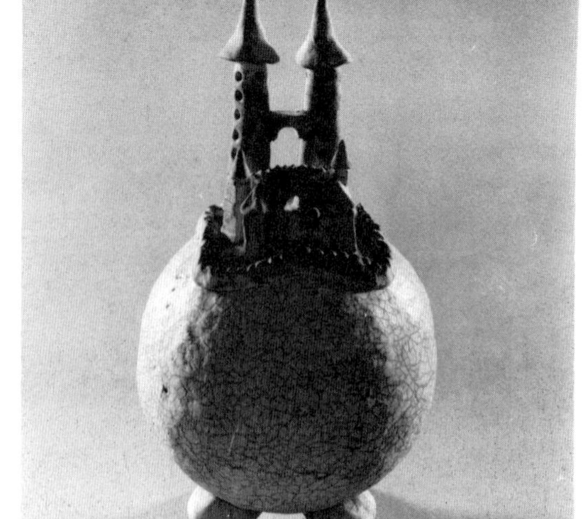

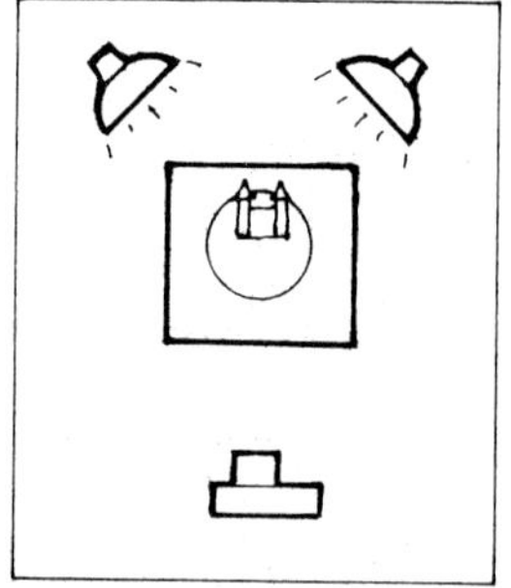

Accent lights

As with a rimlight from the side on a portrait, some products may benefit from extra accent lights introduced to catch reflective or textured oblique surfaces. Almost any number of accent lights may beused, as the effect is more one of reflection than lighting, and it can be controlled with a polarising filter on the camera as well as by varying the accent-light power. True rimlighting is possible with some subjects.

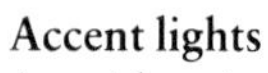

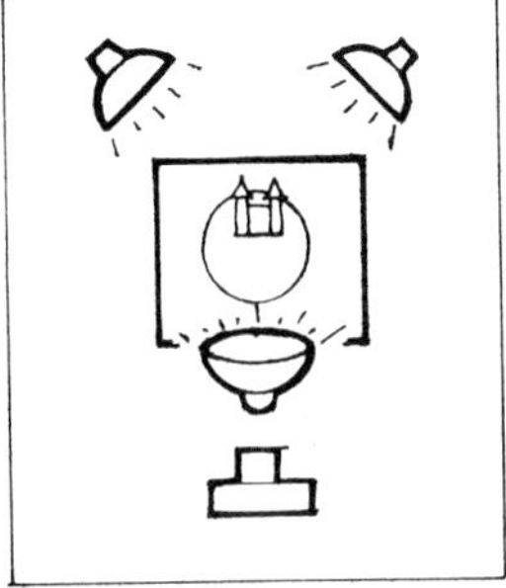

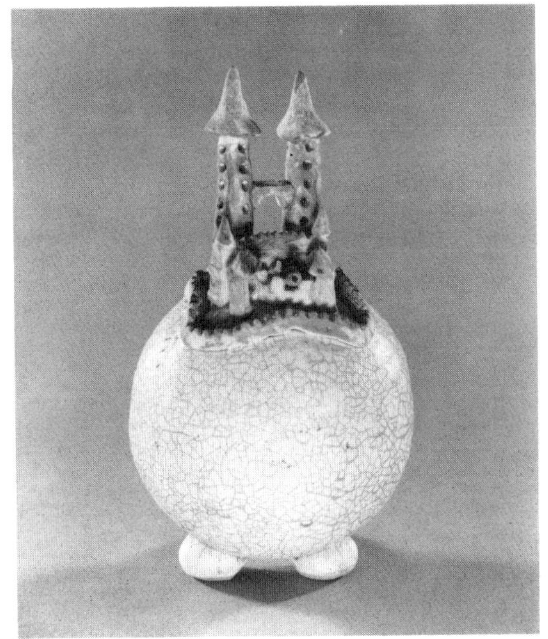

Underlighting
On some still-life subjects, the underside may be important. Often, the use of white background paper will ensure sufficient reflection to fill in the shadows. Where there are steeply undercut parts or cavities in the subject, underlighting with a single light below the camera can help. Reflectors need to be large, and can not always be used in this position. If a small direct source is used the power should be low.

The portrait examples shown on the previous 15 pages have used a limited number of lights, the maximum being four when a main light, fill light, hair light and background light were employed in a portrait set-up. However, three could equally well have been used, as a reflector could have been substituted for the fill light. Even when more ambitious lighting is needed – which will generally only apply to still-life subjects or special techniques – the maximum number of individual light sources needed is not likely to exceed five, as the remaining one is normally a controlled spotlight able to project a small, bright patch.

Video users will find the portrait examples of most use in studio situations, filming talking heads, as they can not easily be applied to moving subjects. The general idea of keeping the main light sources 45° above and to one side of the action area, diffusing them, and adding fill-in does apply. The still-life examples are directly applicable, particularly when shooting short takes for advertising. Still studio lighting techniques are now widespread in film and video, as many still photographers have moved into this area of advertising. The use of diffused single-light sources, diffused backlight, background paper separately lit and underlighting are all advertising still-photography techniques now widely used on consumer products in television commercials.

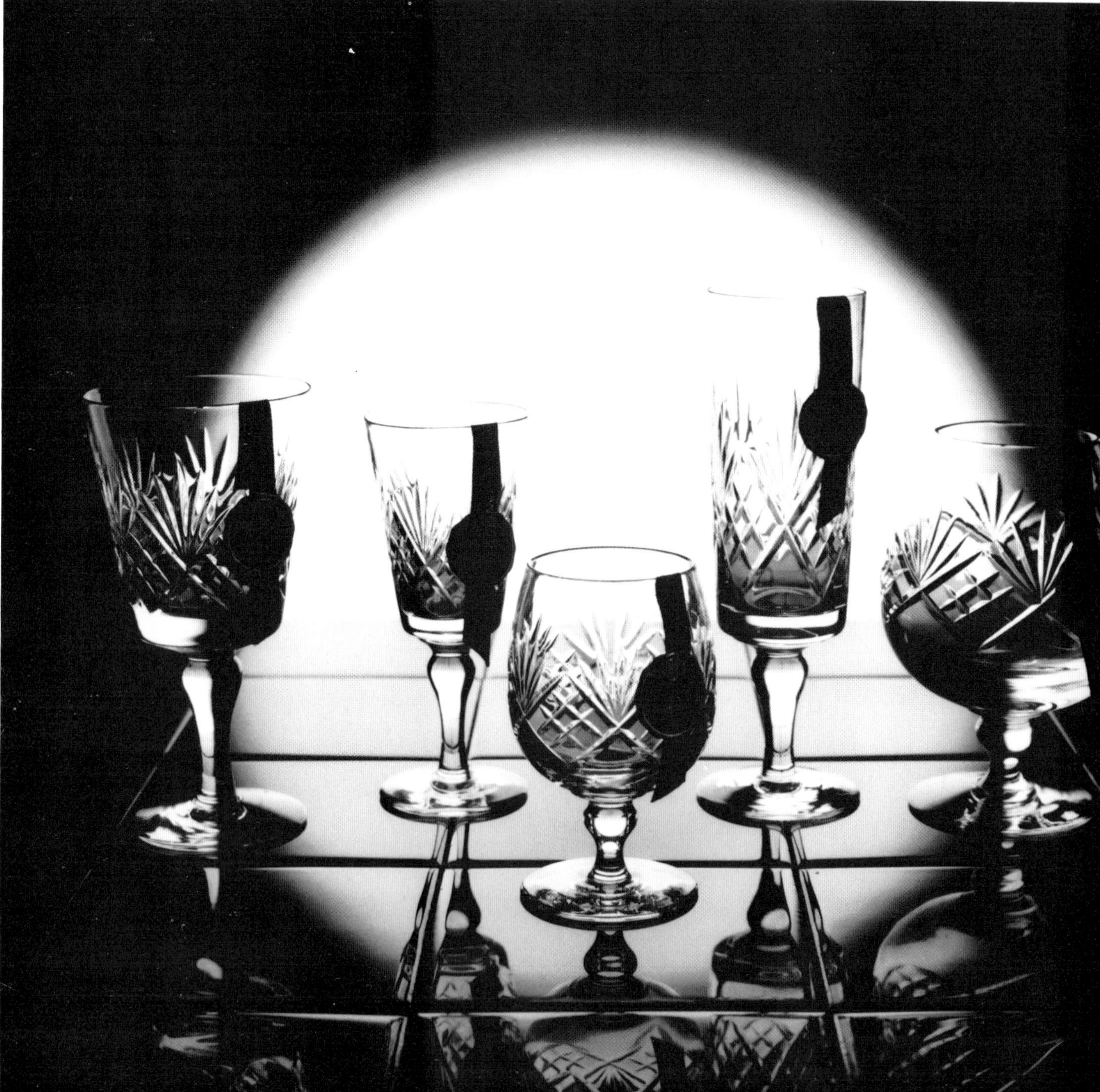

Light-control technology

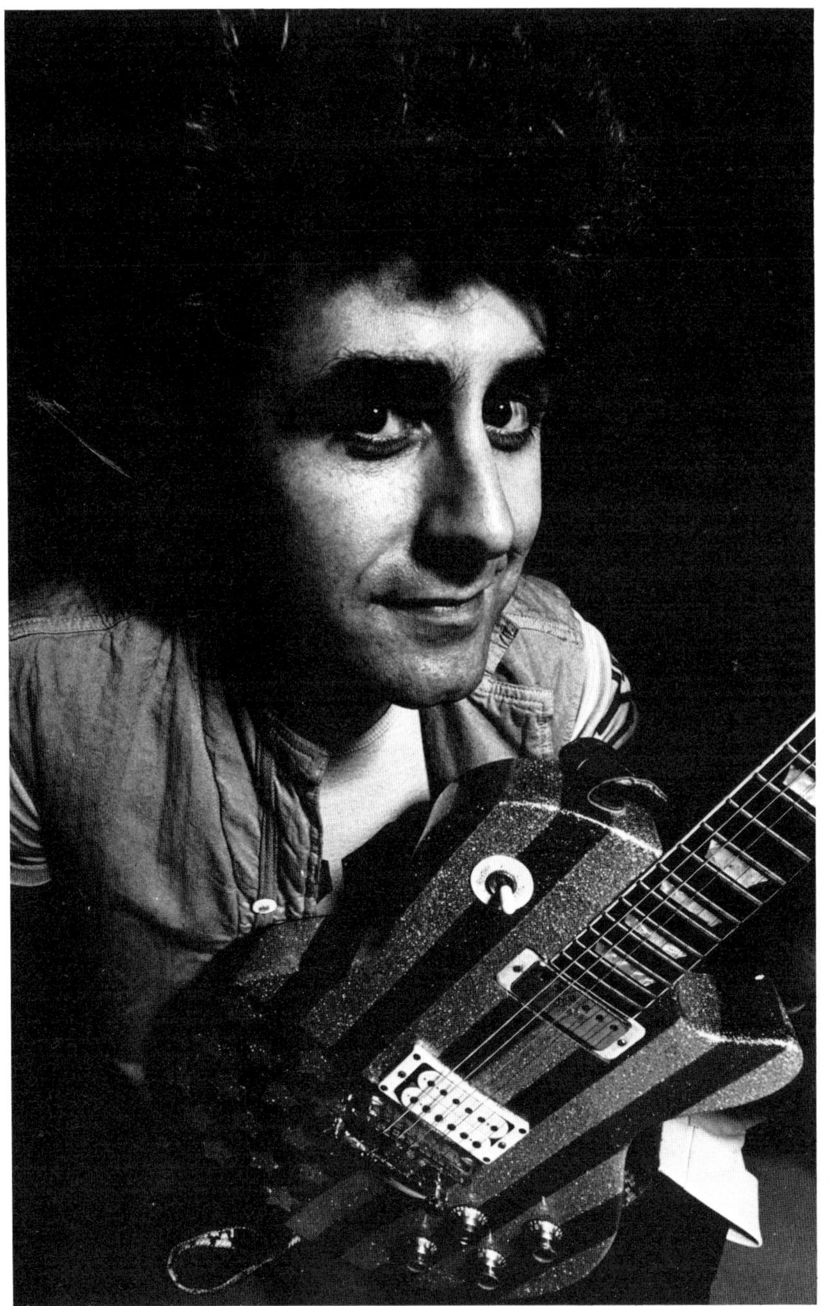

The purpose of studio lighting is to replace daylight, and produce conditions which imitate the ideal daylight circumstances to view a subject. Refinement of lighting technique allows the operator to imitate imaginary lighting conditions as well; light from machines, light cast by a log fire, light in deep space, unearthly light, or perhaps visibly artificial spotlighting.

We have already seen how daylight itself can be categorised, and also how important overcast lighting is. It is relatively easy to imitate direct sun in the studio, because a single light source resembles sunlight, and with careful positioning and fill-in a sunny effect is achieved. Overcast and hazy sunlit conditions are much harder to copy, because the sky is a truly vast light source which extends down to the horizon. In a black studio, it may be necessary to acquire large sheets of white foam polystyrene and suspend them over the subject, bouncing the lights off them. A white studio is easier to work in, since the studio itself can be made to act like the sky.

To control and use light properly, you need more than a selection of conventional lighting heads. How far you go in adding attachments or specialised heads depends on your type of work and budget. Flash systems have more possible range than tungsten systems, but custom-building allows any type of source to be made in either field.

Standard reflectors
The standard reflector supplied with a flood normally has a dish between 20 and 35cm maximum diameter, giving a light spread (even coverage) of between 50 and 70°. Tungsten floods

may have adjustable reflectors, which can be moved backwards and forwards in relation to the bulb, and give a variable angle. Narrow angles give higher light output.

Electronic flash may be fitted permanently with a standard reflector. This reduces its versatility. Better systems have interchangeable reflectors, and the basic one supplied may be termed a 'brolly' reflector or 'spill-kill'. This is a short, small-diameter reflector intended to shield stray light and protect the flashtube and modelling lamp. It rarely gives optimum efficiency, but as it is small it does not obscure light when aimed into a brolly. A larger reflector may get in the way, casting its own shadow on the subject.

For direct flash work, a general-purpose or wide-angle reflector should be bought to replace the spill kill. This will probably have a diameter matched to most add-on light-control accessories in the maker's system, including creative attachments like coloured filter holders. Some makes offer a choice of a 'hard-light' general-purpose reflector with a smooth satin silver inner surface or a 'wide-spread' model, identical in size but with a heavily textured or slightly matt inner surface.

High-efficiency reflectors

To gain maximum output over a narrow field, a deep parabolic reflector of larger size can be used. These may be termed parabolic, high efficiency, or identified by a narrow angle and higher guide number in maker's literature. Typical coverage is around 40°, with minimal light spill, and light output within this coverage is likely to be double that of the general-purpose reflector. Many parabolic reflectors create a hot-spot, or brighter central area, as they tend to focus the rays. The hot spot may be a problem only at some working distances; it can be absent at two metres, serious between three and four metres, and disappear again beyond five metres. It can, of course, be used as a positive feature of the lighting.

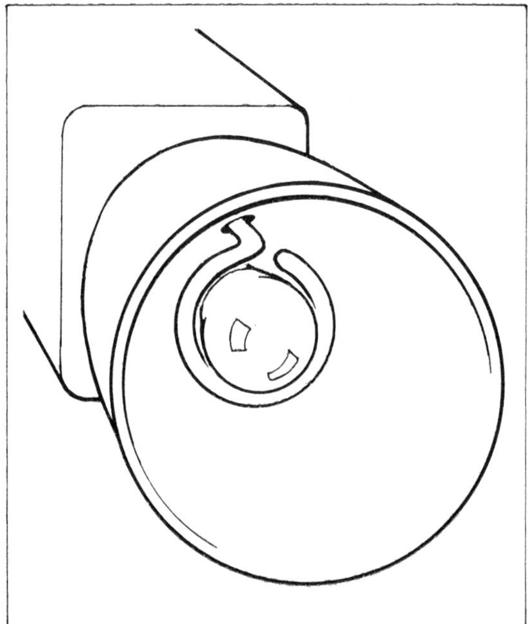

Capped soft reflectors

The opposite of the parabolic reflector is the broad shallow-dish reflector, fitted with a central cap to cover the light source itself. This typically measures 45cm in total diameter. Although you might expect a shallow dish to give a very wide light spread, capping the bulb/flashtube prevents any direct rays from leaving the dish. All the light is either received by the dish direct from the light and bounced forward, or first bounced back to the dish from the inside of the cap covering the light. As a result, the angle is around 70°.

The light output is reduced to around half that of a general-purpose reflector, but as the light source is effectively twice its diameter and there are no direct rays from the bulb or tube, the shadow quality given is much softer. This kind of reflector is sometimes referred to as a 'beauty light' because it gives good directional quality and modelling without harshness. Capped dish reflectors are made in natural metal finish, matt or satin brushed, for

A capped reflector gives a
very soft light flooding a
wide angle.

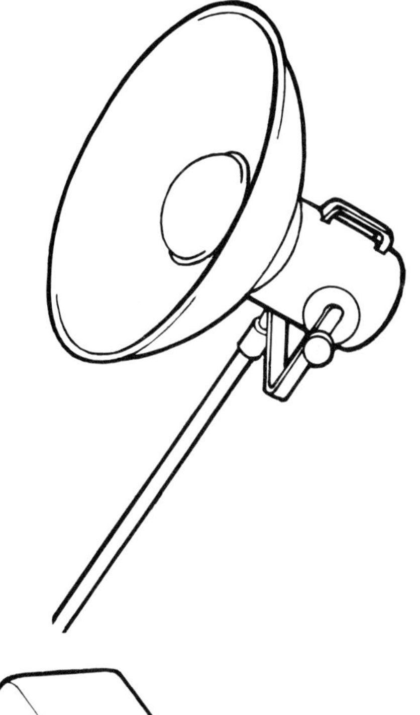

A soft box or hazylight has
a diffuser panel in front and
gives a very soft light, the
diffusion depending mainly
on the size of the front
panel.

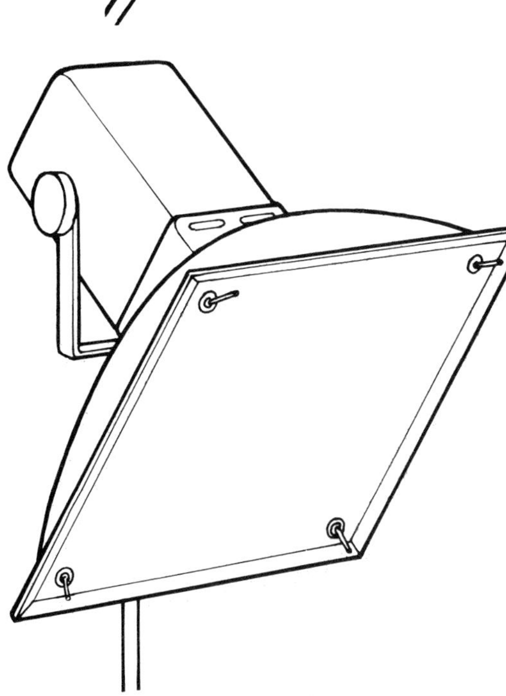

maximum output consistent with light quality;
others are made with a matt white painted interior,
for maximum softness and perfectly neutral light
colour.

Light boxes

To diffuse the light from a general-purpose
reflector and make it resemble the quality from a
capped reflector, though smaller, a sheet of
translucent heatproof plastic scrim can be clipped
to the front, covering it entirely. Care needs to be
taken with parabolic reflectors, and high-wattage
modelling or tungsten lamps, as the concentrated
light may distort and melt flameproof materials.
Covering the front of the reflector this way creates
an enclosed light source. Direct rays from the bulb
or tube can no longer reach the subject. What light
is reflected off the diffuser bounces back off the
reflector and back again, so that a maximum
possible percentage of output finally leaves the
light. This enclosed reflector/diffuser assembly is
the basis of the light box (not to be confused with
light boxes used to view transparencies).

Small light boxes measure about 40cm across, and
may be either round or square. At a distance, the
shape has little effect on light quality, but when
used very close to a subjet there is some advantage
in a square box. The pool of light created has
straight edges, which can be used to produce
graded fall-off. Pieces of card can be clipped more
readily to a square box edge to shield light off from
the camera lens, and a square unit can be made
collapsible. Round enclosed light boxes are mainly
used for portrait and fashion work as an alternative
to the beauty light, and it is considered better to
have circular reflected catchlights in a subject's eyes
than square ones.

Hazy lights

Trade names vary, but the kind of large box 'next
up in size' from the smaller 40cm types is normally
called a hazy, misty, soft-box, or some similar term.

A typical size would be 80 × 80cm square, with a
pyramid reflector box behind the front scrim about
40cm deep. More efficient types take up more space
with a box about 80cm deep. The most expensive
rigid hazy lights have a fibreglass back reflector and
opal acrylic front diffuser. They can be used as light
tables to place subjects on, and are usually
supported on a special heavy duty stand with
geared mechanisms to raise and orientate the box.

Hazy lights are used either as a replacement for a
flash umbrella/diffuser, at a distance, or suspended
over the subject at close range like a flt 'sky'. The
exact quality of light created depends on the size of
the front surface and its diffusing efficiency; this in
turn dictates output. A universal model such as the
Larsen SoftBox has a metallic fabric inner reflector
and a twin nylon diffusing surface. The tube can be
seen clearly through the diffuser and forms a small
but bright spot; the rest of the diffuser is very
evenly lit. This suits low-power units. A heavily
diffused model such as the rigid Broncolor Hazylite
(for flash systems only, unlike the Larsen which is
intended for still or video lighting) has a perspex
front which appears totally evenly lit, with no
hotspot of any kind. A powerful flash is needed to
ensure high output but the light quality is
noticeably less directional and the shadows are
softer.

Window lights
There is little distinction between a window light
and a hazy light in practice. A window light is
either larger (1m × 1.5m, for example) or is
mounted differently, so that it is normally a vertical
light source used to one side. The idea is, as
indicated, to imitate the type of light given by a
large window. A video unit is likely to call all large
square or rectangular diffused lights window lights
unless they fall into the next two categories of
larger light.

Fish-fryer
A fish-fryer is a large hazy, normally 2m × 1m,

108

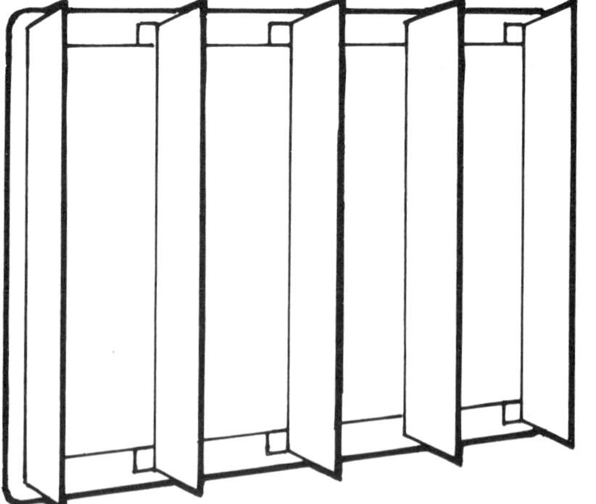

Left: a lightweight fabric
window-light or 'swimming
pool' light on a boom arm.

Left: a hazylight can be
fitted with a slatted blind to
control the pool of light
created.

Right: a very large diffused
light source creates a light,
shadowless and very open
effect for glamour work.

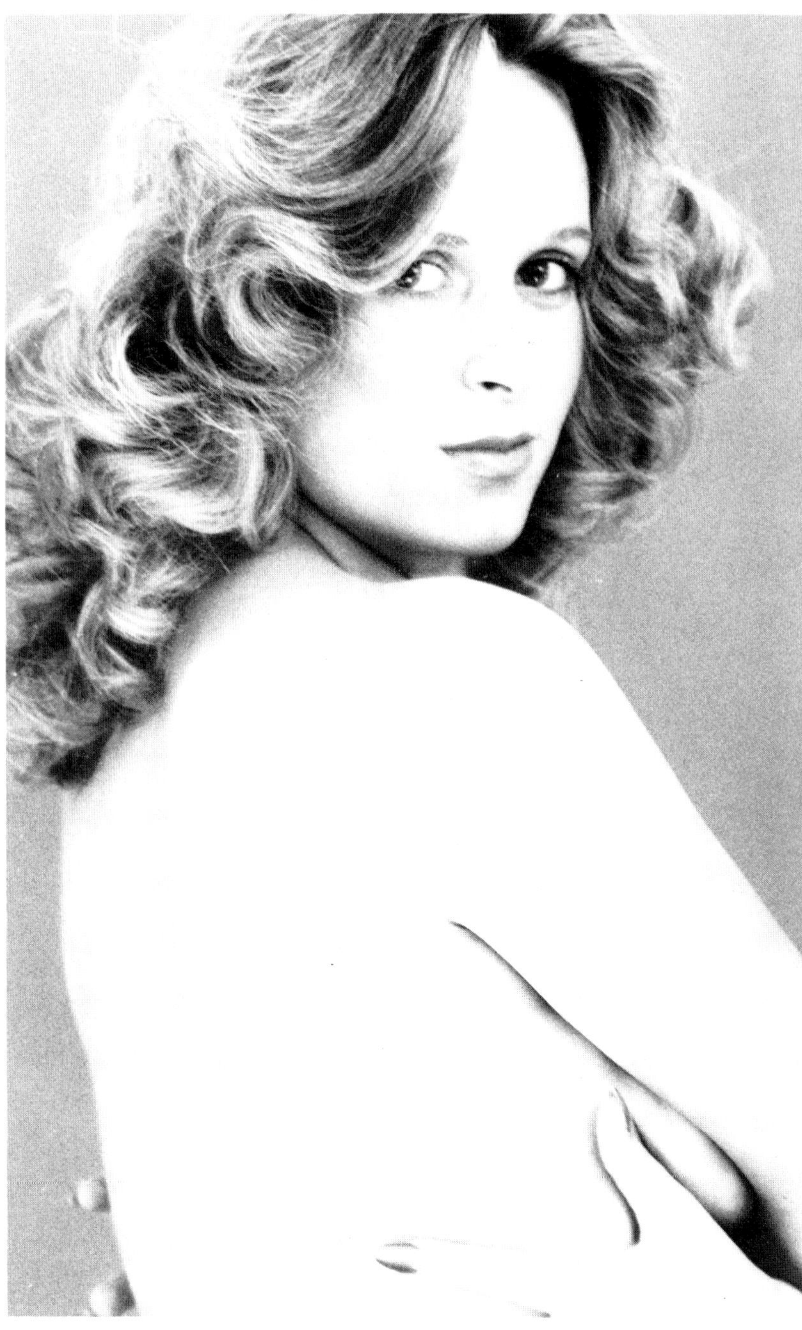

with a removable front panel and a linear lighting tube (whether flash or tungsten). Early models are sheet metal but new flameproof metallised fabrics have enabled lightweight versions with alloy frames to be produced. The fish-fryer may be suspended over the subject for still-life work, in which case it is able to ensure even lighting in depth when the 2m length is aligned over the depth of a subject. For fashion work, the fish-fryer is usually positioned vertically as a side light, about 30cm from floor level and extending to just over head height. This is the only acceptable way to light a full-length figure from a close distance. To go with a fish-fryer, 1m × 2m reflectors on stands are used for fill-in.

Swimming pool
Used more in very large commercial studios and film units, a swimming-pool light has no theoretical limit in size. It may be created by banking window lights or fish-fryers. A size of 4 × 3m can be used to light large subjects, like cars. Swimming pools for film and video may consist of a bank of undiffused floods. In a still studio, one can be created by suspending large high-efficiency reflector panels and aiming powerful tungsten or flash sources from floor level, with parabolic reflectors. This avoids the need to support extremely heavy multiple-flashtube assemblies inside a large light which may be used 3–4cm above the ground.

The purpose of all these progressively larger and more diffused light sources is to create even, soft lighting without harsh shadows. The good qualities of directional overcast daylight, window light or light from diffused rooflights in a daylight studio can be found in some degree in each type. How you select your scale of light remains open, but one immutable law is that big light units needs powerful lights.

A 40cm light box is perfect for close-up photography of jewellery, small animals, or small products. To achieve good results, it has to be close. Sometimes this prevents free positioning of the camera or choice of viewpoint, in which case a 1m square light at twice the distance will give roughly the same overall effect. The 40cm light box would, by comparison, be of little use to provide soft lighting for a product like a washing machine. Even a 1m square hazy would not be big enough to 'wrap' light round the machine from all sides at a reasonable distance. A fish-fryer, used horizontally, would do this job well and avoid the ugly diffused shadow cast by a solid, blocky subject of this type.

There are several other light sources and attachments which are rarely main lights, but are positioned for effect to add rim, back, reflected highlight, spot effects and other kinds of supplementary illumination. Some of these can be home-made and others are mass-produced because the need for them has been proven repeatedly in all kinds of photography.

Striplights

Sometimes a long, thin almost directional light source is needed. Normally, this only applies to still life. The shadows created by a striplight resemble those from a fluorescent tube, and have one directional bias; rotate the light, and the shadow itself changes shape. Striplights can be tungsten (using a linear source) or flash (using one or several linear flashtubes). Normally, they are set into a narrow reflector trough which accepts a front diffuser panel. A typical strip will be 10cm × 1m.

Longlights

Without going to the extremes of a striplight, a normal light source can be converted to a long light. This will probably measure 15 × 50cm, with an opal front and a rigid back reflector. The idea of this is to add fill-in or highlights on still-life subjects, often positioning the light very close. A longlight can be placed immediately under the camera lens, on the background paper in front of the subject, to relieve foreground shadows created by a hazy suspended to the rear of the shot for diffused backlighting.

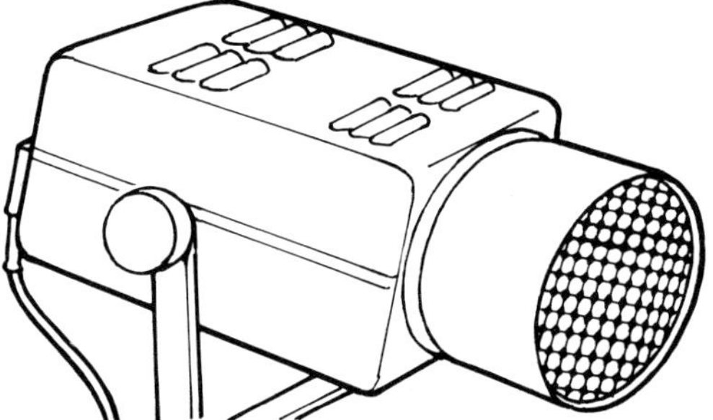

Left: a honeycomb grid spotlight is capable of turning a normal light source into a semi-spot without using lenses. The honeycomb is a tube with hexagonal cells, normally matt black so only direct rays make their exit.

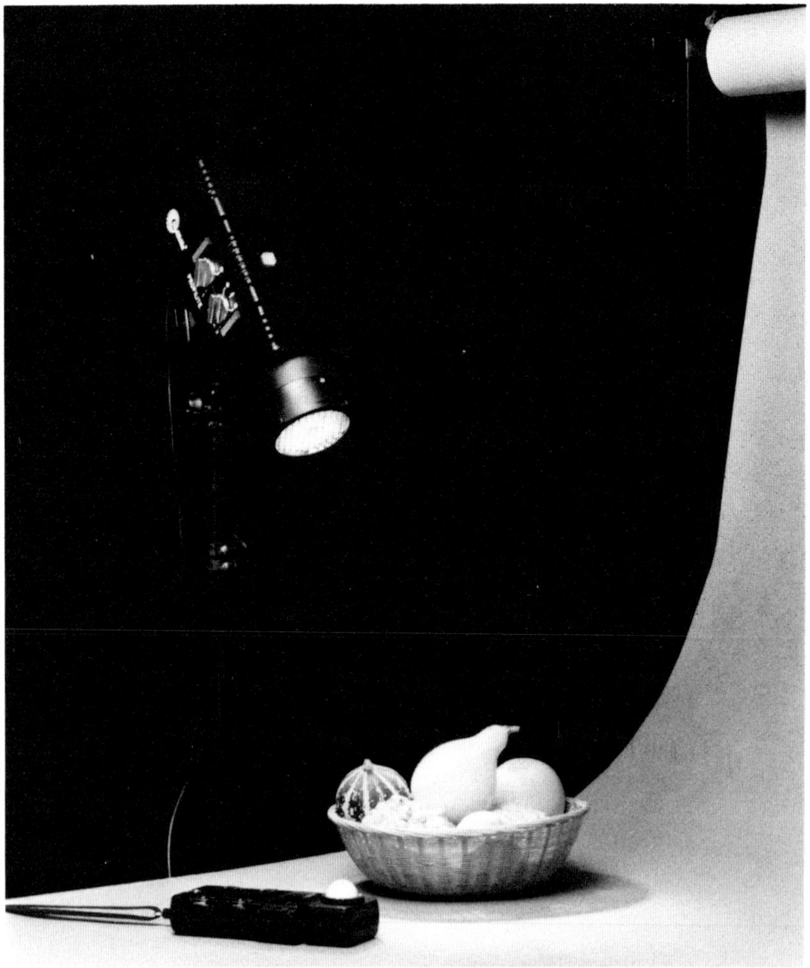

Snoot

A snoot is a long, matt black metal cone or cylinder attaching to the standard reflector to reduce the light source to a small spot, throwing a very restricted circle or patch of light on the subject. Output is normally heavily reduced. A snoot can be made on the spot with black card.

Barn doors

Barn doors are flat metal wings or doors which attach to the front rim of a reflector or the edge of any other light source, like a hazy or longlight. They are hinged, to allow 'closing' either to cover part of the light source or simply shield stray light from the camera or parts of the subject where it is not wanted. Barn doors, like snoots, can be made up on the spot with heavy self-adhesive tape ('gaffer tape') and card. Ready-made metal ones can be purchased singly (clip-on), in opposed pairs, or in a full set of four.

Projection spotlights

In video lighting, small spotlights can be invaluable. These have an optical system using a fresnel lens which can project a hard or soft-edged circle. Inserts may be used to throw patterns of light and shade; coloured gels add interest. The small 'pup' spotlights are suitable for use with 1000–2000W systems, are lightweight, and cost little.

Flash spotlights are different. A special flashtube, giving a near-point-source quality, is positioned as close to a small modelling light as possible. An optical spot attachment using large convex lenses projects the light. A fairly low initial power produces very bright light as it is concentrated. Optical projecting spots will cast very sharp images of pattern foils, transparencies or other artwork introduced into their projection slot.

Honeycombs

Honeycomb grids consist of a metal structure with hexagonal cells, about 2–3cm thick. Each cell acts like a small snoot, around 1cm in diameter. The material used was originally intended to go between two skins of sheet metal to produce lightweight, high-strength body shells for the aerospace industry. It has been 'borrowed' by photography.

A honeycomb can be put over the end of a reflector, and restricts the light to a small pool with very little loss of brightness within that area. It creates a soft-edged spot. Over a light box or hazy, the honeycomb restricts the light to the same shape as the diffused source, with hardly any spread. Small, deep honeycomb sections are used over parabolic reflectors or in the end of a snoot tube to create a 'grid spot', a non-projecting alternative to an optical spot. Matt black honeycombs give the greatest control, but silver honeycombs have a worthwhile effect and actually increase the light level within the restricted angle covered.

Slats

Instead of a honeycomb, a hazy light can be fitted with a series of adjustable black plastic slats about 4–5cm deep which work like a venetian blind. They can control light output, and also prevent spill in one direction only. They weigh much less than a metal grid. The slats are normally used in line with the camera film plane, so that the light is attenuated in front and behind the subject rather than to each side. They act like small barn doors on a large number of striplight sources, by dividing up the square area of the light.

Honeycombs and slats are not often used with reflective subjects, because an image of the pattern may be reflected. When a hazylight is used on a reflective subject, some photographers traditionally put a cross of black gaffer tape over the diffuser panel to resemble the woodwork of a window. When this kind of care is taken, fitting a light-control device which creates a reflection of parallel black lines is out of the question.

Gels

Coloured gels (no longer made of gelatin, but

fireproof polyester) serve to colour the light-sources; grey (ND) gels give control over output. Simple clip-on frames are available to hold 30 or 40cm square cut gels, sold in sets, on to the front rim of normal reflectors. For larger sources, the gel is sold in sheets of 50 × 60cm and rolls. Rolls may be used to cover windows when lighting room interiors with tungsten (see chapter on light and colour) for video or still shots. The maximum effect is always given by pure-coloured gels, and whenever two colours are used in one shot the overlap effect must be considered.

Parabolic reflectors create interesting effects with gels, because of the way they direct light. Light reaching the left-hand side of the subject comes from the right-hand side of the reflector, and vice-versa. Two gels can be placed over the front of a parabolic reflector and three colours will result; the two gel colours at either side, with a third mixture colour in the centre.

Bounce cards

Every studio should have a large selection of sheets of card. Artists' mounting boards are suitable. The white surface can be used as a reflector, or to bounce light off as a kind of makeshift hazylight. Coloured cards add their own slight colour cast to the effect.

French flags

Along with white cards, matt black cards and fabric should be kept. 'French flags' absorb light, as in outdoor light control. The largest (as with reflectors) should be 1m × 2m. Rolls of black fur fabric or velvet can serve as occasional dead black backgrounds, as well as flags.

Perspex and scrim

Diffusers in the studio can be rigid or flexible. Scrim, plastic or nylon fabric, is flexible and needs a frame or line to hang it on. Frames with shrink-stretched diffusing plastic or draughtsman's tracing foil can be made up and stored; they are lightweight and easily handled. The standard

tracing foil to ask for, at any graphic art supplier, is Kodatrace. If this is not stocked, an alternative material will usually be offered. White opal perspex is rigid, and although more expensive to start with, can be used as a very effective reflector or diffuser. A pair of sheets, one 75cm square and the other one metre square, can prove very useful.

Clamps

To support cards, diffusers, gels or perspex the studio should have a good range of clamps and clips. Purpose-made clamps normally have a fitting which will accommodate any normal lighting stand pole, speedframe 25mm structural steel or alloy, down to 12mm shopfitters' tubing. The clamp will probably have a socket to allow a lighting head to be fitted; some are strong enough to be used to position a camera on a ball-and-socket head. Clips, consisting of double bulldog-type spring clips with a joining bar, are for holding lighter accessories like gels and cards. Office clips, workshop G-clamps and clothes pegs can be used.

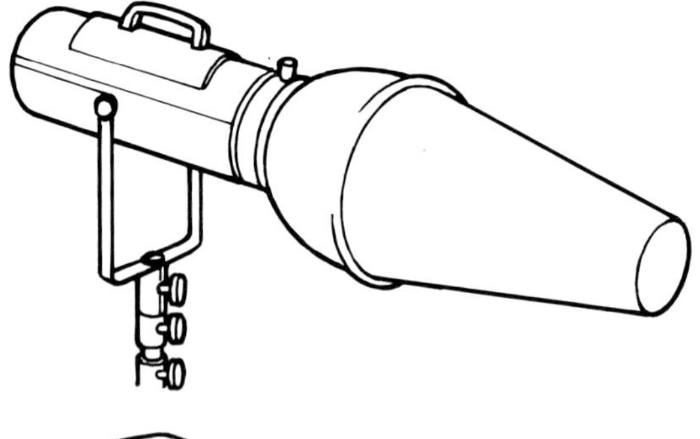

A snoot is a long, often tapered tube which attaches to the front of a light and controls the beam down to a narrow spot for close-range use.

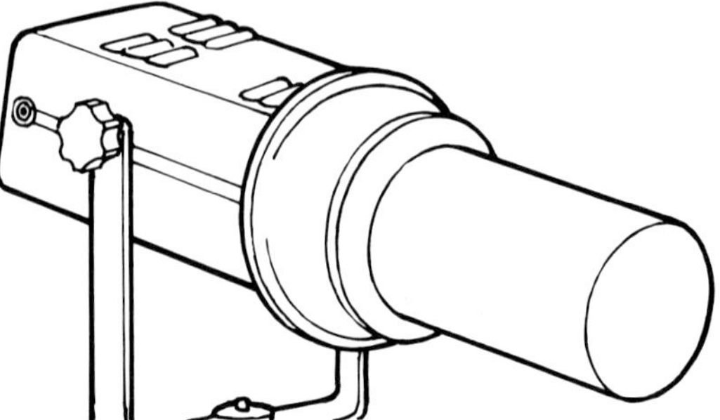

An optical projection spot attachment contains lenses which concentrate the beam and allow it to be used at long range.

Structural supports

A commercial studio should have a stock of structural steel (the type used to make office benches) with corner joints and castors. Black 1 in (25mm) speedframe is recommended. For small subjects, a laboratory framework kit like Climpex is more versatile, allowing elaborate structures and supports to be built up quickly. The structural kit can be used to make tables, stands to support lighting accessories, and special set-ups for unusual subjects (see the chapter on specialised lighting techniques for glassware, reflective subjects, and so on).

Lighting supports

Apart from the basic extending telescopic lighting stand with a tripod base, normally described as a medium-duty portable stand, there are many other ways of making the movement of lights less of an effort.

Castors or a *dolly base* with wheels fit on the stand, and convert it to a mobile studio stand. A heavy dolly base is preferable, because it increases stability. This is very important with large tungsten and flash heads used at 2m height or more. A *heavy-duty stand* will be a better solution, not intended for location use, with a much stronger central column and permanent dolly base.

Boom arms fit on to heavy duty stands and provide a transverse or lateral support, which can be freely angled or rotated. As well as extending the maximum head height by 1–2m, the boom enables lights to be suspended over the subject with the stand clear of the set. Hazylights are normally fitted to boom arms.

Wander arms fit the studio wall, and by clamps or spring tension allow a lighting head to be moved through a wide range of possible aerial positions. They are normally only used for small, light heads.

A wander arm or wall arm will normally hold a tungsten head, or flash head up to 500 joules, together with a lightweight umbrella. The maximum extension is normally 2 metres, subject to a minimum depending on the design; some arms have an elbow, others are just a rotating two-section telescopic boom. The range of possible movement is normally restricted, so that wall mounting can only be used for certain lights or in small studios. The advantages are clear floor spoace and permanently fixed wiring.

Ceiling tracking suits large studios with good headroom, and is universally accepted as the best way to tackle a small video studio. Stands are eliminated, as all light heads are suspended on counterbalanced lazytongs which can be wheeled along two axes on track rails fixed to the ceiling. The lights can be positioned freely, anywhere the track grid extends, from just under ceiling height down to floor level. All but the heaviest units can be used.

Floorlight stands cost very little, and consist of three folding flat legs which raise the light head a few centimetres off the floor. They are essential for underlighting, because normal stands do not allow the light to be much below 1m off the floor.

Apart from these basic types of lighting support, there are many special stands made. Some have motorised movements, hydraulic telescoping arms, or even a fluid-bed suspension to prevent vibration from damaging high-power tungsten filaments when turned on. In the small studio, refinements like this are not needed.

Flash system design

Although it does not affect the performance of the lighting as such, the design of flash systems has a bearing on how the kit is built up, what stands are used, and what lighting control can be added. There are two main types of flash system. Monobloc flash heads are those which are self-contained, and need nothing apart from a mains power supply. In each head, there is a full circuit including capacitors. Each head can be used on its own, independently of the others. The price paid for this is that each head is limited to its own maximum power even though the entire system may have three times this power in total, and each head is also relatively bulky and heavy.

A console, or generator system, uses a floor-standing power unit which contains all the control circuitry and the capacitors to store the energy to produce the flash. From this, heavy-duty cables run to much smaller, lighter flash heads. The power output can be divided as required, in different ratios, between a number of heads. If necessary, the entire power can be outputted through one suitable head. The console system means that there is no need to reach the flash heads to change their power setting, or move from the camera position to do so; all the changes are handled from the console itself. The heads are a fraction of the weight, and easily manoeuvred. Wander arms and tall stands do not present balance problems.

On the other hand, the cables linking the flash heads to the console are fixed in length. Unless special provision is made to include the capacitors in the head (which loses the weight benefit) there is a power loss in the cable, proportional to its length. An output of 1000 joules console may equal 800 joules monobloc. With all the flash heads linked and limited to 5 metres from the console, large lighting arrangements become harder. Often two or three consoles are needed in a big studio, though only one may be used for 90 per cent of the work.

The cables are heavy, as well, and not as easily draped as mains cables to monoblocs. If the console fails or fuses, all the lighting heads are lost. With monobloc flash, the failure of one head rarely ends the day's work. Some console units do not have full proportional control, and can only divide the power between heads in set ratios. On others, the full power must always be used, however it is divided. Monobloc heads allow full control over

individual power (if good controls are fitted) and the use of fractional powers all round when a low total output is needed.

Console units are popular in practice because the power needed for a large hazy or fish-fryer exceeds the 2000 joules maximum found in monoblocs. A typical 1m × 2m light source needs between 3000 and 6000 joules to meet all normal studio demands. If you own a console for this, it makes sense to use

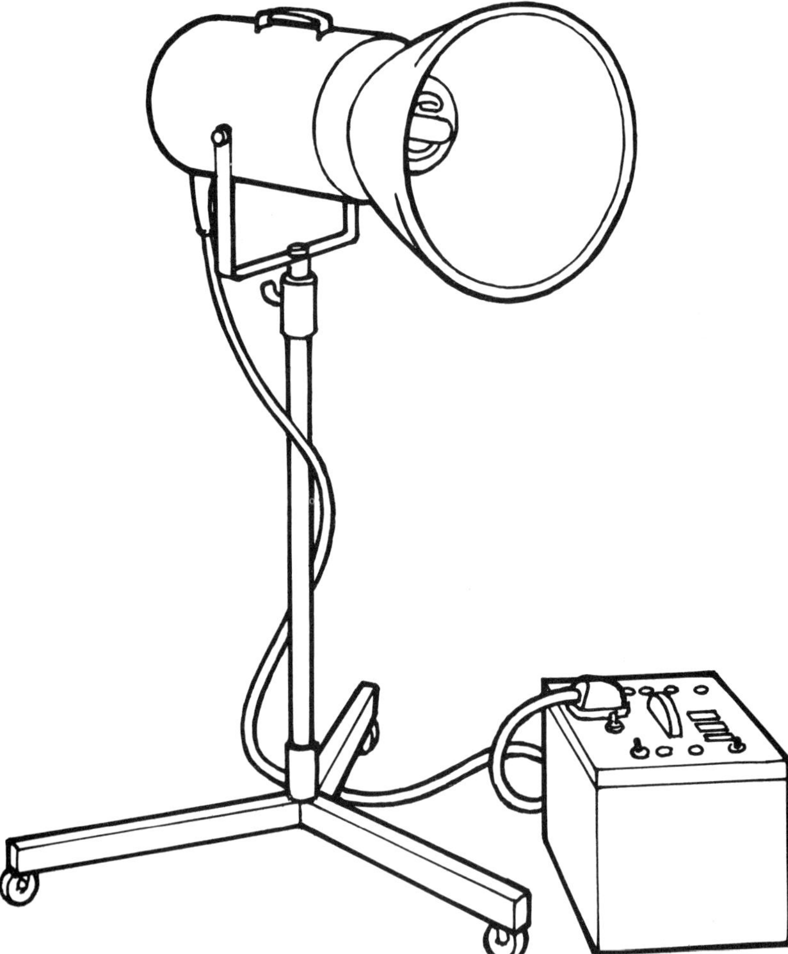

A console-type flash unit with a floor-standing generator and a head containing the minimum of weight is ideal for a large studio. This model has the condensors, bulky but light, in the head in order to cut light loss caused by having a cable between the condensers and flashtube.

the same system for the additional lighting. Owning two consoles solves the failure problem.

Proportional modelling
Within any one studio flash system, the modelling or guide lights on all the flash heads should be fully proportional. This can be tested using an exposure meter and flash meter. When a flash is turned from full to half power, the modelling light should reduce to half output as well. If a 500-joule unit is owned as well as a 1000-joule, the wattage of the modelling lamp in the former should be half that of the latter (at the same voltage).

When thyristor controls are used for varying the modelling lamp brightness, the colour temperature of the light changes. This means that a tungsten-halogen 1000-joule flash with a 650W light used on quarter power produces a very warm yellow light, but a 250-joule flash with a 150W (proportional in effect) modelling light seems blue, and therefore 'brighter' to the eye.

Because of this, and other factors, a reasonable limit of 15 per cent tolerance can be allowed for modelling light proportionality. It is reasonable to fit a 75W bulb to a 200-joule flash and a 150W bulb to a 400-joule head, and accept the result, even though the 150W bulb may not give exactly twice the light of the 75W. It is wrong to mix tungsten half-watt (domestic) bulbs with either enlarger bulbs (slightly over-run) or photoflood bulbs (highly over-run). Nor should tungsten-halogen bulbs be mixed with these; the wattages and outputs are disparate.

Other flash features
Different makes of flash have different built-in features. With monobloc heads, there is normally a built-in *slave cell* or photocell which responds to any other flash firing, and fires its own head simultaneously. This avoids wired-up connections. Some makes have no cell, but a socket for one supplied separately. A cell which can be switched off is an advantage, and not all offer this option.

Most console units have a cell on the console to allow firing via the flash from a main console.

Flash-ready is indicated universally by a light which comes on, a second or two after the last shot, to show that the flash unit has recharged fully and is ready for use. The position and brightness of this signal can affect working ease greatly. In some makes, the light comes on at 90 per cent full charge, and flickers when 98 per cent (or theoretical maximum) charge is reached. An audible bleep signal is fitted to many makes, and avoids the need to glance at heads.

Flash-fired signals are rarer. They can take the form of the modelling light switching off momentarily, though this shortens the life of the light. A separate flash-fired light may be fitted. In others, the audible recharge warning doubles as a flash-fired signal; it buzzes as the flash recharges, and goes off when the recycling is complete. As it is up to the maker to decide which features to include, these minor points may affect choice of flash when other features appear equally balanced.

Infra-red cordless firing is a feature which may be built-in or can be added to most units. A small firing transmitter is fitted to the camera's flash-synchronisation socket or accessory shoe, and a receiver box on to the console or one flash head. An invisible infra-red emission triggers the flash when the shutter is pressed, without annoying cables. Most systems have two or three channels, so that there is an option to fire different flashes selectively. When ordinary slave cells are fitted, remote triggering can also be rigged up using a small camera-top battery flash-gun. At the kind of apertures used with studio flash, aiming such a gun at the studio ceiling will have no effect on the shot, but will trigger the main flash.

Flash metering
A flash meter is like an ordinary exposure meter; most operate by incident light only, and will only take readings when coupled by cable to the flash.

Better models will take a reading when positioned
in the subject plane, without cables, responding to
the flash automatically. The most sophisticated
types can take incident, reflected, spot or probe
readings and combine any number of consecutive
flashes, ambient daylight and different shutter
speeds to give a reading accurate to 1/10th of an
f-stop. Whatever type you can afford, a flash meter
is essential for accurate studio flash exposure. It is
not possible to rely on analagous modelling-light
metering or calculations, even when you know your
flash system thoroughly.

Simple flash meters have a limited range. Normally,
this means they will give readings at ISO 100/21°
from *f*/2.8 to *f*/32. This corresponds with the likely
maximum range of a small studio set-up and 35mm
or 6 × 6cm camera. Meters like this are not suitable
for large-format (5 × 4 in) work. Instead, a meter
with a range covering to *f*/128 should be
purchased; at the very least, *f*/90. The smallest stop
on most large-format lenses is *f*/64, but a meter has
to be able to read beyond this to indicate
overexposure at this setting. This often means the
meter will not give readings wider than *f*/5.6, but
such wide apertures are hardly ever used on
large-format cameras.

Cheaper meters also have various shortcomings.
Some are sensitive to ambient light, and have to be
zeroed or switched on immediately before the
reading is taken. The cheapest makes call for the
modelling lights to be turned off when the reading
is taken. Others will only give accurate readings if
the flash duration is longer than 1/1000 second,
and can not be pressed into service to take readings
from portable flash units which may give times as
short as 1/50 000 second.

Check exposures

With tungsten lighting, test shots are hardly ever
needed. Video offers the facility to take a test and
preview it directly; the lights can be adjusted and
the effect seen on the monitor screen. Flash, with
relatively imprecise modelling light and occasional

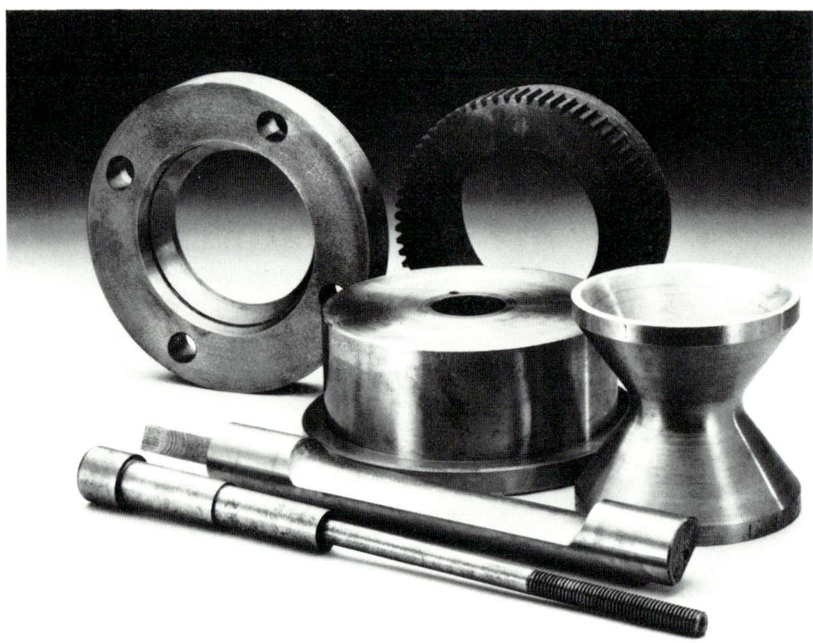

doubt about exact exposure effects, is best tackled
with test shots. A studio in a large city embarking
on a major shoot may test using the film batch
selected for the job, thus checking two variables at
one go. The reversal film can be taken down to the
lab and processed within two hours, or done on the
spot and seen in an hour.

For routine single shots, a polaroid instant-picture
test is cheaper and quicker. Black-and-white
polaroid tests lighting ratios and exposure
adequately, either using an older polaroid camera
with full exposure controls, or an adaptor back to
fit a rollfilm, 35mm or large-format camera.
Colour polaroid gives some idea of final results but
the colours do not resemble other films. At the best,
polaroid tests show if the desired effect has been
achieved. They can not check exposure precisely.
Often they can reveal an unwanted reflection, a
flash head failing to fire, or a fault in the
modelling-light ratio which leads to one head being
too bright or dim.

Above: a typical polaroid
instant test shot shows
roughly what the light effect
and exposure will be. Right:
the final enlargement
reveals far more depth of
tone and detail, but is
essentially the same.

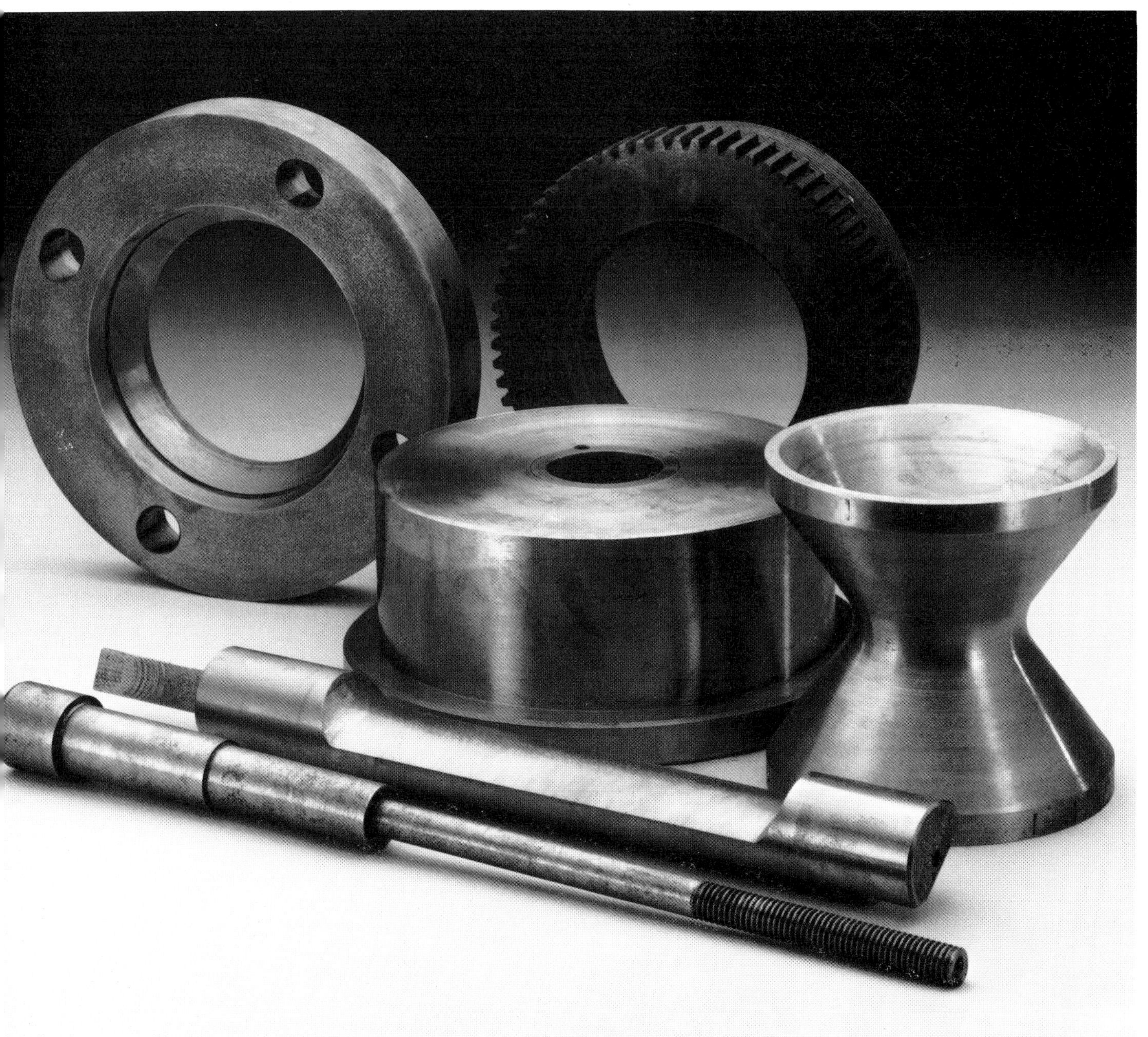

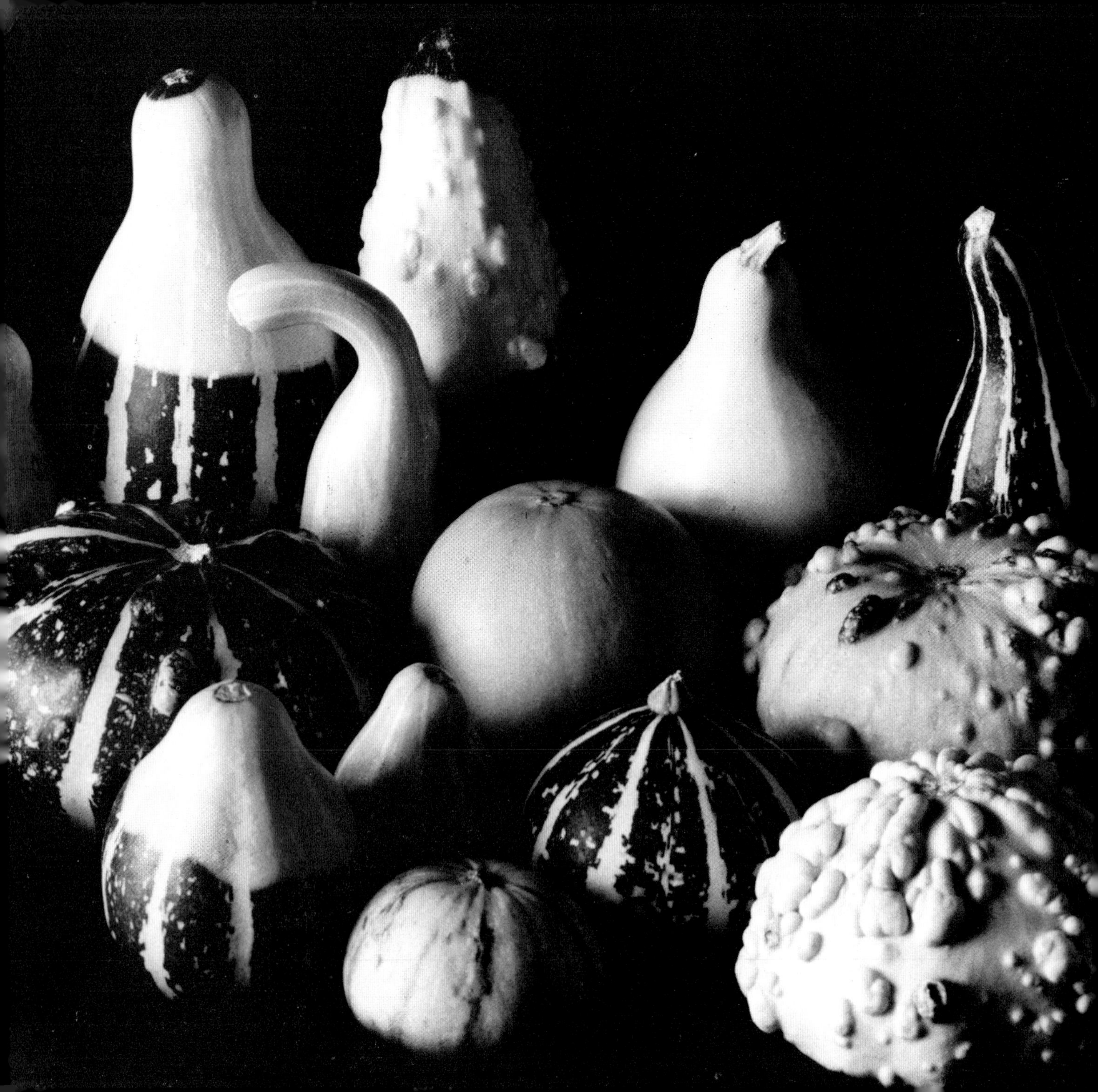

Light and colour

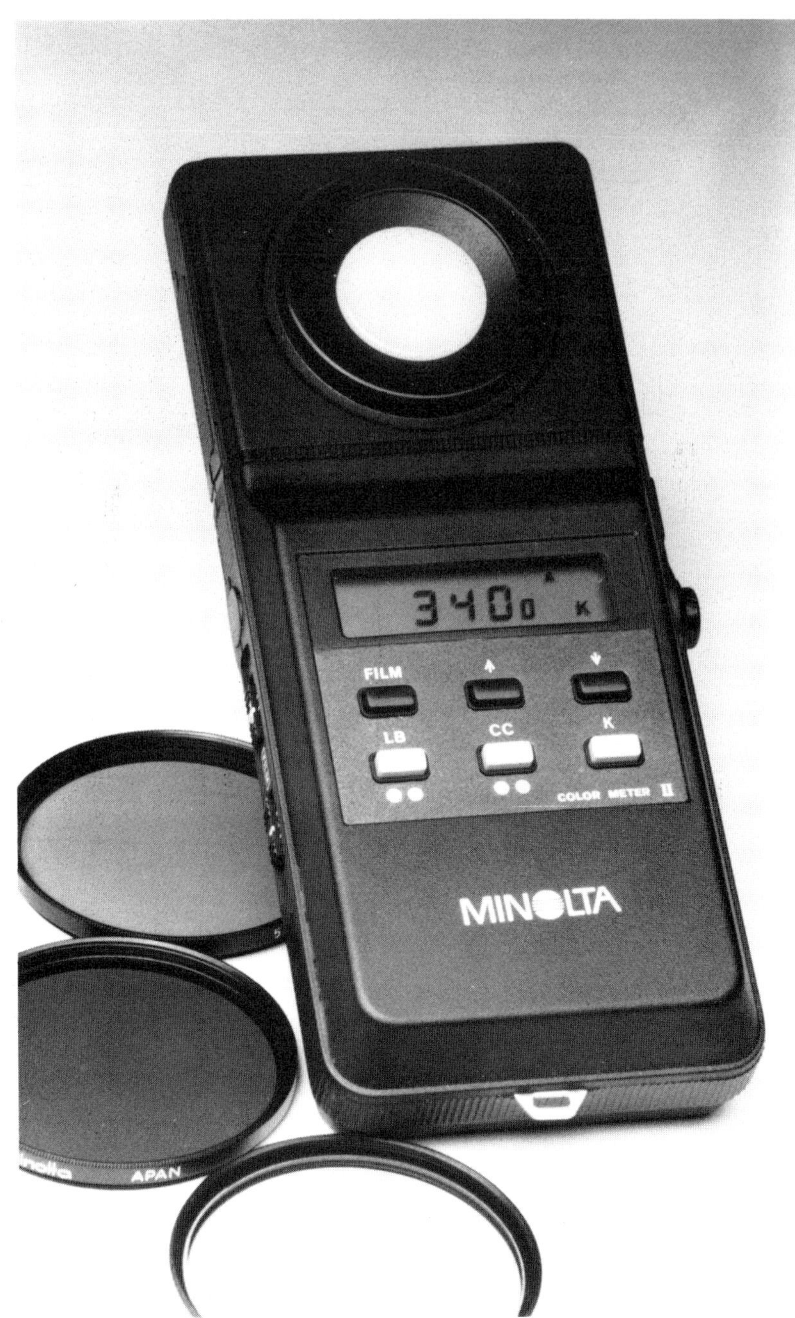

White light is composed of a mixture of wavelengths from 440 to 700 nm (nanometers). That, at least, is the standard explanation. In fact, there is no such thing as white light; the human eye merely responds to wavelengths within this range, and attributes a neutral balance to the mixture inherent in sunlight. There are wavelengths both longer and shorter than this which are invisible to the eye, and the distribution of wavelengths within 'white' light is not totally even.

The theory of colour forms a subject of its own, dealing with perception, psychological values, aesthetics and so on. For lighting purposes, this side of colour does not have to be considered; it is strongly influenced by the subject matter and the purpose of the shot, and therefore can never be quantified. Technical accuracy of colour recording, on the other hand, can be. White light, or average daylight, can have its colour content measured. All other forms of light, whether continuous or instant, can be matched or compared with this. The scale used to measure the simple colour content of light is called the Kelvin scale. It is based on the colour of wavelengths emitted by a black body at different temperatures. As this theoretical body is heated, it first glows dark red, then orange-red, through orange and yellow to white, and then on to blue-white and blue. The scale used is written in 'Kelvins' (*not* 'degrees Kelvin', a common mistake) from 0 to 20 000 or more.

The range of colour temperatures commonly encountered is from around 1800K (light from oil lamps, flames and candles) to 20 000K (blue northern sky). All sources contain, to some extent, all the colours of the spectrum from violet to red. The central colour of the wavelength range 400 to 700nm is green, and this is the element of light least affected by changes in colour temperature.

Colour-temperature changes result from shifts in the relative amount of blue-violet or orange-red included.

Most colour films today are balanced for 5600K. This is a compromise between European daylight, which is standardised at 4800K, and American daylight at 6000K. A film balanced for 6000K will show English daylight as comparatively warm in colour; a film balanced for 5000K would show American daylight as blue. These 'daylight standards' are simply agreed figures, and do not imply that all daylight in the USA is bluer than all daylight in the UK.

Mean noon sun is 5000K, and this is the colour balance used for many professional reversal films. Tungsten lighting has a colour temperature of 3200K and professional tungsten-light films match this. Some may be sensitised to 3100K (Agfa) or 3400K (Kodachrome Type A, a film balanced for over-run photofloods and now obsolete). Tungsten-balanced film is called Type B, and daylight-balanced film Type D. Artificial light, in general, is referred to as A because the now-discontinued Type A films used this designation.

Effects
When a film is used in light with the correct overall colour temperature, the results are neutral. Colours are rendered as they would appear to the eye. The eye is able to compensate for changes in colour temperature between around 3000K and 10 000K; film is not. When the colour temperature of the light is higher than the balance of the film, the result appears *blue* or *cold*. If it seems paradoxical that a high temperature should produce a cold result, remember that it is the film giving a cold rendering, not the light producing cold colours. If the colour temperature of the light is lower than the balance of the film, the result will be too *yellow* or *warm*.

Coloured filters can be bought to fit over either the light or the camera lens to correct this. The standard filters, with fixed values, are D-to-A and A-to-D. A-to-D is a filter to use daylight film in artificial light, and is medium blue in colour (Kodak/Wrattan filter series No 80B). D-to-A filters do the reverse, allowing artificial-light film to be used in daylight (amber colour, Wrattan 85). When mixed-light sources are used, large sheets of 80B filter material can cover tungsten lights to match existing daylight, or sheets of 85 cover windows to make daylight match tungsten. Flash can be used with a Wrattan 85 filter in combination with tungsten light.

Mixed colour balance can look attractive. A blue outdoor snow scene photographed at dusk is enlivened by the warm, yellow light from the windows of a cottage. Any attempt to 'correct' this would be destructive. When a domestic lamp appears in a room interior lit by flash, it is normal to allow it to record a warm colour. Artificial-light scenes shot on daylight film look inviting and glowing, particularly when warmth, winter evenings or firesides are evoked.

Measuring light colour
It is impossible to assess colour temperature by eye, and unless you know the pedigree of the light source a colour temperature meter is needed. These are expensive. The meter will take a reading in Kelvins, but unfortunately a difference of 500 Kelvins at 3000K is not the same as a difference of 500 at 10 000K. To produce a scale where the same change numerically always needs the same filter to balance, the colour temperatures must be converted to mireds (*micro-reciprocal degrees*).

To obtain a mired value for a colour temperature, divide the Kelvin figure into 1 000 000. Daylight at 5000K becomes 200 mireds and tungsten light at 3200K 313 mireds. The change from daylight to tungsten is +113 mireds; to correct this, a filter with a value of −113 mireds is needed. Amber filters have + values and blue filters − values. The 80B A-to-D filter has a value of −112 and is therefore the correct one to use.

The tables supplied by filter manufacturers often give the plus or minus mired values for each filter, and the tables supplied with a colour meter should list popular filter serial numbers. The Minolta Color Meter II, which accepts an attachment for measuring the colour content of flash, gives readings via a microprocessor in Kelvins, or mired shift, and has a simple table on the back to show which Kodak Wratten series filter is required. The most useful filters to have to hand are the full conversion filters 80B and 85, a mild warm-up filter 81A, a weak blue 82A, and perhaps two intermediate ones: 81D amber, and 82C blue. You will then have mired values of +18, +42 and +112; −21, −45 and −112 respectively. Domestic lightbulbs have a mired value of 360; the filters needed for daylight film are −160, to an 80B plus 82C blue will do, adding up to −157. For Type-B tungsten light film, the required shift to match domestic lightbulbs is −47, so the 82C at −45 can be used.

Light from a blue sky, as found in open shade, has a mired value of about 80. A warm-up correction of +120 can restore accurate skin tones, and that means using an D-to-A filter type 85 with normal daylight film. On an overcast day, with a mired value of around 125, a filter of +75 would be correct. In practice, an 81D amber filter will restore part of the correct colour balance with its +42 shift, without making the picture seem artificially 'sunny' and over-corrected.

In practice, you can soon recognise when to use different amber or blue filters to correct known conditions. It is better to err in favour of excess warmth where skin tones are concerned, but to avoid the indiscriminate correction of lighting conditions which may add a great deal to the mood of the final picture.

Green shift

The colour-temperature scale and the mired values take no account of the changes in green content in light. With daylight and tungsten light, green stays fairly constant and needs no correction. Sometimes there is a problem, and a colour meter will detect a green shift. The opposite colour to green, in filter terms, is magenta (a mixture of red and blue, which are at opposite ends of the spectrum). Green and magenta filters have no effect on colour temperature, but do change the colour balance.

Unless you own a colour meter, the first experience of a green cast in a picture is likely to be from fluorescent light. This may look white, and has a measurable colour temperature around 4800K. It is deficient in magenta (red and blue content) and therefore gives a green cast to pictures. The normal correction is a special filter, called FL-D. This pinkish-brown filter is balanced to correct an 'average' fluorescent tube to daylight film. In practice it works well. Type FL-B filters allow the use of tungsten-light film under fluorescent tubes.

Colour correction or compensating filters, in magenta and green, are available in a range of strengths expressed as 'CC' values. CC30M is a magenta filter of 30 units density, CC10G a green of 10 units density. As a green correction is not often thought desirable, most photographers keep one or two magenta filters handy. Colour-compensating filters are also made in red, blue, yellow and cyan (green-blue).

Testing film and lights

Without a colour meter, most studios occasionally test their film stock and light sources (including control attachments and reflectors) using a colour wedge. The Kodak Colour Patch and Grey Scale is an example; so is the MacBeth Color Checker. These are flat, printed colour specimens with accurate solid colours, which can be photographed and later compared with the results.

By viewing the transparencies through different

filters and carefully assessing the rendering, you can establish whether your lenses, light and film give accurate colour rendering. If not, you can estimate which filters are needed. Often it is simply a case of finding that one flash head is slightly blue, checking it and discovering that unlike all the rest it has been fitted with an uncorrected tube giving out too much ultra-violet. Or perhaps one seems too warm, and you find that the envelope covering the flashtube and modelling lamp has become discoloured and scorched.

You may find that a particular reflector or a sheet of perspex warms-up colour, or that one umbrella introduces an unwanted green shift. Lenses, which may alter colour rendering, can be tested. In video, the colour checker can be lit using your regular lights and the colour controls adjusted carefully to match (using two identical monitors and a VTR) the checker recorded as neutrally as possible under daylight conditions. Settings can be noted, and every time you return to the same lighting system these settings are repeated so that skin and clothes do not appear to change colour.

Correction later on

Perfect colour balance is not vital for video work, as corrections can be made later on. It is only essential in transparency photograhy because there is no printing stage. When colour negative film is used for ciné shoots, or for colour prints, it is not vital to correct for colour. It can improve results and make printing easier if conversion filters are used for daylight and tungsten changes, but fine-tuning is not required.

There are some conditions where reversal film is undesirable, as colour can not be predicted or assessed. A factory lit by fluorescent tubes with some tungsten, large sodium roof floods and added mercury vapour lamps presents an impossible problem. The light is totally mixed and there will be massive, invisible, colour shifts.

To ensure that a good result can be obtained,

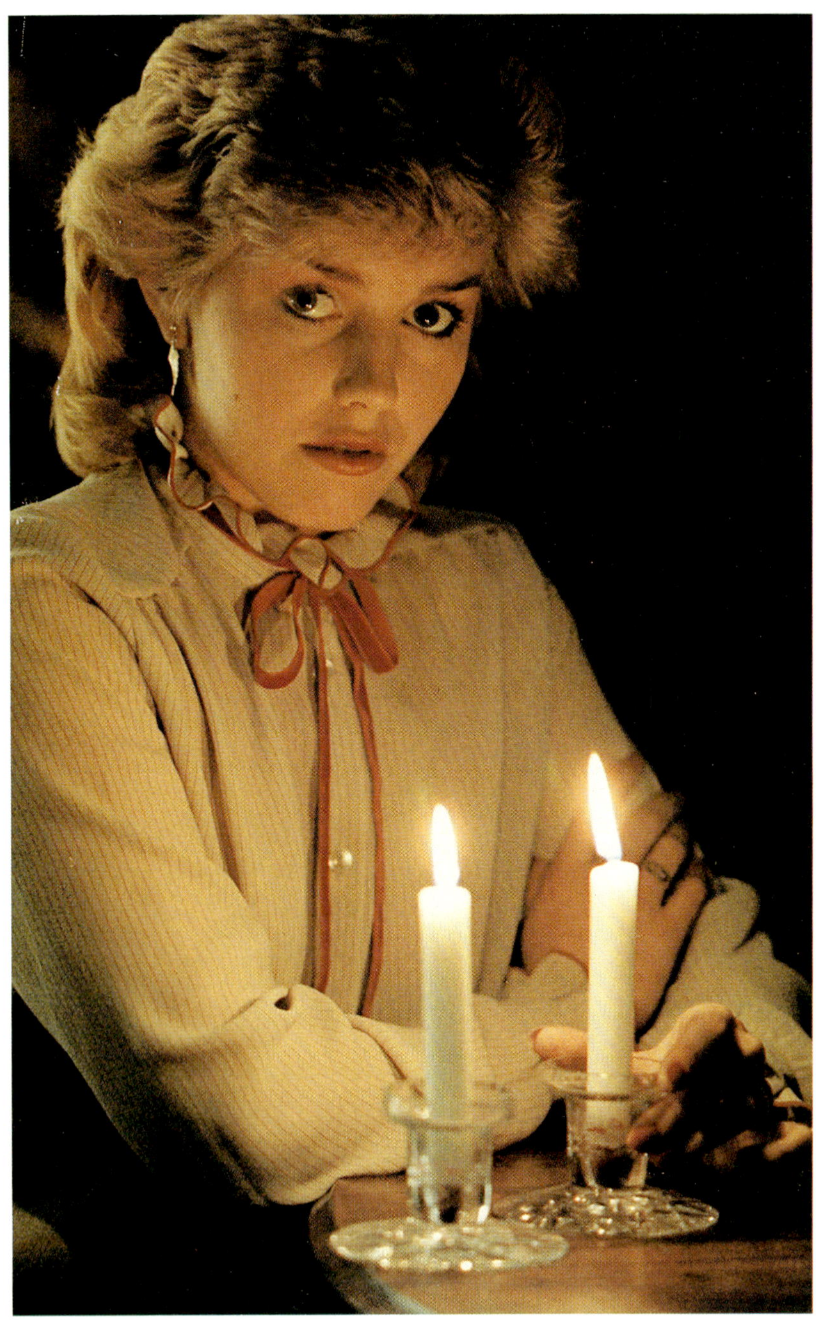

colour negative film should be used. A fast film, with high colour latitude, offers the best hope of securing a pleasant overall balance when printing. Plenty of exposure should be given, to ensure that wavelengths which are under-represented record sufficiently strongly to be usable. It is easy to filter out the excess colour from predominant wavelengths as long as there is a good image present from the impoverished sections of the spectrum. If normal exposure is given, then this may mean that the green- and blue-sensitive layers of the film receive 130 per cent of the amount needed for minimum detail, but the red layer only receives 50 per cent. An exposure meter will call that 'correct'. It is vital to make sure in this case that the red layer gets 100 per cent of the required exposure for adequate detail, even if the other two layers are overexposed at 260 per cent of required minimum.

This is the only way of ensuring that a clean print, with good shadow detail and a full range of

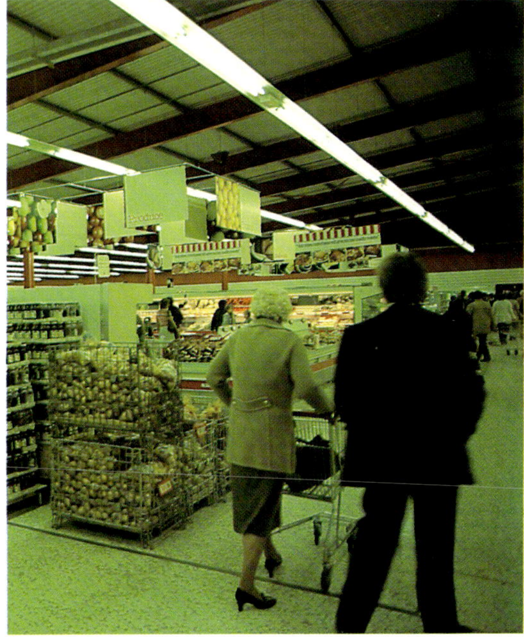

colours, can be produced under mixed non-continuous spectrum lighting. There are limits to corrections possible, as video users find out; it is not practical to expect neutral colour under sodium street lights any more than you would expect to be able to balance back to 'white' after shooting through a dark green filter. The alternative is to accept factory lighting in all its contrast and colour clashes, and use it creatively, working by natural light. The results can be vivid or lurid depending on conditions.

Studio colour

Colour balance and content does change the feel of pictures. It is sometimes wrongly assumed that all light sources are accurately matched in colour. This is not so. In electronic flash, one make may have colour temperatures from 4500K to 5000K and another consistently produce from 5600K to 6000K. There is always a slight variation between units, just as there is when changing power. Similar differences can be found between different tungsten-halogen lighting units, depending on the reflector, bulb type, operating voltage, and the age of the bulb itself.

Unless the colour balance is tested or known, a studio may produce inferior results over a long period, having nothing else to compare them with. One photographer may change filmstock or equipment, searching for a solution to the problem that 'film X is always too blue' without considering the possibility that the lighting system is blue, not the film.

Maximum saturation and control over colour are only possible when the balance is near-perfect. This does not worry the social photographer taking portraits on negative stock, the film crew testing every shot and having the processing modified to correct, or the video operator able to correct on the spot. For the advertising photographer using reversal stock exposure is of prime importance and must be studied, in theory and practice.

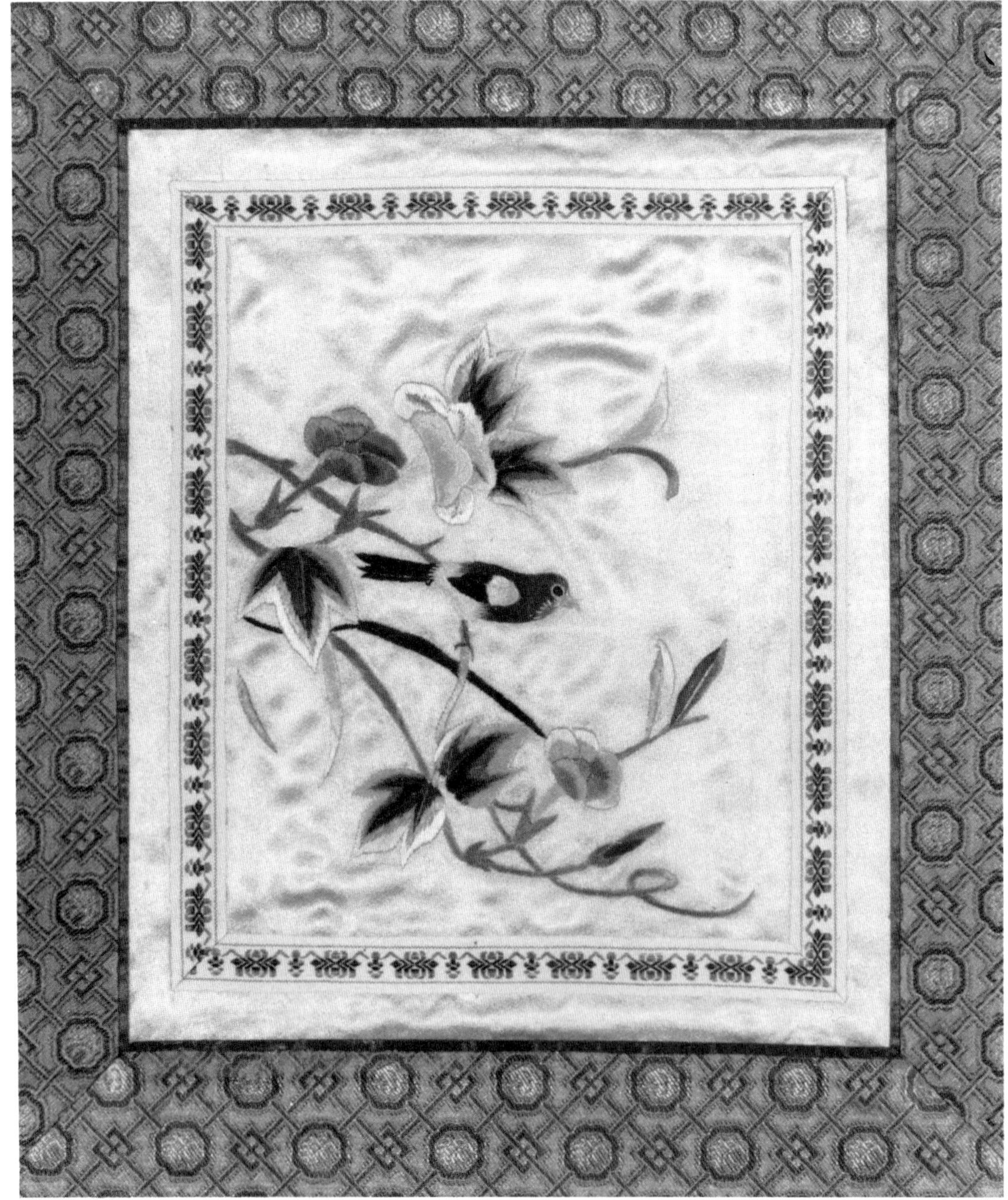

A silk picture is copied without removing it from its frame, at the same time revealing the texture and sheen of the material. Two lights at 45° angles were used. *Richard Bradbury/A1 Studios.*

A strong crosslight from a point source picks out the relief of coins in a close-up study. *Richard Bradbury/A1 Studios.*

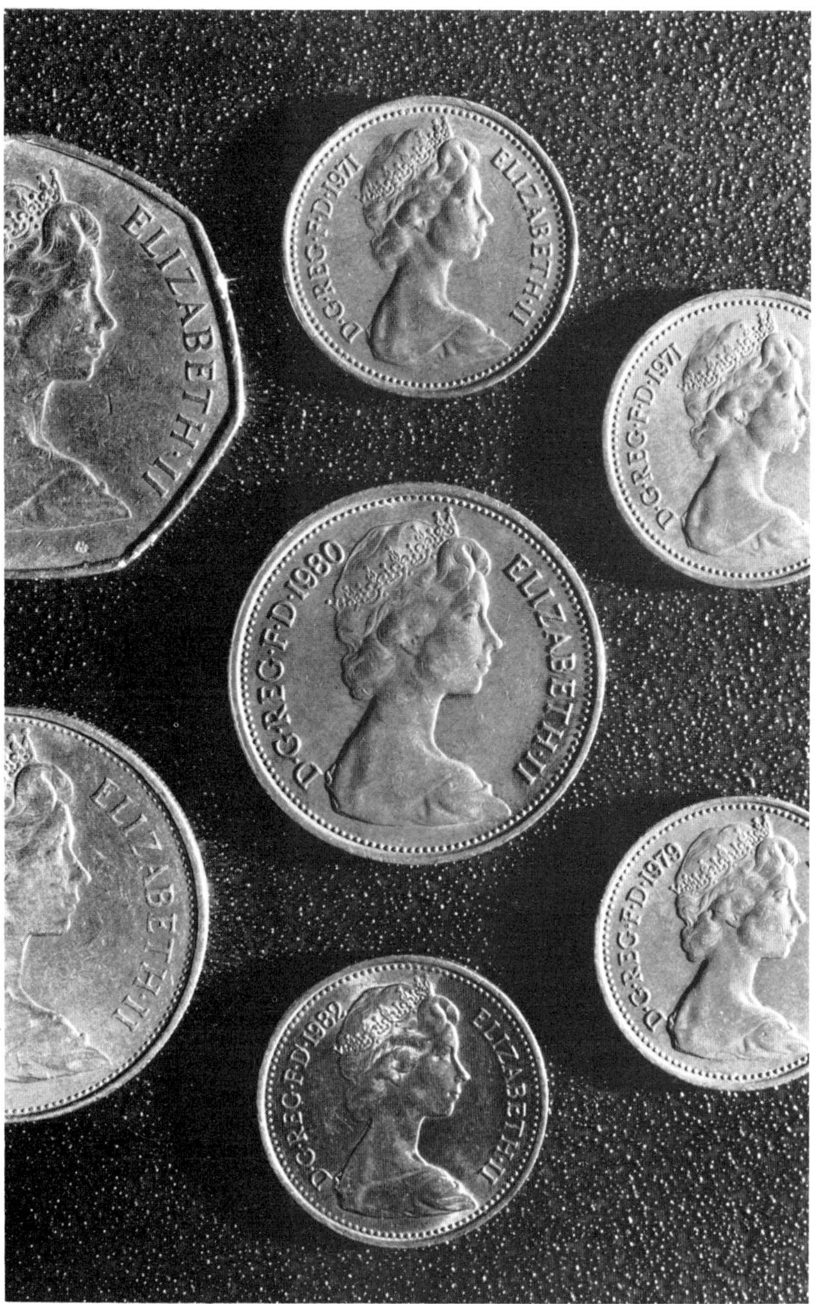

Specialised lighting techniques

There are some tasks where routine lighting set-ups fail because of special problems. Often, these are common standardised jobs and once the basic technique is learned there is no further creative thought to be exercised. Copying and rostrum work fall into this category. There are times when a studio may be fully occupied with nothing but copy work or rostrum filming for weeks.

Flat copy
Flat copy is a term used to describe any kind of original which is two-dimensional. The range could be from a postage stamp to a poster, and the possible applications include full colour reproduction, copy slides, line negatives for black-and-white reproduction on artwork, and rostrum zoom and pan work from artwork for television advertising.

The basic requirement is to light the original evenly from corner to corner, with no local hot spot or variations. It should be possible to hold it flat, so the lights must not cast shadows of clips. Normally, it is desirable to lose any textural detail except when photographing fabric or an oil painting where the texture is part of the artwork or subject. Flat copy work imposes camera alignment and support demands which have nothing to do with lighting. We will assume that a stand is used, or that the photographer is able to align camera and copyboad accurately.

The first rule of flat copy work is to have the camera as far from the original as possible. This entails using a longer lens than normal, or a relatively long zoom setting. Extra working distance does three things: it reduces the apparent effect of any misalignment, leaves more room for lighting, and helps avoid reflections on the surface reflector with a card snoot will suffice. The light is brought closer, until the illuminated subject looks correct in relation to the card, and the exposure is read from the card.

With luminescent subjects, the amount of lighting added from the camera position determines surrounding shadow detail. The subject itself will not be affected, because it is normally transparent.

As an example, an electronic device may have a light-emitting diode display or a video display screen. The main subject has to be lit with flash, but a 'soak' exposure must also be given in total darkness to record the illuminated area. To find the correct exposure for this, the modelling lights are adjusted so that the display seems just brighter than the overall lighting. A reflected-light overall metered exposure for this condition will give correct rendering to the display or screen. With video screens, it is important to avoid direct illumination of the screen surface, as this is grey. Full contrast will not be visible in the combined shot if the main lighting reaches the screen.

Assuming the metered exposure for the display is 1 second at $f/11$, there is a choice between making a single flash and time exposure, or two separate ones. As most shutters will fire the flash at the start of a long exposure, it is just as convenient to use a single shot, and there is less risk of moving the camera. To do this, the flash has to be adjusted or controlled to need $f/11$. If the flash is so powerful that $f/32$ would be needed at minimum power, it may be better to make two exposures. This should only be done if the lens is focused precisely on the illuminated display; when the aperture is changed from $f/32$ to $f/11$, exact image size may change fractionally, and this can move the position of the second image enough to make it seem that the camera has been moved. This only applies to details out of the plane of correct focus; sharply focused detail remains stable when the aperture is changed with all but the poorest lenses.

Transparent subjects

When the subject is transparent, or virtually so, it can not be lit from the front. Instead, the background must be illuminated. Because most transparent substances are capable of refracting and 'piping' light, it may be possible to put extra light into them by aiming a small spot source into the material from the rear or below. This leads to two options, mainly concerned with glassware and liquids in bottles. Plastic has such a low refractive index that background illumination and internal lighting rarely work.

The simplest set-up for glassware photography is a white background, lit by one or more lights which are to the side, above or below the subject area. The glassware is positioned so that it is seen against this illuminated backdrop. Careful choice of camera angle will show the shape and quality of the glass as a silhouette; edges become distinctly black, and thick areas may show graduations of grey. The surface on which the glass is placed can change the effect. If this is a clear glass table or shelf, the appearance will be different from a shot using a matt black shelf. To make glass shots more interesting, the background can be grey or coloured, and a diffused light added near the camera to create white direct reflections on the glass surfaces and edges. This combination of colour, crisp shadow outlines and pure white reflection highlights is very effective.

When the glass is thick, it can be placed on an opaque background with normal illumination, and light introduced from the base of the item. The background is cut out, to fit the shape of the product, and a diffused light source positioned underneath the cut-out. The light is piped through the glass, and gives it a suffused brightness. This works best with a dark background and can be dramatic against pure black. The main problem is that any flaws in the glass, or minute dust particles in liquids if a full bottle is involved, show up strongly from this internal illumination.

Some liquids naturally pick up light, so that when placed on a transilluminated surface like a perspex table they will stand out even against distant parts of the background which are graded off to a shadow tone. When photographing glasses and bottles which do not have the right shape to refract light this way, a small piece of white card should be cut and placed behind the glass. If possible, position this a few centimetres behind, so that it is not sharply imaged. Plastics, with low refractive indices, are best shown by inducing reflections and setting them against a neutral or dark background. If there is a clear plastic panel in a product, position the camera and hazylight to give it a sheen; the detail behind will still be visible.

The impression of smoothness, finish and quality in any product is enhanced by using graded light. If the background in a glassware shot can be made to fall off gently to shadow at the top, or edges, the viewer will think the glassware has the same smoothness.

Polished and reflective subjects
Cutlery and silverware, machined bright metal, jewellery and mirrors all present special lighting problems. The common factor is that any reflective surface can not be lit by aiming a light-source at it. If you aim a spotlight at a silver teapot, a single very small spot of light will show, reflected in a black teapot. Polished metal objects are only visible because of the reflection of their surroundings seen in the metal. In everyday circumstances, we take the surroundings into account and see the object in its own right. In the studio, an objective rendering of the subject is needed; we expect to see silverware looking like silver, cutlery looking like steel, and a mirror looking like a mirror. To produce contours and give clues to shape, there must be some lines or patterns produced by variations in the reflected surroundings. But in silverware (for example) these should be relatively fine dark lines with most of the subject almost white. A hint of gradation and tone is needed, to avoid the appearance of a line drawing.

To light a flat reflective surface like a mirror, set up the subject and camera. Through the lens, examine the area of studio visible in the subject. Then suspend a roll of white, pale blue or grey seamless background paper to cover this area fully. The further away it is from the subject, the larger the area to be covered. If the camera is close to the subject the same applies, so it helps to use a long lens from a distance. You will rapidly find out how much more space is needed than you think if you set up a simple trial project to photograph a wall mirror. The main lighting should be based on the mirror frame and background, and have no effect on the glass surface or the suspended 'reflected background'. This will be lit separately, by a head carefully positioned not to appear in the reflection.

If the seamless paper is evenly illuminated, the level of illumination determines the apparent colour and brightness of the mirror. Too little light will tend to show any slight flaws in the paper, and unless the paper is tinted blue or grey, the colour may be unpleasant. Too much light will reduce the mirror area to plain burned-out highlight. The correct solution is either to light the paper evenly and spray a 'shade line' diagonally across it with light grey or silver paint spray, or to light the paper to produce a gradation. Then the mirror will look natural.

A three-dimensional reflective subject presents greater problems. Cutlery can be photographed using a single large hazylight, suspended over the items and slightly to their rear, so that the diffused light source is seen reflected in the flat faces of the blades and handles. Because there are curves, some parts of most designs will not pick up the light and will record as black. Where this is unwanted, reflectors or white cards are positioned by trial and error.

Trophies, jewellery and other complex surfaces may need surrounding entirely with light. A $1m^2$ hazylight suspended above the subject can be backed up by identical units on both sides, and a white card with a small hole cut in for the camera

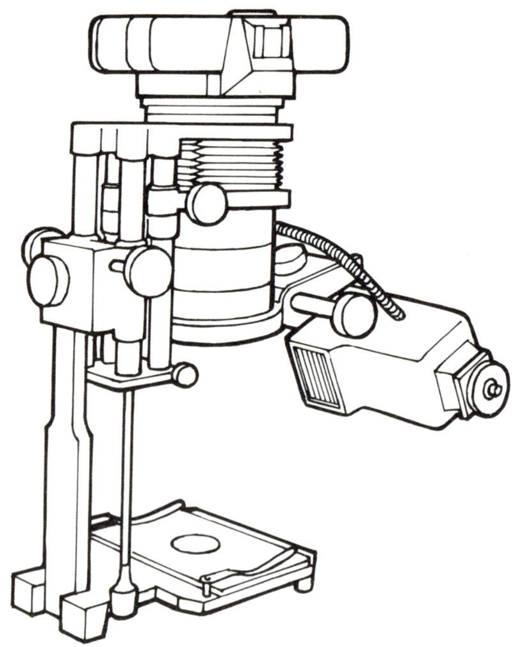

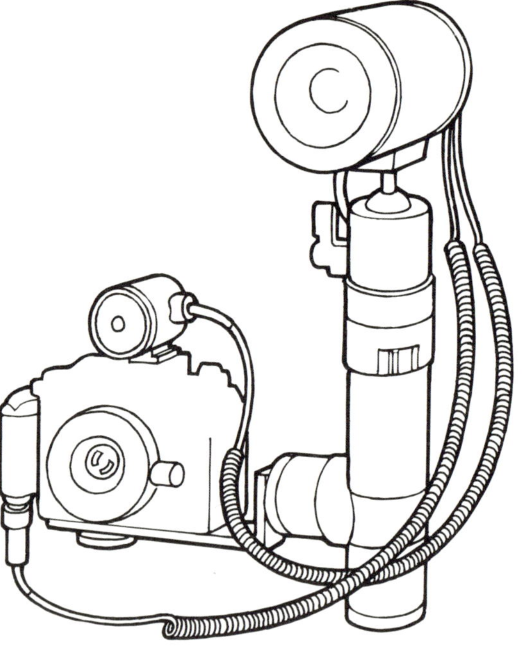

Special types of lighting equipment. Far left: a macro set-up using a flash on a special bracket to create textural lighting on small subjects. Left: an underwater flash unit attached to an underwater camera and sealed at all points.

When setting-up lighting for multiple exposures or superimposition, the use of large light sources may be ruled out unless you have very effective french flags or mask-off at the camera. Camera masking involves the use of a deep lens hood with provision for fixing or inserting mattes, which are cut cards used to obscure parts of the frame. Even black fabrics do not show as totally black when photographed, so it is not enough to cover areas of the set with velvet. Spotlighting and tight light control can not prevent bounced light from the subject itself reaching other parts of the shot. So a combination of camera masking, careful lighting and use of light absorbing panels may be needed.

Exposure is cumulative, so that a part of a subject which receives 50 per cent of maximum exposure and renders mid-grey will appear white if given a second exposure. It is better to keep contrast high and shadows dense when making multi-exposure shots. Simple double exposure should not present problems, but four, eight or 16 shots on one frame may introduce a kind of shadow degradation in areas you think are completely black.

Lighting interiors
Room sets for advertising work are often not real rooms, but stage sets made of flats, doors, windows, wallpaper and carpet in the studio. They have no ceiling, unless called for, and light can be introduced from above. When the ceiling is absent, the basic technique involves as large as diffused light source as possible from above, slightly towards the camera. This should 'lift' all shadows so that no part of the room set is too dark.

To give atmosphere, diffused sources can then be concealed behind the windows, which are normal window frames fitted with tissue paper rather than glass. The level of these is adjusted until the tissue burns out as a pure highlight, which in turn produces pools of 'window light' near the

windows. A light-blue filter on these lights can give
a feeling of open daylight. Within the room, special
bare-bulb flash heads may be positioned in
domestic light fittings, covered with a light amber
filter to give the effect of tungsten light. In a studio
with full black-out, real tungsten lights may be used
with a second exposure.

The idea is to provide lighting which shows detail
in fabrics, furniture, wallpaper, kitchen units, or
whatever points are most important. If the main
subject is a leather settee, woodgrained kitchen
cupboards or a ceramic-topped table the best
lighting will be diffused backlight, to bring out
sheen and texture. The fake window should
therefore be behind the main subject. To bring out
textures like bedlinen, or create more atmosphere,
the main fill-in light can be omitted, and all the
light supplied through the windows. A window
light source positioned where another window
would be (even if the wall is absent) adds realism.

In genuine rooms, existing daylight may be the best
choice, because the room has been designed to use
the qualities of natural light. To prevent deep
shadows, a fill-in light aimed at the ceiling above
the camera should be balanced to avoid killing the
daylight effect. Where tungsten is involved, filters
can be fitted over the light or the windows (outside,
not in) to match colour temperatures. Where
window light is not adequate, bouncing lights off
the ceiling still produces the most natural effects. If
the ceiling is slightly coloured, the resulting cast
may suit the decor. By aiming the bounced lights at
points just above the windows, where the ceiling
naturally reflects most window light, a natural
effect can be achieved, but only when the windows
are close to the picture edge and the light can be just
out of shot.

Very large interiors call for more lighting.
Balancing the interior light level with outdoor light,
so that a clear view is seen through the window,
instead of burned-out blur, also needs power unless

you wait for dull light or dusk. In churches, halls
and cathedrals there are often pillars, coves,
archways or doors where lighting can be concealed,
aiming into the view as a localised cross light. The
resulting pools of light with balancing areas of
shade emphasise space. The same technique can be
used in factories, hiding lights behind machinery; it
is not necessary to diffuse the source, as direct light
seems appropriate in industrial shots.

Much depends on whether you are looking for
detail or effect. If detail is the main concern, the
added lighting should counteract the effect of
existing light, filling in the shadow areas.
Atmospheric shots may be better with the artificial
light aiding and abetting the architect's intentions.
Industrial shots benefit from the use of coloured
filters for effect lights, as there is often so little
colour present. Blue makes metals look metallic,
red and yellow indicate heat processes. Green,
purple and cyan do not generally suit industrial
shots.

Finally, there is a good argument in major buildings
for abandoning artificial lighting of any kind. The
light within a building is part of its integrity, mood
and design. The windows and interior spaces are
just as important, architecturally, as facades and
details. The quality of light is part of the plan, and a
photographer making the decision to re-light a
great interior tampers with aesthetics.

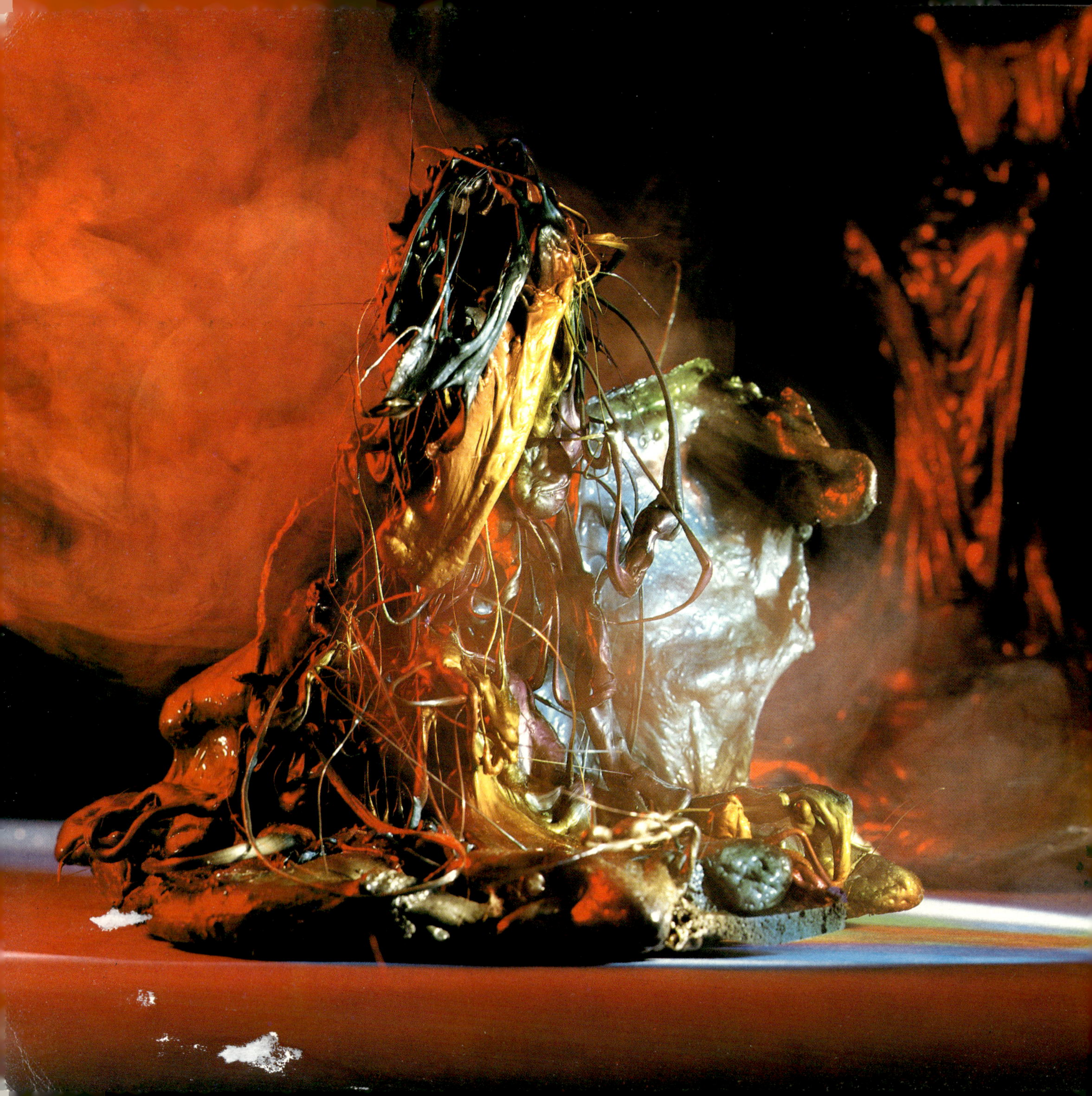

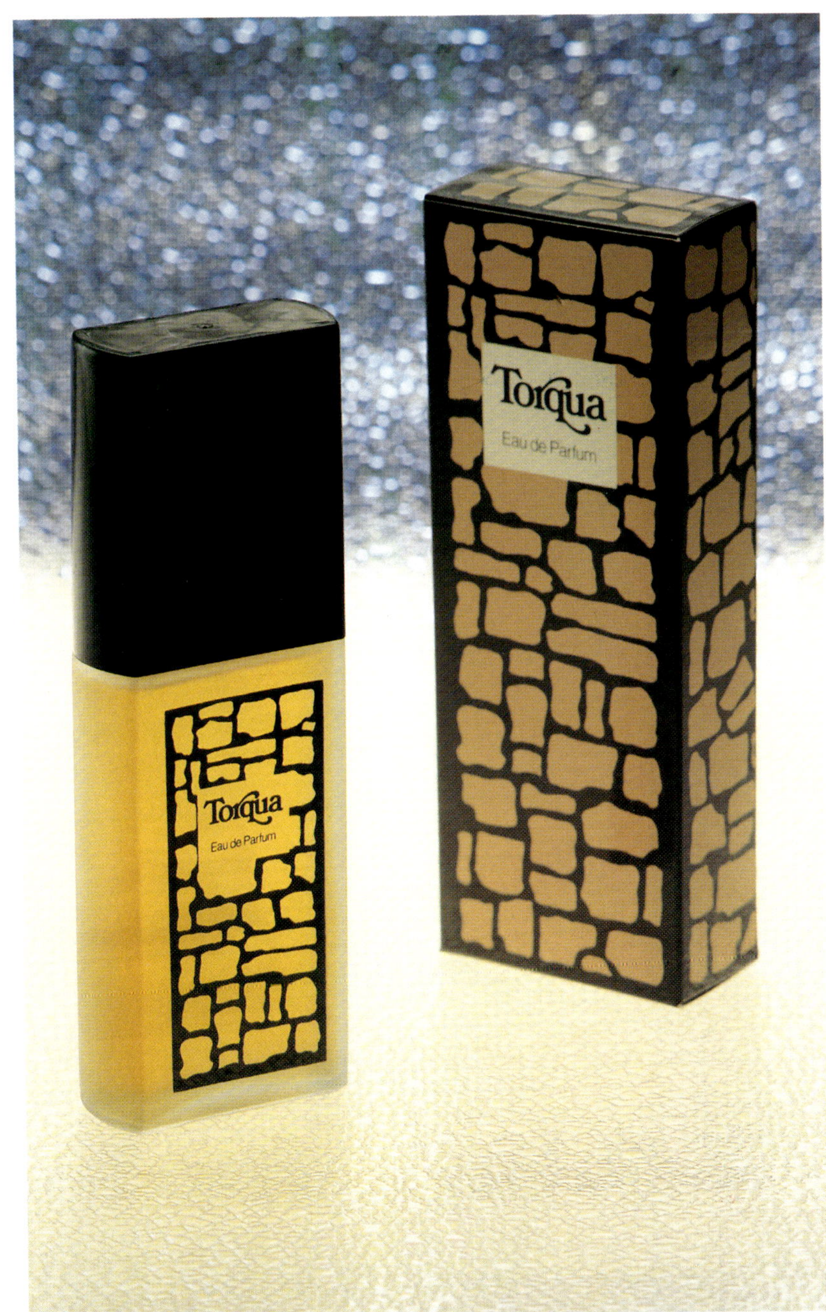

Advanced techniques

Coloured lighting

When coloured light is used as a main light source, rather than for effect, exposure is particularly difficult to calculate. A direct reading, whether incident or reflected, tends to cancel the effect of the colour by recommending more exposure than necessary. To understand this, imagine a scene photographed normally. To make it appear red, a red filter should be placed over the light or the camera lens. There does not need to be an exposure change, or only the shadows will appear red; the metering will try to create a full range of tones including highlights, which will be white or very light red.

Exposure for coloured light should therefore be based on the exposure without the coloured filter in place. In practice, slightly more exposure is given; if the filter indicates a three-stop change in exposure, a one-stop adjustment will give a clean result with good colour saturation. Where coloured lights are used with complementary (opposed) colours, the effect is diluted where the light is superimposed. A red light and a blue light create something close to white. Coloured light is therefore best restricted to crosslighting, rim light, or backlight and only one main coloured light. Two opposed contrasting crosslights can be used, or a main light with a contrasting backlight from the opposite side, hitting a shadow area.

Polarised lighting

Instead of using a polariser on the camera, polarising filters can be used over lights. This helps control reflections and sheen from backlight except in metallic or mirror subjects. If a camera polariser is used as well, the exposure may be increased out of proportion to the value of the effect. There is not much point in using a polariser on a front light, as the glare-cutting properties depend on angles of incidence and reflection which are not encountered from lights near the camera. Because of the high cost of polarising material, it is unusual to cover a hazylight or other large source. Normally a polariser will be used on a small flood or spot. There are some methods which call for polarised light in order to achieve a specific effect, and with these, all the lighting has to be polarised.

Dark ground lighting
Dark ground lighting is a term covering any technique which, by transillumination or sidelight, sets subjects against a solid black while giving them luminosity. Polarised light can be used to produce dark ground illumination with any translucent subject. A sheet of polarising material is placed below the subject, and under this a diffused light source which serves as the background. The specimen is normally placed on glass. A second polariser is then placed over it (or over the camera lens).

When the light is turned on, all light reaching the subject from behind is polarised. When it passes through the translucent subject, it is scattered again, and depolarised. Light passing beside the subject remains polarised. If the second polariser is rotated to 90° opposing the first, all that light is stopped, but the random light leaving the subject is partially transmitted. The final effect is a glowing, transilluminated subject against solid black. The technique can be used with slices of fruit, seafood, plastics, fabric and, most effectively of all, with crystals and rock slices. This is because crystals, minerals, and some plastics rotate the plane of polarised light and may introduce colours depending on the stresses and structure within the sample.

There are some polarising materials which change colour according to orientation, and these can be used to make dramatic 'coloured ground' shots,

with the specimen shown in brilliant red against deep blue (or another combination).

Front projection
The ability of polarising filters to accept or reject light according to orientation allows a simple form of direct image superimposition, similar to electronic colour keying in video. An aluminium screen has the property of returning a projected image, if polarised, with identical polarisation. In a front-projection system, a semi-silvered mirror is used to project a polarised image of a background transparency along the same axis as the camera lens, aimed at the screen. The model or subject stands in front of the screen. Lighting for the subject is also polarised, but rotated to oppose the background shot's orientation.

Through the same polarising filter and semi-silvered mirror the camera lens receives back the background image in full, and a proportion of the random unpolarised lighting reflected back from the subject (which scrambles the polarisation of the main lights). Any stray light falling on the background screen has no effect, because it is opposed to the polariser and blocked entirely. Thus the subject appears, without any shadows, against an apparently natural backdrop. Clever choice of props and slides is essential to get the best results.

The latest generation of front-projection systems eliminates the need for polarised light by using a high-gain screen which returns light in full (like a cat's eye) only when perfectly aligned. As the projection and camera lens axes are concurrent, this happens with the projected image, but the subject lights, even when they light the screen, have no visible effect.

Back projection
Back projection is easily handled in a small studio, but it is only suitable for small subjects and

Page 134: an experiment with coloured light and cigarette smoke using a pure grey 'sculpture' created by the waste from a plastic moulding machine. *David Kilpatrick/A1 Studios.*

Page 135: a background with partial transillumination, partial reflection and separate lighting for the main subject. Courtesy Azure Perfumes Limited, *David Kilpatrick.*

portraits. A rear-projection screen is needed, along with a slide projector. The projector stands behind the screen, the studio is blacked out, and the subject is placed well in front of the screen so that none of the main lighting degrades the projected image. Unless a special flash projector is built, this remains a tungsten-light process, and exposures of one or two seconds may be needed at apertures small enough to render the background slide sharp. For portraits, it is best used to create abstract effects. In place of expensive rear-projection screens, Kodatrace can be used, stetched on a home-made frame.

This system is entirely suitable for video use on head shots, and inset pictures can be projected (as in television newscasts) using a small rear-projection screen set into the studio set back flat. The light from a projector matches the colour temperature of tungsten heads, so there is no problem of compatibility.

Multiple strobe flash

In video, electronic editing can produce multiple stop-action overlays and composites from original movement. Still photographers have to rely on multiple exposure to create multiple images, and the best way to freeze action on a single frame is strobe flash. Like a disco strobe light, strobe flash gives a series of high-speed light pulses, each less than 1/1000th of a second in duration. A typical small unit gives from 2 per second to 30 per second, triggered when the camera (set on a suitable exposure time like 1 second) is released.

Basic lighting technique involves setting the subject against a distant, dark background so that no cumulative flash effect degrades the contrast. The subject should be light, or reflective, and movement must relate to the strobe interval; too close an overlap of images double-exposes them on top of each other, and results in overexposure. Some

popular flashguns for camera-top use, and one or two special studio flash units, can be used for short bursts at 5 frames per second. This can be controlled either with a multi-flash attachment (electronic) or by using a motordrive camera set on multi-exposure, so that the film does not advance. Sequence operation is normally provided only at low powers – one quarter output or less – in both flash types.

Flash and time

Combined flash and time exposures, in still photography, produce fluid movement trails with a single sharp frozen image. The exposure is fairly easily balanced, by setting an aperture one stop smaller than needed by the flash and a shutter speed to give half the necessary exposure at that aperture, metered from the available light. Two halves thus make a full exposure. If the background is very dark, normal exposure for the subject and flash should be given. The method only works reliably when the subject is lighter than the background, or the light detail over-rides the dark subject and wipes it out. Camera movement can be combined with subject movement for abstract effects.

Most camera shutters fire the flash, when connected via a synch lead, at the start of the exposure. This means that if the technique is used to show a car speeding forwards, the movement streaks will appear in front of the car instead of behind it. The car has to be driven backwards to create motion blur behind it, and the trails produced should go beyond the edge of the frame. An alternative is to pan the camera, leaving the subject stationary against a dark plain background, to produce the streaks. If neither solution works, then a means to fire the flash reliably at the end of the exposure has to be contrived. This normally means modifying the camera or shutter so that the shutter closure activates the flash.

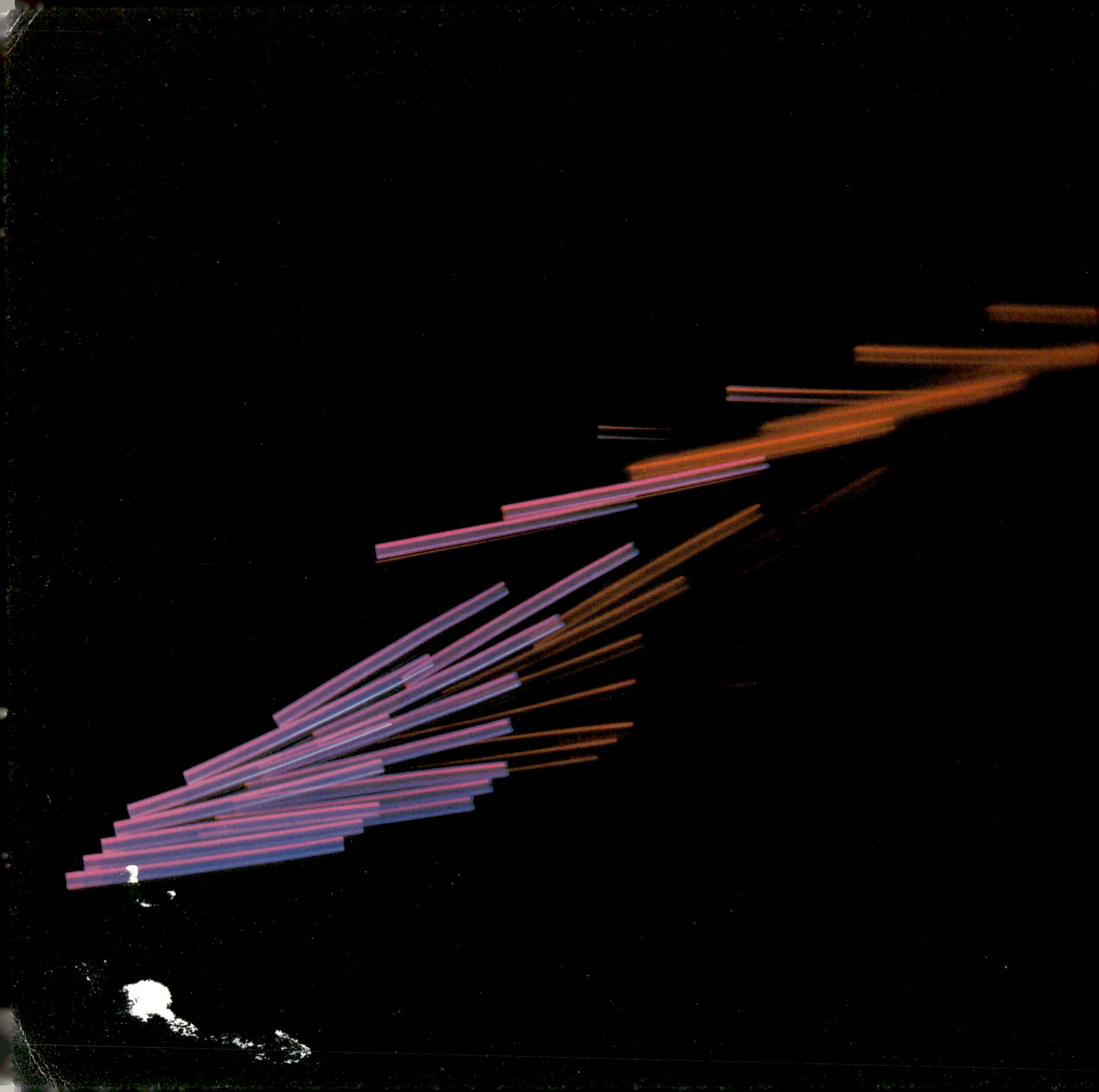

Multiple exposures can be created optically using prisms to overlap the image rather than separate exposures. In this case one facet of the prism is coloured yellow and the subject, pipette tubing, has been lit with deep blue and red light on a glass table with a black ground. Courtesy Wragby Plastics Ltd, *David Kilpatrick*.

Multiple colour exposure

The rules governing multiple exposure using different-coloured lights or filters are similar to those for mixing coloured lights. Where complementary colours overlap, much of the colour is lost in the mixture produced. Green and purple may be strong colours individually but produce a murky white when overlaid by multiple exposure. If a set of filters matched to produce a perfect integrated white is used, with correctly balanced exposure, the whole scene will appear neutral but with parts which have moved between the exposures rendered in different colours. Filters called 'tricolour', normally used for printers' colour separations, consist of a set of red, blue and green. Two-colour separation filters are usually green and orange, and do not give as good a neutral effect. You can also take two exposures, one through an A-to-D conversion filter and the second through a D-to-A.

Holography

Three-dimensional hologram technique goes beyond the scope of this book, since the lighting used does not follow the guidelines for stills and videos. When setting up a studio, however, it can be worth bearing in mind the requirements of a holographic system. A black studio with total blackout is needed, and vibration has to be damped down. This means avoiding city centre locations and major roads or rail routes. The floor should be solid concrete and the bed for setting up the holographic system will probably be concrete and steel. The positioning of holographic apparatus has to be worked out exactly, and consists of a large geometric shape with mirrors precisely aligned. This is one reason why normal photographic and film studios take little interest in holography.

Video effects

Video, unlike still photography, can be subjected to all kinds of distortion and optical trickery without recourse to lenses or films. Because of this, very few video operators now use the complex lens attachments which once used to feature in television studios. All the colouring, splitting, overlaying, distorting and multiplying necessary can be done electronically. This does not rule out the use of coloured lighting, polarisation or projection. Effects produced visually, and photographed without modification, look most realistic. Despite the sophistication of electronic image manipulation, the results can be identified, particularly when popular systems are used rather than broadcast standard video and professional editing suites.

Since many video effects use either colour identification or light and shade contour division to change the image (turning shadows one colour, mid-tones a second, highlights a third, an so on), lighting does have a bearing on the use of after-treatment. If you know that colour-key background drop-in will be used, where a particular colour of background is replaced electronically by a new scene, avoids this colour or anything close to it in clothes, props or lighting. A special effect with part of the subject itself replaced by background needs deliberate use of the same colour instead. Where the image is posterised, or broken down into tone and colour bands divided by sharp contours, the lighting must give smooth gradations. When it is reduced to 'line' (pure black-and-white) the lighting can be very high contrast, and directional.

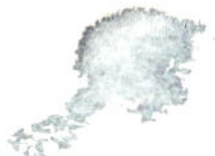

Technical hitches

A professional camera user should learn to recognise situations and conditions likely to degrade (or lose) results. Most of these are common enough to be learned quickly.

Adverse light

When the light is generally in front of the camera, rather than behind it, exposure metering is always uncertain. Whatever the composition, there is a strong chance that some adjustment must be made, and automatic exposure will cease to work correctly. The light can be overcast, sunny, or in a studio. The simplest way to back up your visual diagnosis of adverse light is to swing the camera (or meter) round through 180° and take a reading in the opposite direction. If there is any significant decrease in the amount of light metered, the light is clearly directional. From here, continue on the basis of selective, close-up, incident-light or manually adjusted exposure increase to ensure full detail in the scene originally metered.

Imbalance of tones

The second major reason for apparent 'lighting' failure is an imbalance of tonal values within a picture. This may either be an overall bias towards dark or light tones, or strategically misplaced areas which clash with the camera's exposure metering system. This applies to average, or integrated, metering. The meter expects the scene to integrate to 18 per cent grey, but for practical reasons its receptive field is limited. A camera's meter may take 60 per cent of its reading from the centre of the picture, biased towards the bottom of the viewfinder, and 40 per cent from the edges in a gradual roll-off.

If the whole scene is light (snow) or dark (granite rocks) then, as we have already seen, an adjustment must be made to the exposure if the result is to resemble the original. When anomalous tone area falls on the most sensitive areas of a camera's metering pattern, similar results happen without being as easily diagnosed. The greatest deviations from correct exposure are caused when a small but brilliant light source is included in the frame, and hits the maximum sensitivity point exactly. Video cameras do not suffer badly from this since their exposure is controlled by integrating an electronic reading from the image tube, but ciné cameras panned across a scene may suddenly cut the exposure as a bright highlight or light source passes a sensitive highspot.

Incorrect spot readings

A hand-held narrow angle meter, called a spotmeter, may be used for critically accurate readings from a distance. A typical spotmeter has an acceptance angle of only 1°, with an optical focusing viewfinder and lens. Some cameras also have 'spot' reading systems, either fixed or available by switching from the average metering system normally used. These are not as narrow in angle.

The principle of spotmetering is to aim the meter at an area corresponding to 18 per cent grey, a mid-tone. If a spotmeter is aimed at a different tone, the reading will have to be adjusted. For a highlight tone (white or just off-white), the exposure has to be increased by 5X (2.3 exposure values). When the shadows are metered, the indicated exposure should be cut by 6X (2.7 exposure values). Failure to make these adjustments will result in wrong exposure.

Lens flare

In adverse light, lens flare may veil the picture with an even haze of diffused light. Although this may not have serious local effects, because the flare covers the whole picture, it reduces contrast and colour. This flare may turn into localised patches when the lens aperture is closed down. As ciné and still SLR cameras view at open aperture, and only close down for shooting (unlike video, which works at stopped-down aperture all the time) these patches may not be seen until too late, when the film is processed. It is therefore important to examine the viewfinder image carefully, and use a stop-down preview if fitted, when shooting against the light or towards bright light sources.

Internal reflections

Stopping the lens down cannot help you to spot internal reflections, produced inside the camera body by light sources just inside the camera body by light sources just outside the picture. Often the picture is composed so that a light-source is sufficiently far outside the frame edge to avoid lens flare. This may place it ideally for internal reflection, which is only visible on studio view cameras where a ground-glass back is used for focusing. The ultimate cure is a perfect lens hood, matched to the shape of the image frame, which can be adjusted to suit each lens or focal length exactly. Hoods like this are sold for all the major 16mm ciné systems, Hasselblad and similar still cameras, and larger video cameras. Some cameras are prone to internal reflections and others are not. If you are lucky enough to have a camera with a well-designed and matt-finished 'dark chamber', all the better. You may never encounter the problem or have to find a solution.

Low light problems

Both film and video systems run into trouble when the light is unusually low. Video tubes continue to respond but the need to amplify the image more and more finally produces a recording which is little better than monochrome. Colours degrade, and 'ghosting' effects of light-trails when the camera pans past a bright detail become predominant.

Low-light cameras, fitted with highly sensitive image tubes, are needed to retain the quality. Simple single-tube cameras are rarely much good; broadcast-quality three-tube cameras are much better. Sharpness, contrast, colour and freedom from image break-up and 'snowstorms' all go by the board when small video cameras are used at the limit of their sensitivity. Photographic film, by contrast, continues to record with constant sharpness regardless of the exposure time, and any light which can be seen by the human eye can be recorded easily. However, contrast, relative sensitivity and colour rendering are not as immutable. With exposure longer than 1 second, the reciprocity law (which states that half the light needs double the exposure time) breaks down. If an exposure of 1 second at $f/8$ is indicated, reciprocity says that 2 seconds at $f/11$ or 4 seconds at $f/16$ will give identical results. In practice, 3 seconds at $f/11$ or 8 seconds at $f/16$ may be needed.

Every film varies: special tungsten films need less correction than daylight films, slow films often need less than very fast ones. There may be an increase in contrast, and colour rendering can shift, usually towards greenish shadows and magenta highlights. Manufacturers issue tables, on request, for professional emulsions. These give curves or data for increased exposure at long times and recommended trial filter packs also adjust colour.

When low light is also unusual in colour, bigger problems can arise. The normal reciprocity law failure correction may not be enough, particularly when the light colour is one to which the film's sensitivity is now effectively reduced. If the opposite applies, and film which will tend towards magenta with long exposures is used in magenta lighting, then a very strong filter pack and greatly extended exposure will be needed to achieve correct balance. As with mixed industrial lighting, the best solution is fully exposed colour negative film, used later on to make transparencies or projection copies, and colour corrected at the printing stage.

Flash failure

The 'flash fired' signals on studio flash, audible warnings, and lights in the viewfinder of SLR cameras are all intended to check that your flash has fired. With SLR cameras, the mirror flips up

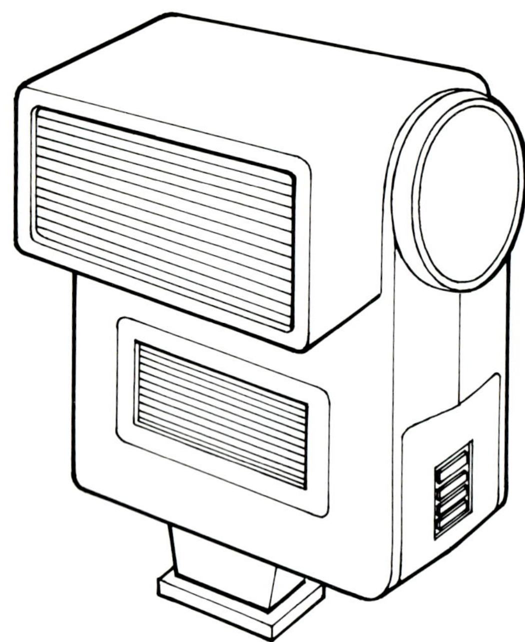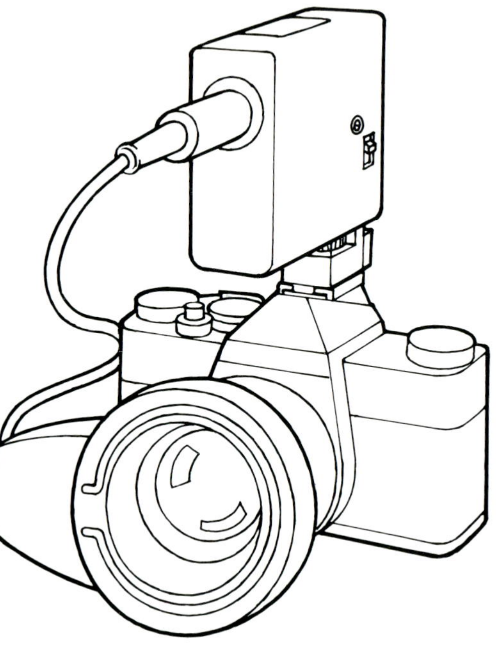

and blocks out the viewfinder at the moment of exposure, so you may not be sure. Sometimes the flash fires but no picture is recorded. The fault is not found until blank film is returned from the processor. The main reasons are incorrect flash synchronisation or shutter operation. This may be a mechanical fault, in which case it will happen suddenly. It can be checked for by opening an empty camera and looking through the film gate, releasing the shutter, with the lens taken off or at full aperture.

Incorrect setting or connection is much more likely. Electronic flash, the only type of flash discussed here, should always be connected to the socket marked X. If there is a single socket, and a switch, the switch should be set to X. Settings marked FP or M, intended for flashbulbs, now virtually obsolete to the extent that professional bulbs are normally imported to special order. Electronic flash synchronised at FP or M settings will fire before the

shutter opens and the film will not be exposed. Partial exposure of a frame is caused by setting a shutter speed faster than the maximum X synchronisation speed on an SLR with a focal-plane shutter. The flash fired, but the film was half covered by the shutter, so that only a strip of picture appears.

Lighting ratio failure

Although everything seemed correct visually, the final picture (by studio flash) is not properly lit. This is a disappointing experience, and happens to every photographer. There are two main causes: fitting the wrong modelling lamp so that the ratio of modelling lighting does not match the final flash output, or misuse of controls.

Many flash units allow the modelling lamps to be switched to full power, regardless of flash output setting, for focusing. Careless use can lead to the scene being lit on this setting, when the flash is at different true settings on each head. Other units allow the flash and modelling lamps to be switched on independently. Failsafe designs have a single switch, with positions for off, flash only, and flash plus modelling. This avoids the chance of setting modelling only, without flash. Heads which do permit this may be set up in difficult positions, such as under a perspex table-top for transillumination or very high as a top light, and the failure to switch on the flash circuit may not be spotted. In a multi-head set-up it is rarely clear that one head has not fired.

The only answer is to establish a set routine before the first exposures are made, checking each flash head in turn. Another way of making sure that hidden or remote heads are not accidentally switched off is to connect the flash synchronisation lead to one, instead of to the obvious main flash. Console flash units often have an individual warning light for each head, so you can see at a glance whether they have fired and when each has recharged.

Flash meter failure

Flash meters are supposed to be accurate, because they are used by professionals who need precise control. In practice some are influenced by static, modelling lights, exhausted power cells, or the exact method of use. Holding a meter vertically or horizontally may change the reading given. A new meter should be tested with and without modelling lamps, in normal room or daylight, hand held and resting on the subject, as well as in different positions. The reading should be checked against a known accurate meter at different distances, and the new meter then calibrated. If no meter is available, calibration can be carried out using a roll of film for test shots at different settings. The meter reading is compared with the exposure found to be best, and the meter adjusted to match if necessary.

Cast shadows

When flash is used in bright ambient light, the effect on the subject and background may not be obvious. The modelling lamps are often too dim to overcome the existing light level. The final picture can show ugly shadows cast on the background which were not visible at the time of taking. To check for this, close one eye, and look steadily at the subject. Fire the flash manually (all systems have an open flash button, to operate without the camera connected). You should be able to see the lighting effect clearly enough to spot shadows despite the very short duration of the flash.

Red eye

In direct flash-on-camera shots the subject's eyes may appear bright red. This applies just as much to professional flash units as small snapshot cameras. The best solution is to diffuse the light, by bounce flash or the use of a special reflector attachment. Failing this, the flash must be moved off the camera to at least 30cm from the lens, preferably twice this.

Low power, bright ambient light

Sometimes you want to light the subject mainly with flash, but it is distant, and the flash is not powerful enough. In the studio, the standard practice is to black out entirely, open the shutter, and fire the flash several times without touching the camera. On location, this may not be possible. Multi-exposure is needed, with the shortest possible shutter speed each time. With a leaf shutter, the normal maximum speed of 1/500 will still synchronise electronic flash, and present few problems unless the existing light is very bright. Focal-plane shutters can make this type of work impossible, with synchronisation speeds of 1/30, 1/60 or 1/90 in most makes. The maximum available is likely to be 1/200 in special high-speed shutters.

There is no solution to this. As when tryin[g ...] light an outdoor scene with tungsten, the on[ly ...] sheer power – or the ability to see, recogn[ise,] use the qualities of light as well as to handle lighting systems. That is the ultimate secret of good lighting: understanding light.

Index